DRAWN TO THE WORD

BIBLE AND ITS RECEPTION

Robert Paul Seesengood, General Editor

Editorial Board:
Brennan Breed
Stephen R. Burge
Lesleigh Cushing
J. Cheryl Exum
Michael Rosenberg

Number 4

DRAWN TO THE WORD

The Bible and Graphic Design

Amanda Dillon

Atlanta

Copyright © 2021 by Amanda Dillon

All rights reserved. No part of this work may be reproduced or transmitted in any form or by any means, electronic or mechanical, including photocopying and recording, or by means of any information storage or retrieval system, except as may be expressly permitted by the 1976 Copyright Act or in writing from the publisher. Requests for permission should be addressed in writing to the Rights and Permissions Office, SBL Press, 825 Houston Mill Road, Atlanta, GA 30329 USA.

Library of Congress Control Number: 2021948716

For my darling mother,
Janet Dillon
with love and gratitude.

Contents

Acknowledgments ix
Figures xi
Abbreviations xiii

1. Introduction 1

2. Biblical Reception History: Charting the Field 25

3. A Social Semiotics of the Visual 55

4. Liturgy and Lectionary in Biblical Reception History 81

5. Color 105

6. Silhouette 133

7. A Semiotic Analysis of the Graphic Design *Easter*
   by Nicholas Markell 155

8. A Semiotic Analysis of the Graphic Design *Christ
   Yesterday and Today* by Meinrad Craighead 191

9. Conclusion 215

Appendix 225

Bibliography 231
Ancient Sources Index 251
Modern Authors Index 255
Subject Index 259

Acknowledgments

The original sketches of this project began to take shape in my imagination long ago. This book is the realization of a dream to bring together two great passions of mine: the Bible and graphic design. There is much more to be done in this field, this is only a beginning, but I am truly thrilled to see it realized. I wish to thank the Mater Dei Educational and Research Trust for awarding me with a Dermot Lane Scholarship without which it would not have been possible to achieve this. I am truly appreciative of the privilege of having Brad Anderson as my PhD supervisor on this academic journey. I greatly benefited from his enthusiastic and thorough engagement with my work. Of the many persons who at one stage or another have been of assistance, Martin O'Kane, and Cheryl Exum are due special mention for having both been of great inspiration as well as welcoming me to ISBL meetings and supporting my research with well-placed critique and encouragement over the years.

My appreciation goes to Rhonda Burnette-Bletsch, Nicole Tilford, and the editorial board for the opportunity to publish in this new series with SBL Press: The Bible and Its Reception. I wish to thank Theo van Leeuwen and Gunther Kress (RIP) for giving of their time on the respective occasions I had the good fortune to be in their company, graciously listening to my description of this particular interdisciplinary dialogue that I was proposing and offering useful questions and flags to my fledgling attempts with their methodology.

In between wonderfully distracting conversations about "life, the universe, and everything," three librarians—June Rooney, Anne O'Carroll, and Áine Stack—were always helpful in finding elusive papers and facilitating frequent and fruitful raids on the Jesuit Library, Milltown. Thanks also to Gesa Thiessen for kindly fielding questions about Lutheran liturgical practice and welcoming me to St. Finian's Lutheran Church to inspect the Evangelical Lutheran Worship Sacramentary. Linda King lent her expertise in design history and research to early iterations of the manuscript—thank you.

Bernadette Flanagan, and Michael O'Sullivan, Waterford Institute of Technology, and SpIRE Spirituality Institute; Fáinche Ryan, Loyola Institute, Trinity College Dublin; Mary Madec and Mary Mullen, Villanova University; Sabine Schratz, Lumen Dominican Centre, for the many lecturing opportunities afforded me, I thank you all.

Finally, much gratitude to Paddy Dundon, Margery Povall, Kathleen Fitzpatrick, Patricia Keating, Helen O'Keeffe, Roisin Hickey, Anthony Fay and Breda O'Neill, Sean and Ger Goan, Candace and Keith Malcomson, Tom Whelan, Kieran O'Mahony, Breda Gahan, Des and Jon Clark, Sarah and John Richards, Roy and Jo Emmerich, and Christine and John Valters Paintner for engaging (and often extremely long) conversations, generous hospitality, friendship and favors, long drives, ridiculous giddiness, intercessions, books, walks, wine, meals, mad music, movies, and moral support.

Figures

1.1. Nicholas Markell, *Easter*	7
1.2. Nicholas Markell, *Easter*, with labels	8
1.3. Meinrad Craighead, *Christ Yesterday and Today*	12
1.4. Meinrad Craighead, *Christ Yesterday and Today*, with labels	13
1.5. Detail from *Christ Yesterday and Today*, by Meinrad Craighead	14
1.6. Detail from *Christ Yesterday and Today*, by Meinrad Craighead	14
1.7. Detail of Text from *Christ Yesterday and Today*, by Meinrad Craighead	16
1.8. Nicholas Markell, *Christ*	19
2.1. A diagrammatic outline locating this study	26
4.1. Evangelical Lutheran Worship Lectionary, Year C, gold-foiled and stamped (leaf pattern) cover and title page	96
4.2. The Evangelical Lutheran Worship *Worship* pew edition, and double-page spread detail showing lectionary readings	97
4.3. *The Sunday Missal* and internal double-page spread	101
4.4. Detail from the Evangelical Lutheran Worship *Lectionary* cover showing gold-foil cross design	103
5.1. Double-page spread in *The Sunday Missal*	122
5.2. Double-page spread in *The Sunday Missal*	122
6.1. Meinrad Craighead, *Christ, Image of God* (Col 1:15)	141
6.2. Meinrad Craighead, *Give Witness* (1 John 5:8)	141
6.3. Meinrad Craighead, *Bread of Life* (Matt 6:11)	142
6.4. Meinrad Craighead, *Bread and Wine* (Heb 4:16)	143
6.5. Meinrad Craighead, *Through Him and with Him* (Eucharistic Prayer 3)	146
6.6. Meinrad Craighead, *Hail Mary* (Luke 1:26–38)	148
6.7. Nicholas Markell, *Lent*	150

6.8. Nicholas Markell, *Moses* — 150
6.9. Nicholas Markell, *Easter Vigil* — 151
6.10. Nicholas Markell, *Holy Baptism* — 152
7.1. Nicholas Markell, *Easter* — 156
7.2. *Easter* with labels — 157
7.3. A simple diagram of a vector — 159
7.4. Diagram demonstrating how the figure of Christ may be read as a vector — 162
7.5. Detail of the *Vine* and the *Fish* — 165
7.6. Detail showing the *Waves/Net* episode — 169
7.7. Detail showing the *Emmaus* episode — 171
7.8. Detail showing the *Light* episode and the optical illusion of vibration set up by the high contrast between red and white — 178
7.9. Diagram showing perspective lines created by the *Wave* pattern that create a vanishing point in the lower central disciple of the *Tiberias* episode — 181
7.10. Diagram showing the second vanishing point created by the *Emmaus* road — 181
7.11. Detail showing the *Tiberias* episode — 183
8.1. Meinrad Craighead, *Christ Yesterday and Today* — 192
8.2. *Christ Yesterday and Today* with labels — 193
8.3. *Christ, Image of God*, by Meinrad Craighead — 195
8.4. Detail from *Christ Yesterday and Today* showing a section of the *Outer* and *Inner Strands* — 197
8.5. Detail of text from *Christ Yesterday and Today* — 201
8.6. Detail of text from *Christ Yesterday and Today* — 204
8.7. Intersemiotic systems within the ideational metafunction — 213

Abbreviations

1 Apol.	Justin Martyr, *First Apology*
1QapGen	Genesis Apocryphon
1QH	Hodayot
1QIsa[a]	Isaiah[a]
2 Bar	2 Baruch
2 Esd	2 Esdras
2Q14	Psalms
4Q11	Paleo-Hebrew Genesis–Exodus[l]
4Q17	Exodus–Leviticus[f]
4Q26	Leviticus[d]
4Q27	Numbers[b]
4Q270	Damascus Document[e]
4Q502	papyrus Rituel du mariage
11QT[a]	Temple Scroll[a]
AB	Anchor Bible
ABD	*Anchor Bible Dictionary*. Edited by David Noel Freedman. 6 vols. New York: Doubleday, 1992
ACE	*Art and Christian Enquiry*
AcT	*Acta Theologica*
ArtB	*Art Bulletin*
Bapt.	Tertullian, *De baptismo*
B. Qam.	Bava Qamma
BibInt	*Biblical Interpretation*
BlTh	*Black Theology*
CLE	*Children's Literature in Education*
CompLit	*Comparative Literature*
CrQ	*The Critical Quarterly*
CurTM	*Currents in Theology and Mission*
DSD	*Dead Sea Discoveries*

DV	*Dei Verbum*. Pope Paul VI. November 18, 1965. https://tinyurl.com/SBL6701h
EBR	*Encyclopedia of the Bible and Its Reception*. Edited by Hans-Josef Klauck et al. Berlin: de Gruyter, 2009–
ELW	Evangelical Lutheran Worship
ER	*Encyclopedia of Religion*. Edited by Lindsay Jones. 2nd ed. 15 vols. Detroit: Macmillan Reference USA, 2005
ETPC	*English Teaching, Practice and Critique*
HB	Hebrew Bible
HBAI	*Hebrew Bible and Ancient Israel*
ILCW	Inter-Lutheran Commission on Worship
Int	*Interpretation*
JBRec	*Journal of the Bible and Its Reception*
JSNT	*Journal for the Study of the New Testament*
JSOTSup	Journal for the Study of the Old Testament Supplement Series
JSportsSci	*Journal of Sports Sciences*
JWCI	*Journal of Warburg and Courtauld Institutes*
KJV	King James Version
LBW	*Lutheran Book of Worship*
LNTS	Library of New Testament Studies
MS	*Milltown Studies*
NIB	*The New Interpreter's Bible*. Edited by Leander E. Keck. 12 vols. Nashville: Abingdon, 1994–2004
NIDB	*New Interpreter's Dictionary of the Bible*. Edited by Katharine Doob Sakenfeld. 5 vols. Nashville: Abingdon, 2006–2009
NT	New Testament
NTS	*New Testament Studies*
OBO	Orbis Biblicus et Orientalis
OT	Old Testament
PCNT	Paideia Commentary on the New Testament
PIBA	*Proceedings of the Irish Biblical Association*
SC	*Sacrosanctum Concilium*. Pope Paul VI. December 4, 1963. https://tinyurl.com/SBL6701g
SJT	*Scottish Journal of Theology*
SP	Sacra Pagina
Tg. Ps.-J.	Targum Pseudo-Jonathan

THL	Theory and History of Literature
VisCom	*Visual Communication*
WBC	Word Biblical Commentary
WC	*Written Communication*
WUNT	Wissenschaftliche Untersuchungen zum Neuen Testament

1
Introduction

> Every scribe who has been trained for the kingdom of heaven is like the master of a household who brings out of his treasure what is new and what is old.
> —Matthew 13:52

Biblical reception history is now a rapidly expanding area of biblical studies that concerns itself not only with how biblical texts have been received historically but also with how they are received in the contemporary era and in diverse cultural contexts such as art, popular culture, politics, fashion, and sport. My interest is in how the biblical text is received within the prevailing cultural shift toward the visual. The field of biblical reception and the visual arts has seen much excellent work done on easel paintings, probably the most appreciated and well-preserved art form (in the West) of the last five hundred years. The work of graphic designers—the likes of Ade Bethune, Rita Corbin, and Fritz Eichenberg and their inspired work for *The Catholic Worker* newspaper in New York, and Frank Kacmarcik's imprint on so many publications of Liturgical Press of Collegeville, Minnesota, prime examples among so many others—has been somewhat neglected thus far.[1] It would be fair to say that neither art-and-design historians nor

---

Unless otherwise stated, all biblical translations follow the NRSV.

1. Ade Bethune's archive is held at St. Catherine University, Minnesota. See her artwork at "Ade Bethune Drawings," St. Catherine University Library and Archives, http://content.clic.edu/cdm/landingpage/collection/abcorig. A small selection of Rita Corbin's designs may be seen at "Gallery," Rita Corbin, http://ritacorbinart.com/calenders/. Unfortunately, no single website or archive exists for Fritz Eichenberg's work, but a sample may be viewed at "William Greenbaum Fine Prints: Fritz Eichenberg Prints," https://tinyurl.com/SBL6701a. Some samples of Frank Kacmarcik's artwork can be seen at "Frank Kacmarcik—Uncle Frank," Pinterest, https://tinyurl.com/SBLPress6701a. An archive of his work, including his iconic covers of the journal *Wor-*

biblical reception scholars have paid contemporary graphic design illustrating the Bible its due attention. Adorning and embellishing the everyday, an illustration alongside a column of text or the cover of a monthly journal, graphic design plays a profound semiotic role in creating and advancing the meaning not only of particular articles and issues but of the cultural artifacts themselves, the organizations behind them, and the community of readers they address. Bethune's design for the masthead of *The Catholic Worker* has never been replaced and is now iconic, continuing to embody the driving core principles and identity of that organization. Such longevity is exceptional in an age of frequent rebranding. Similarly outstanding graphic design explicitly interpreting the Bible is to be found in the liturgical books used by Christians in the context of their Sunday corporate worship. Two examples, Nicholas Markell's recent work for the Evangelical Lutheran Church of America's Worship series (2006) and Meinrad Craighead's designs for the Roman Catholic *Sunday Missal* (1975), stand out as perceptive engagements with the biblical texts surrounding them.

This study sets out to explore and reveal how graphically designed images function semiotically in the reception of biblical texts and to open up this arena of the visual arts, graphic design, to the field of biblical reception history. The semiotic approach developed by theorists Gunther Kress and Theo van Leeuwen will be brought to bear on the reception of the Bible that occurs in these designs—as they are found illustrating lections in the liturgical books of the church.

My own experience as a biblical scholar with a long background in graphic design has led to my endeavoring to understand how biblical texts are received in graphically designed images. While there has been a growing interest in the visual reception of the Bible in recent years, little attention has been given to the actual inner workings of the image, the fact that every aspect—medium and color, opacity and saturation, strength or weakness of mark, vigor of stroke, directionality and compositional con-

---

ship, and his vast collection of twentieth-century design is held at the Hill Museum and Manuscript Library at Saint John's University, Collegeville, Minnesota. See "Saint John's University. Arca Artium," Collection at the Hill Museum and Manuscript Library, Saint John's University, https://hmml.org/collections/repositories/united%20states/saint-john-s-university--arca-artium/. Other graphic designers who have illustrated biblical texts and are of particular interest include Eric Gill, Caryll Houselander, Barry Moser, Benton Spruance, Blair Hughes Stanton, Clemens Schmidt, and Placid Stuckenschneider.

figuration—is a choice that has been made by the artist with the intent of communicating something about the biblical text. All of these dimensions of a design collude to make meaning. As I will outline below, these elements are an important part of the discourse surrounding analysis of graphic design more generally, and this study will bring these dimensions to bear on the analysis of biblical images.

Graphic design is the holistic integration of spatial, textual, typographical, and illustrative elements in a way that best communicates an intended message to the viewer/reader. One of the primary impulses of graphic design that distinguishes it from some other visual art forms is its communicative function over personal self-expressive concerns. Graphic design is always explicitly oriented toward the viewer with the intention and desire to impart meaning. Design theorist Jessica Helfand writes,

> Designers are, by their very nature, emissaries of all that faces outward: makers, doers, propagators seeding the future. Their focus is on identifying and, by conjecture, improving the conditions that frame our experience, bringing order and efficiency, comfort and delight, entertainment, information, clarification to all that eludes us.[2]

The task of the graphic designer is to hold the viewer/reader in mind throughout the process of designing. Paul Rand, one of the foremost graphic designers of the late twentieth century, defines design thus: "To design is much more than simply to assemble, to order, or even to edit; it is to add value and meaning, to illuminate, to simplify, to clarify, to modify, to dignify, to dramatize, to persuade, and perhaps even to amuse. Design broadens perception, magnifies experience, and enhances vision."[3] The question remains, How does one describe the dynamics at work in an image? Beyond a personal apprehension and description of an image, how may one make a claim for the inner workings, the visual dynamics (much of which may often be perceived unconsciously) of the artwork? How does one give an account of all the visual givens that designers assume when designing? How does one describe how meaning is made visually? How does one assert what a designer has achieved visually—in terms of meaning—in theoretical discourse?

---

2. Jessica Helfand, *Design: The Invention of Desire* (New Haven: Yale University Press, 2016), 19.

3. Paul Rand, *Design: Form and Chaos* (New Haven: Yale University Press, 1993), 3.

Here semiotics, a social semiotics of the visual, to be precise, provides a powerful resource. This is an emergent theoretical approach developed and advanced by Kress and Van Leeuwen. Both are former students and colleagues of British-Australian linguist-semiotician Michael A. K. Halliday, renowned for his paradigm-shifting *Systemic Functional Grammar*.[4] Their approach, articulated primarily in their groundbreaking *Reading Images: The Grammar of Visual Design*, explores and describes the inner workings of visual artifacts.[5] A social semiotics of the visual offers a vital methodology for scholars working in the area of biblical reception, and a route of access into the meaning-making potential and qualities of images. Thus, this study brings together a new methodological approach, a social semiotics of the visual, and a new area of focus, graphic design, to the field of biblical reception history.

I have chosen to concentrate here on the artwork of two contemporary designers: Markell and Craighead. Both of these artists have created designs that have been featured in Christian literature of varied forms. In making works that are intended for the faithful, often in a liturgical context, the designer hopes there will be an aha moment of recognition; an indelible insight, a spark of convergence that serves to "broaden, magnify and enhance" their "perception, experience and vision."[6] This study sets out to understand how Markell's and Craighead's designs function semiotically as interpretations of the (Easter) biblical lections in the iconic liturgical books of the Evangelical Lutheran Church of America *Lectionary* (in the Worship series) and the Roman Catholic *Sunday Missal*. I will briefly introduce the designers and the primary artworks (figs. 1.1 and 1.3) drawn from the range of designs made for the respective books.

1.1. Nicholas Markell

1.1.1. Biographical Notes

Nicholas T. Markell, born in 1961, was raised in Owatonna, southern Minnesota, where he developed an early love of art—most especially depicting

---

4. Michael A. K. Halliday and Christian Matthiessen, *Halliday's Introduction to Functional Grammar*, 4th rev. ed. (London: Routledge, 2014).

5. Gunther Kress and Theo Van Leeuwen, *Reading Images: The Grammar of Visual Design*, 2nd ed. (London: Routledge, 2006).

6. Rand, *Design*, 3.

the natural world, the fish and fauna of the countryside around him. Upon finishing high school, he entered the University of St. Thomas in St. Paul, Minnesota, and earned a bachelor of visual arts. He then worked for several years as a graphic designer and art director, guiding creative projects for several prominent Minnesota organizations.[7] However, his inclination toward the spiritual led him to join the Paulist Fathers as he explored the possibility of a religious vocation in the arts. He explains,

> In 1987 I decided to study for Christian ministry, earning a Master of Arts degree in Theology and a Master of Divinity degree from the Washington Theological Union, now located in Washington, DC. I planned to be an ordained priest, but my future took a different direction. For the past 15 years or so I have operated an ecclesial arts studio, creating stained glass and iconography for worship and graphics for religious publication.[8]

The Markell Studio "is an ecclesial arts consultancy dedicated to iconic imagery in glass, pigment and graphics"—the primary art forms to be found in church buildings.[9] Markell has been granted numerous awards and accolades, "most notably those given by the Washington Building Congress, PRINT publications and ministry and Liturgy magazine."[10] He is a recognized master iconographer in the Byzantine and Romanesque iconographic traditions, and lectures and instructs on iconography, liturgical art, and Christian imagery.[11]

Markell's intention is to serve the ecclesial community through the creation and promotion of iconic imagery. As the artist's website states, "Nicholas' images explore art's full spiritual potential, revealing dynamics of contemporary human experiences as they are shaped by the wisdom and inspiration of both our religious and cultural heritage." Markell endeavors to create iconic images focusing on the three principles of beauty, mystery,

---

7. "Nicholas Markell," Markell Wildlife Art, https://tinyurl.com/SBL6701b.

8. "Nicholas Markell."

9. Markell has created stained-glass windows for St. Mark's Episcopal Cathedral in Minneapolis; Saint Michael Catholic Church in St. Michael, Minnesota; and St. Thomas More Chapel at Ohio State University. See https://www.markellstudios.com.

10. "Nicholas Markell," Gray's Sporting Journal, https://www.grayssportingjournal.com/nicholas-markell/.

11. Markell is a long-standing member of the Liturgical Commission for the Roman Catholic Archdiocese of Minneapolis and St. Paul.

and meaning. His images are intended to communicate multiple levels of meaning in a simple way: they offer "a visual meditation, complementing songs and text while simultaneously standing alone as confessions of faith. Created in a spirit of simplicity, they are meant as a prayer guide."[12]

1.1.2. The Graphic Design *Easter* by Nicholas Markell

Visual social semiotics refers to the distinct narrative elements or objects in an image as *episodes* or *represented participants*.[13] These will be named here and marked throughout this book in italics. Reference to an object or visual element in this way alerts the reader that an *episode* is being discussed.[14] Markell's *Easter* (fig. 1.1) features a large central silhouette of the risen *Christ*. His arms are diagonally outstretched, and his hands reveal the wounds of crucifixion. The head of *Christ* is crowned with a *Halo* created of thin, sharply pointed red wedges (fig. 1.2). Over the left arm of *Christ* is a thin, black *Cross*, from which flies a red-and-white resurrection banner and two further red banners lower down the cross.[15] In the symmetrically corresponding place on the right-hand side, a black, three-leafed *Sprouting Vine Shoot* emerges, with a red semicircular blossom above and three red circles or grapes below it.

On either side of *Christ*, below his outstretched arms, a semicircular flourish of red fish and black fish appear to leap out of the water in an animated way. The pattern is symmetrically and vertically flipped but does not correspond exactly color-wise. If each of the vertical side panels of *Fish* is understood as forming three clusters (four at the top, eleven in

---

12. "Nicholas Markell," Markell Wildlife Art, referring to images produced for David Haas, *Biblical Way of the Cross, Based on the Stations Led by Pope John Paul II* (Chicago: GIA, 2005).

13. Figs. 1.2 and 1.4 provide a detailed legend of these episodes and represented participants, as they are referred to throughout this book.

14. I have named these episodes or represented participants, as seen in Markell's *Easter* (fig. 1.2), for example, and the other labeled designs. This is therefore an act of interpretation in itself.

15. A resurrection banner is a red banner featuring a white cross along its length. It is a motif in Christian art that dates back well into the Middle Ages and can be seen most frequently and prominently in Renaissance art. These banners form part of the episode that is the *Cross*. The *Cross* here refers to Christ's Passion, the crucifixion from which he has risen—embodied in the central silhouette, and so it is simply a cross without a corpus. Rather, banners signaling victory over death fly from the cross.

Fig. 1.1. Nicholas Markell, *Easter*. © 2011 Evangelical Lutheran Church in America, admin. Augsburg Fortress. All rights reserved.

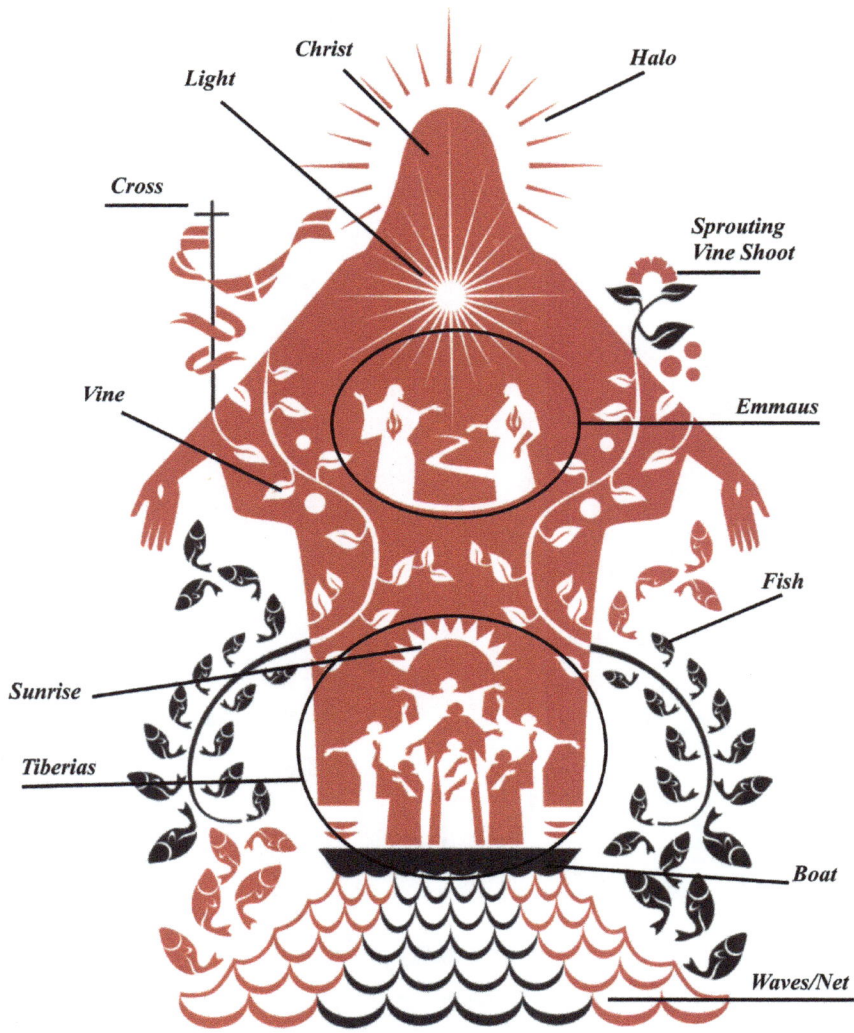

Fig. 1.2. Nicholas Markell, *Easter*, with labels. © 2011 Evangelical Lutheran Church in America, admin. Augsburg Fortress. All rights reserved.

the middle, and five at the bottom), one may perceive a diagonal correspondence of two clusters, the four fish at the top and the five fish at the bottom—in terms of the color switching across the image—in a way not dissimilar to a chiastic structure in literature. At the base of *Christ* is the thin black horizontal, roughly rectangular shape of the *Boat*. Beyond this, five rows of linked semicircular shapes of decreasing depth stretch below the figures at the bottom of the image. These may be interpreted as either *Waves* of water or the *Net* that has been cast into the water from the boat to catch the *Fish*. The silhouette functions as a container for reversed-out episodes, white on red, six in total: the *Light* in the top third of *Christ*; the two figures on the road to *Emmaus* in the center; the two almost-identical, symmetrical *Vines*, vertically flipped on either side of the figure; a further *Sunrise* episode; and the ensemble of figures in the boat on the Sea of *Tiberias* at the bottom of the figure. There are three episodes—*Halo*, *Light*, and *Sunrise*—with strong sun or light symbolism that may form a trinity of light through the vertical center of the design. Markell has achieved his intention of communicating multiple levels of meaning in a simple way. There are many instantly recognizable biblical motifs operating in this design: the risen *Christ*, the *Vine*, the *Fish*, the *Cross*, the three different light symbols noted above, *Halo*, *Light*, and *Sunrise*. There are also the two clearly indicated gospel resurrection narratives of the road to *Emmaus* (Luke 24:13–35) and the appearance to the disciples at the Sea of *Tiberias* (John 21:1–14).[16]

The perfectly formed straight lines and smooth edges to all the shapes composing this illustration indicate that it has been created mechanically in a digital illustration program such as Adobe Illustrator, most probably using a stylus and tablet. It is composed of digitally generated vectors that allow for the formation of smooth curves, for example, that can be repeated at preset intervals to create a pattern such as that of the *Waves/Net* at the bottom of the image. Likewise, they can be collectively and uniformly stretched, as seen here. No doubt, there were many hand-drawn sketches of initial ideas and preparatory plotting of the illustration before it was brought to the computer and modeled up in Illustrator. Beyond the smooth curves and clean lines, the symmetry that is created both in the silhouette shape of *Christ* and the *Fish*

---

16. These episodes shall be referred to as *Emmaus* and *Tiberias* respectively and indicated in italics.

and *Vine* episodes is easily and well achieved in a vector-based illustration application. The digitally generated clean, crisp appearance of these lines and shapes gives the design a contemporary feel and facilitates the complexity of the design.[17]

1.2. Meinrad Craighead

1.2.1. Biographical Notes

Meinrad Craighead, born in 1936, was raised in Chicago and then Little Rock, Arkansas.[18] As a child, she took to drawing and exhibited a natural inclination for art.[19] In 1960, Craighead received a scholarship to study art at the University of Wisconsin. After teaching for two years in Albuquerque, she received a Fulbright scholarship to study and teach art in Florence, Italy. She returned to the United States twenty-one years later.[20] In the meantime, in 1966, after a period at Montserrat in Spain, she entered the Benedictine monastery of Stanbrook Abbey in England.[21] She remained there for the next fourteen years and continued her artistic work publishing her first book, *The Sign of the Tree*, and becoming the subject of a number of documentaries filmed by Italian, British, and US television.[22] Craighead then left religious life and after

---

17. This image is discussed in chs. 6–7, and an in-depth semiotic analysis is found in ch. 8.

18. Meinrad Craighead's first name was Charlene. On entering monastic life at Stanbrook Abbey, she took for her name in religious life "Meinrad," the name of her great-great-uncle, a Swiss Benedictine monk, Brother Meinrad Eügster (1848–1925) of Einsiedeln monastery in Switzerland. See Meinrad Craighead, "Lodestone," in *Meinrad Craighead: Crow Mother and the Dog God; A Retrospective* (San Francisco: Pomegranate, 2003), 17. Craighead died on 8 April 2019 in Albuquerque, age eighty-three.

19. Craighead discusses her early artistic activity and spiritual experiences in the documentary made of her life and work, *Meinrad Craighead: Praying with Images* (Durham, NC: Resource Center for Women and Ministry in the South, 2009).

20. Rich Heffern, "Art and Spirituality: In the Name of the Mother," *National Catholic Reporter*, 18 July 2008, https://tinyurl.com/SBL6701c.

21. A reflection on Meinrad's time at Stanbrook has been written by Rosemary Davies, "The Struggle for Solitude," in *Meinrad Craighead: Crow Mother*, 129–53.

22. Craighead has produced a number of publications of her work. These include Craighead, *Meinrad Craighead: Crow Mother*; Craighead, *Sacred Marriage: The*

three years in London returned to Albuquerque, where she lived near her beloved Rio Grande River until her recent death. Her large body of later artwork has been the subject of greater focus and appreciation from art historians, scholars, and those in the field of female spirituality and ministry.

1.2.2. The Graphic Design *Christ Yesterday and Today* by Meinrad Craighead

The Craighead image being explored in depth in this volume is a black-and-white design (fig. 1.3) that features a small central silhouette of *Christ* bearing the five wounds of crucifixion. These wounds are reversed-out white, and the wound in the side of *Christ* may be said to be subtly heart-shaped even though it is on the right side of his body. This silhouette appears in a white, spherical shape that I will name *Light* for the purpose of this analysis (fig. 1.4). This *Light* is contained within a black circular shape that forms the center of a *Cross* that serves to divide the upper half of the composition into five distinct areas. *Strands*, like ripples of light, reverberate outward from the central *Light*. These vary greatly in thickness and do not necessarily correlate exactly on either side of an arm of the *Cross*. I suggest there is a set of *Inner Strands* and a set of *Outer Strands*: those closest to the *Cross* and those further out, respectively. The *Inner Strands*, the central eye of the *Cross*, *Light*, and *Christ* form a cohesive group that dominates the vertical center. I will refer to this collective, grouped participant as *Flame* (fig. 1.5).[23]

Wisdom of the Song of Songs (London: Continuum, 1997); Craighead, *The Litany of the Great River* (Mahwah, NJ: Paulist, 1991); Craighead, *Liturgical Art* (Kansas City, MO: Sheed & Ward, 1988); Craighead, *The Mother's Songs* (Mahwah, NJ: Paulist, 1986); Craighead, *The Sign of the Tree* (London: Beazley, 1979); Craighead, *The Mother's Birds* (Worcester, UK: Stanbrook Abbey, 1976).

23. In the technical language describing images, rather than using the term *element*, for example, favored by earlier art historians, Kress and van Leeuwen use the term *participant*. Every semiotic act involves two types of participants, interactive participants and represented participants. "The former are the participants in the act of communication—the participants who speak and listen or write and read, make images or view them, whereas the latter are the participants who constitute the subject matter of the communication; that is, the people, places and things (including abstract 'things') represented in and by the speech or writing or image, the participants about whom or which we are speaking or writing or producing images" (Kress and van Leeuwen, *Reading Images*, 48).

Fig. 1.3. Meinrad Craighead, *Christ Yesterday and Today*. © Meinrad Craighead. All Rights Reserved.

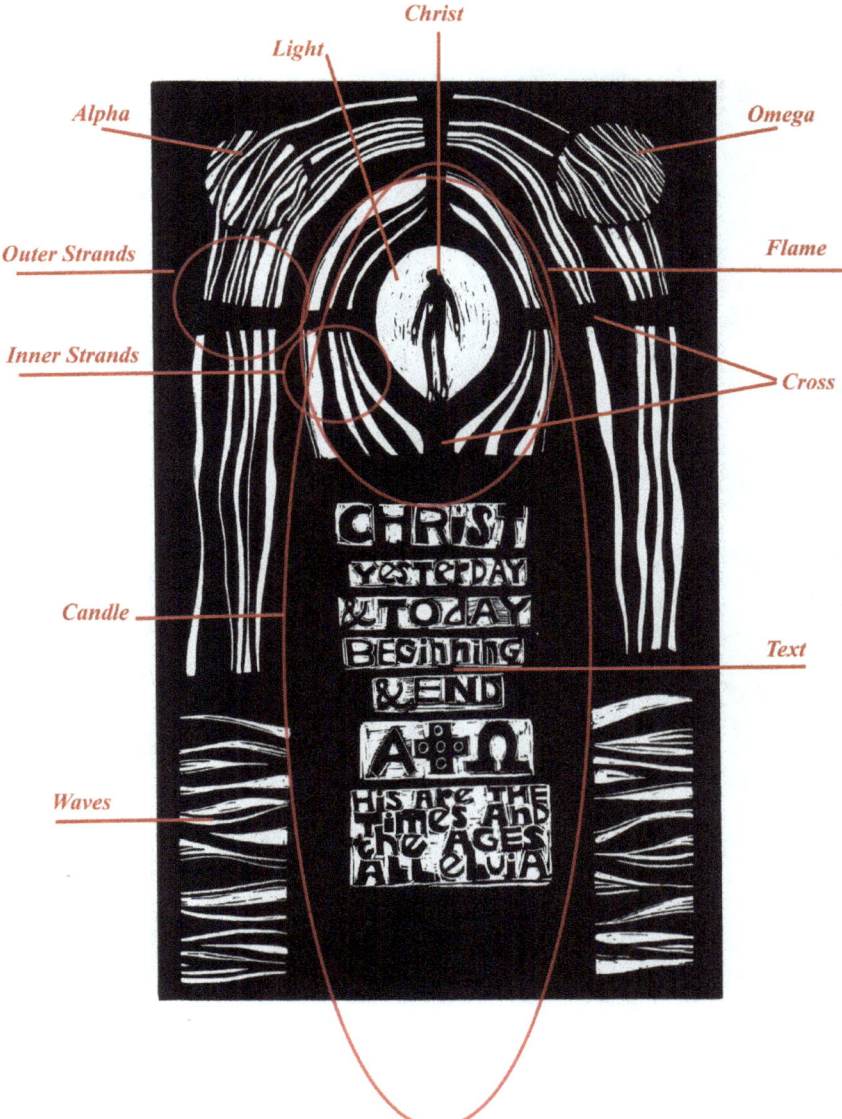

Fig. 1.4. Meinrad Craighead, *Christ Yesterday and Today*, with labels. © Meinrad Craighead, All Rights Reserved.

Fig. 1.5. Detail from *Christ Yesterday and Today*, by Meinrad Craighead. I will refer to this collective represented participant (*Christ*; *Light*; *Cross Inner Strands*) as *Flame*. © Meinrad Craighead, All Rights Reserved.

Fig. 1.6. Detail from *Christ Yesterday and Today*, by Meinrad Craighead. © Meinrad Craighead, All Rights Reserved.

In the outer, upper two quadrants, there are two further discs, one on the left and one on the right, with many lines within them; they almost seem like magnifications, a view through a microscope, of the *Outer Strands* beneath them or within which they are placed (fig. 1.6). I label these two discs *Alpha* (left) and *Omega* (right) and will elaborate on this in chapter 9. The *Outer Strands* that curve around the top, in the upper quadrants, flatten out to become vertical stripes down the sides of the composition in the lower quadrants. In the bottom third of the composition are similar horizontal stripes or *Waves*. The design is predominantly black. The figure of *Christ* is a black silhouette, as are the letters in the *Text*.

1. INTRODUCTION

Centrally placed, in the lower half of the page, beneath this silhouetted *Christ* is a body of *Text*, an integral part of the carved woodcut (fig. 1.7).[24] There appear to be three different segments within this body of *Text*. There are two short sentences: "Christ Yesterday & Today Beginning & End," and, "His Are The Times And the Ages Alleluia." Sandwiched between these is a graphic element featuring the symbols A + Ω, the Greek letters *alpha* and *omega*. The plus sign stands in for the *and*; it is also a cross patterned with five small circles.[25] The five circles signify the five grains of incense inserted into the wax at the cardinal points of the cross during the ritual blessing of the Easter candle. Almost all of Craighead's woodcuts for *The Sunday Missal* contain sections of biblical text.[26] The words of the *Text* are placed in white horizontal rectangles and are made up of a mixture of uppercase and lowercase letters, apparently randomly mixed together in words, along with ampersands and a plus sign replacing the word *and* in three instances.

It is important to note here that both artists featured have had much personal exposure to Christian social life and liturgical practice. This experience no doubt influenced how they understand both the Scriptures they are illustrating as well as the liturgical context for which they were intended. However, a social semiotic of the visual approach, as chosen here, enables the artworks to be analyzed in their own right, as it were. It is not necessary to inquire into the intentions of the artist, to which, of

---

24. The text is taken from Heb 13:8, "Jesus Christ is the same yesterday and today and forever." "Alpha and Omega" appears three times in Revelation, once as a self-designation of Christ (Rev 22:13; see also 1:8; 21:6).

25. Traditionally, the Easter Vigil begins outdoors with a brief Service of Light, the blessing of the Easter fire, and the blessing and lighting of the Easter candle. The celebrant, in an eight-part sequence of moves, cuts a cross in the wax of the candle with a stylus, then traces the Greek letter alpha above the cross, the letter omega below, and the numerals of the year in between the arms of the cross. Then he blesses the candle. All this is accompanied by saying, "[1] Christ yesterday and today [2] the beginning and the end, [3] Alpha [4] and Omega; [5] all time belongs to him, [6] and all the ages, [7] to him be glory and power, [8] through every age and for ever. Amen." When the cross and other marks have been made, the priest may insert five grains of incense in the candle. These are symbolic of the five wounds of Christ. See *The Sunday Missal* (London: Collins, 1975), 209.

26. These texts are either Scripture passages taken from the readings of the liturgies they accompany or, in a few instances, from the prayers of the Mass, for example, the design *Through Him and with Him*, which appears on page 42 of *Sunday Missal*.

Fig. 1.7. Detail of *Text* from *Christ Yesterday and Today*. © Meinrad Craighead, All Rights Reserved.

course, the vast majority of viewers will never have access. A social semiotic of the visual approach sets out to explore how the inner workings of the image—composition, texture, color, directionality, framing, angle, form, among many others—afford semiotic meaning potential to the image. This approach does not seek to discover *the* meaning of the image but rather to uncover its meaning potentials as construed through the internal relationships between the many aspects of the image. Moreover, within a social-semiotic perspective, the meanings of images, objects, and events are not fixed, but rather the meanings arise within the situational and cultural context in which the image or object appears, according to cultural conventions that are largely recognized by members of a group or community.

1.3. Considering *Christ*, a Brief Application of a Methodological Approach

By way of a brief introduction, and aware that much ground will be covered before reaching the full-length and in-depth thorough analyses of the graphic designs already introduced, an abridged taster or teaser is offered here—an analysis of Markell's *Christ* design—as sustenance for the journey. Without overburdening this very brief introduction to a social semiotics of the visual analysis with a surfeit of technical terms, it is necessary to state at the outset that this, *Christ* (fig. 1.8), is a *conceptual* image. It is replete with readily recognized symbols further identifying it as a *symbolic process*. There are a number of immediately striking features, not least the commanding, central robed figure—which we identify as Christ (given this context of the ELW liturgical books)—crowned with a halo and facing out to the right. The crucifixion is implied in the gesture of his outstretched arms and the small cross-shaped, star-shaped wounds in the palms of his hands. *Symbolic processes* are about what a visual participant *means* or *is*. Here, the Christ figure is a *Carrier* in a relationship with various *Symbolic Attributes*.[27] In a conceptual image, the *participants* are not *doing*—interacting—with other participants. Rather, this type of image is

---

27. Kress and van Leeuwen, *Reading Images*, 105. Symbolic attributes are characterized as follows: they are made salient in the work, for example, through exaggerated size, conspicuous color, or being foregrounded in the design; they look out of place in the whole in some way; and they are conventionally associated with symbolic value.

about the way participants *fit together* to make up the larger whole. In this sense, one may say it has the structure of a map.[28] The larger participant, the *Carrier*, represents the whole (say, Ireland) and the other participants, the *Symbolic Attributes*, represent the parts (counties, rivers, etc.). The Christ figure functions as a *Carrier*, and the sun, moon, stars, and trees function as *Attributes*, in this instance *Symbolic Attributes*, the parts that lend meaning to the whole.

In the upper half of the circle is a pattern comprising a tree motif repeated four times in different color combinations using the color triad of red, black, and white. The color changes depict different seasons of the year: a white, snow-laden tree set against the dark night and snowfall of winter; the spring energy of new life coming to bud and bloom against a bright dawn; the full red heat of summer; and then the leaves turning red against the pale sky of fall. The tree with its raised branches is the same tree moving through the cycle of the four seasons and so representative of earthly time. Interestingly, this tree is not in a state of perpetual bloom, it is not an evergreen: it is subject to the vicissitudes of the seasons and climate. Significantly, the allusion to the four seasons of the year also connotes the yearly cyclical nature of the lectionary and the liturgical seasons of Advent, Christmas, Lent, Easter, and so forth.[29]

The lower half of the circle is a sweep of the figure's layered robes—like priestly garments. Draped around his shoulders is a mantle featuring symbols of the cosmos: sun, moon, and stars, set against the primordial black of the universe. Christ presents himself, opening out in this broad gesture, and held in the swath of his garments are those symbols that most readily identify him. The largest of these cosmic elements is the central white star—the upper vertical ray of which is also a subtle cross, hinting at both the star heralding his incarnation (Matt 2:2–10) and his death on the cross, which is clearly reiterated in his bodily gesture and the wounded hands. The lower body of Christ also forms the trunk of a tree. The simple white lines cleverly suggest the soft folds of fabric falling over a knee, or a cord hanging down, or a knot in a plank of wood, or a gnarl in a trunk. Cross, tree, and wood are beautifully and subtly layered together, different associations rising to the surface and falling back as another comes to the fore.

---

28. Kress and van Leeuwen, *Reading Images*, 50.
29. A fuller exploration of the lectionary can be found in ch. 4.

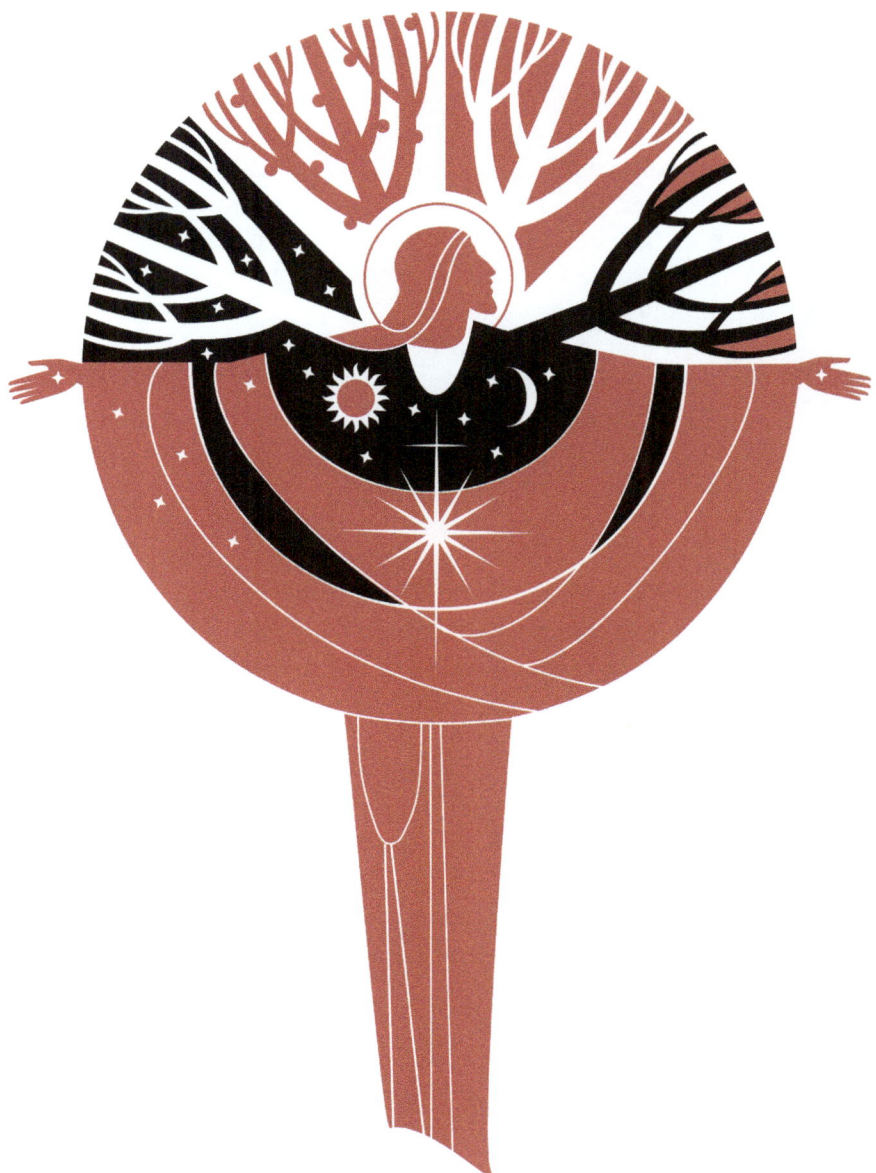

Fig. 1.8. Nicholas Markell, *Christ*. © 2011 Evangelical Lutheran Church in America, admin. Augsburg Fortress. All rights reserved.

Here Christ is the tree of life. His body forms the trunk, and his arms are like branches, and indeed branches radiate out around him. Within the Hebrew Bible and the New Testament there are many tree symbols and metaphors, from the earliest chapters of Genesis (Gen 2–3), right through to the closing chapter of Revelation (Rev 22:2, 14, 19).[30] Furthermore, personified Wisdom is "a tree of life to those who lay hold of her" (Prov 3:18). Feminist biblical scholar Carole Fontaine notes, "Woman Wisdom is identified with the Torah and redemption of the Jews in history (Sir 24:8–12, 23–29; Wis 10:15). She is also associated with 'glory' or 'spirit,' 'discerning comprehension' (see e.g., Wis 1:6; 9:6–16; Sir 1), concepts that later link female Wisdom to the Logos prologue to the Gospel of John and to Trinitarian theology."[31] Psalms liken the righteous to a tree. They are described as flourishing "like the palm tree and grow[ing] like a cedar in Lebanon" (Ps 1; 92:12, 14).[32] Daniel (4:10–12) and Ezekiel (17:22–24; 47:12) both speak of life-giving trees. The expanse of Christ's gesture is also linked to these other symbols of time, seasons, and Scriptures. His reaching gesture encompasses the beginning of time in one direction and the end of time in the other. The crucified one is also Lord of the cosmos, holding the stars in the palms of his hands—hands that reach out beyond the boundary of the containing circle—into the sacred space, into another spatial and temporal register, signified in the white space.

This is a crucifixion pose, but this figure of Christ is very much alive, with his head held high and with an open-handed gesture that connotes hospitality, invitation, and embrace. This is reiterated in his gaze past the edge of the circle into a further, more distant space. Christ has his head turned facing to the right. He is gazing into the beyond. There are two important and noteworthy aspects to this: first, the body of Christ here is in a frontal position, facing the implied viewer, yet his head is turned

---

30. Nancy Declaissé-Walford, "Tree of Knowledge, Tree of Life," *NIDB* 5:659–61. Tree imagery is also found in nonbiblical early Jewish literature and in the iconography of many other religions.

31. Carole R. Fontaine, "Sophia," *NIDB* 5:356–57. See also Elizabeth A. Johnson, *She Who Is: The Mystery of God in Feminist Theological Discourse* (New York: Crossroad, 1995), 86–100.

32. See Gail Ramshaw for a reflection on the tree symbol in the Revised Common Lectionary: *Treasures Old and New: Images in the Lectionary* (Minneapolis: Fortress, 2002), 393–400.

away. The visual proposition here is one of offer rather than demand. Christ presents himself for contemplation, but no demand is being made of the viewer. Second, his implied gaze is directly linked to the material format of the codex book. The convention in Western countries is that a book opens from right to left. Situated at the beginning of the volume, this illustration is an invitation to physically turn into the forthcoming pages. The visual allusion is that more of this revelation, on offer here in this image, is to be found in the pages of this book.

This design is essentially symmetrical but for the little touches of asymmetry that lend it great dynamism without detracting from the power of the central focus. One small example is the large star in the center of the image. Its lower-central vertical ray crosses over folds in the robe. There is a fold slightly to the left that might have been brought over to intersect perfectly behind the star ray—but it does not. Resisting the urge to arrange everything in perfect symmetry, which would have depleted the dynamism of the design, invests it instead with energy and a poetic quality.

This Christ figure has no feet, as his robe ends in a curved flourish. Visually, the elongated length of the body prevents it being top-heavy and lends it a certain lightness and altitude. The impression is subtle and almost unnoticed, but this footless figure levitates in the white space, clearly marking it out as a resurrection image. This simple curving of the bottom edge lends dynamism to the figure, preventing it from becoming static. The strong central vertical axis and the lower point on the right set up a potential pivot around which he might spin like a whirling dervish. This Christ figure is elevated and suspended in the surrounding white space, which is not meaningless, but instead functions here to connote sacred space and/or the divine light of God.[33]

In this systemic approach to composition, the various areas of the artwork are invested with conventional relational connotations.[34] This composition has strong balancing vertical and horizontal axes. It is dominated, however, by the circle in the center. Circles are associated with values of wholeness, completion, continuity, harmony, unity, and balance,

---

33. See ch. 5 for an elaboration on the role of white space on the page.

34. The compositional values of top = ideal as to bottom = real; left = given as to right = new; and center as to margin/polar are dealt with in detail in chs. 7–8. See also Kress and van Leeuwen, *Reading Images*, 179–214.

and "a sense of permanence goes with the central position."[35] This composition is about the primacy of this central figure. The turning of Christ's head toward the right is the visual-hermeneutical key to this entire design. This one small gesture, the focal point of the image, is the visual proposition that creates coherence between all of the many symbols, signified values, and gestures throughout the piece. This turn of Christ's head to the right signifies a turn toward the new, toward the future, toward possibility and potentiality, a new thing: person, object, or event. Theologically, one may see Christ, here the center of origin and prime mover of communication, Lord of the cosmos, indicating himself as having set in motion the new thing to which he turns: "See, I am making all things new" (Rev 21:5). Christ is the mediator of the new (Luke 22:20; 1 Cor 11:25; Heb 8:8, 13; 9:15; 12:24).

This new creation is enhanced in the very unusual inversion of the top-bottom/ideal-real convention. In the circle, the top half relates to the real world—the ground, the trees of the earth, and the seasons. The bottom half relates to the ideal—in religious art conventionally the heavens, the skies, the cosmos, life beyond our reach and all of its connotations of God's acts of creation. Christ's robes form the inverted heavenly dome of the ancient Hebrew cosmology, where the firmament was a contained vault through which the sun, moon, and stars, hung in place by God, moved on fixed tracks (Gen 1:1–2:4; Ps 8:3; Jer 31:35; Job 38:4, 19, 38; 2 Esd 6:45). In Christ, the relationship between heaven and earth has been reordered. This radical spatial disruption further strengthens this visualization of a paradigm shift: the advent of "a new heaven and a new earth" (2 Pet 3:13; Rev 21:1). The open invitation extended to the viewer is to become a part of this new creation (2 Cor 5:17; Gal 6:15; Col 3:10).[36]

Echoes of countless refrains heralding Christ as the Word of God, through whom all things came into being (John 1:1–5), and Sophia Wisdom, the tree of life (Prov 4:13), with God in the beginning (Prov

---

35. Rudolph Arnheim, *The Power of the Center: A Study of Composition in the Visual Arts* (Berkeley: University of California Press, 2009), 73.

36. Almost every lection cited here forms part of a liturgical text and may be found in the Revised Common Lectionary. See an excellent digital resource for checking the place of a particular lection in the liturgical calendar: "Revised Common Lectionary," Vanderbilt Jean and Alexander Heard Libraries, Divinity Library, https://lectionary.library.vanderbilt.edu//search.php.

8:22–31; 9:1–6), resonate profoundly with this image. It might be said this graphic design is a visual paean to Col 1:15–20:

> He is the image of the invisible God, the firstborn of all creation;
> for in him all things in heaven and on earth were created, things visible and invisible, whether thrones or dominions or rulers or powers—all things have been created through him and for him.
> He himself is before all things, and in him all things hold together.

Markell's *Christ* sets the tone, informing us that each of these Evangelical Lutheran Worship volumes has a christological focus, consistent with the hermeneutical agenda of the lectionary itself. A lectionary is a curation of diverse biblical texts often organized around theological themes pertinent to a liturgical season and arranged around a perceived intertextual connection. The graphic designs in the lectionary reflect this. In a sense, this is a masthead design, the signature graphic that defines the visual register and modalities for the entire series of liturgical books. It functions as a graphic legend of sorts for the illustrations that appear throughout the Evangelical Lutheran Worship series, through the treatment of the human form, the use of silhouette, color, line, central composition, and other consistent aspects of style, issues to which we will return in the following pages.

1.4. Outline of Study

The past pages have provided a brief introduction to some of the ways graphic design of the Bible works and have offered suggestions for how to read a biblically based graphic image. The chapters that follow set out to reveal, clarify and demonstrate the visual meaning-making at work, offering the reader the reader a comprehensive introduction to graphic design as a form of biblical reception. Chapter 2 seeks to situate this project within the context of the current emerging field of biblical reception history research. Having perceived certain gaps in this area presently, as discussed above, I lay out the relevance of my proposed methodological approach and subject matter in relation to the broader field, its methodological and hermeneutical concerns and debates. In chapter 3 I focus specifically on semiotics and expand on the social semiotics of the visual approach advanced by Kress and van Leeuwen. Chapter 4 considers the iconic liturgical books of the lectionary and the missal as a site of reception of the Bible. What are these books, and how did they emerge out of ancient Jewish and Christian reading practices? What is their function in Christian liturgies today?

One historical and traditional design pattern that is repeated in contemporary lectionaries is the color triad of black, red, and white, a triad that is brought to wonderful intersemiotic expression in the work of Markell. Craighead's illustrations, on the other hand, are black and white—but within this long-standing triadic color formula of liturgical books and Bible printing. Silhouette is a graphic device deployed to great effect by both designers, in thoroughly different ways but toward the same theological ends. Color and silhouette are the subjects of chapters 5 and 6 respectively. Finally, in chapters 7 and 8 I turn to the graphic designs in question, briefly introduced here, and offer a thorough semiotic analysis of these two key works, one by each artist.

This study suggests that both graphic design and liturgical contexts are untapped areas of investigation for those interested in biblical reception and that social semiotics may be a valuable resource for those engaging with visual reception. May this short introduction serve as an invitation to delve into this book and the approach I am advancing for the biblical reception history project.

2
Biblical Reception History: Charting the Field

> Scripture ... is constantly liable to be discovered somewhere other than where we thought we had put it for safekeeping.
> —Ben Quash, *Found Theology*

How do graphically designed images function semiotically in the reception of biblical texts? This is the searching question at the heart of this exploration. In this chapter I situate the quest for an answer within the broader discourse of contemporary biblical reception history studies. This project draws, theoretically, from two established strands of academic theory: hermeneutics and semiotics (fig. 2.1). The academic areas—biblical reception history and a semiotics of the visual—may be visualized as siblings on a family tree descending from these two parents, hermeneutics and semiotics. Hermeneutics, the philosophy of interpretation, has given rise to an area of interpretation studies known as reception history: the study of the reception of texts by individual readers and in turn, in societies, cultures, and epochs. Semiotics, on the other hand, is the field of examining the meaning-making structures, dynamics, and functions operative in all forms of communication.[1] In this sense reception history

---

1. Those to first formalize semiotics, in the European context most especially, have historically understood themselves foremostly to be linguists and have placed semiotics within their field of linguistics, Saussure being the preeminent example. Contemporary semioticians (Eco, Kress, van Leeuwen, Hodge, Jewitt), linguists (Halliday), and cultural theorists (Bal) have argued for an inversion of this understanding, tending to favor an understanding of semiotics as the larger category in which linguistics is to be found. This is a corrective to the perceived hegemony of language in efforts to theorize about communication generally—the "verbocentric dogmatism" (Eco) or "linguistic imperialism" (Mitchell) that has prevailed heretofore. See Umberto Eco, *A*

and a semiotics of the visual are metaphorical siblings of a sort, employing different methodologies, yet concerned with meaning and how meaning is made and received by readers and viewers. These four areas—hermeneutics and reception history, semiotics and a semiotics of the visual—form the foundation of this endeavor. My methodology for analyzing the graphic designs will be drawn from semiotics, and the context in which these images occur, illustrating lectionaries and missals, places them in the social context of the church and within the reception history of the Bible.

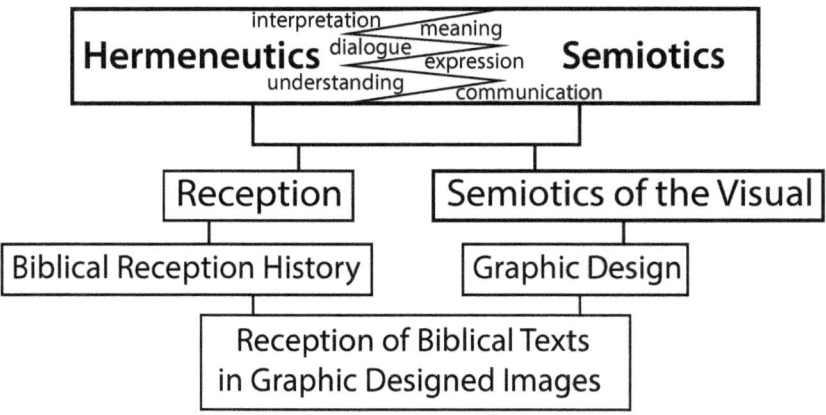

Fig. 2.1. A diagrammatic outline locating this study, a reception of biblical texts in graphically designed images, within the hermeneutical frame of reception history (left) and the methodological frame of semiotics (right).

This chapter focuses on biblical reception history. It is necessary at the outset to consider the foundational influence of the two major theorists, Hans-Georg Gadamer and Hans Robert Jauss, on whom biblical scholars draw. Following that I will offer an overview of the broader field of biblical reception history within which this study is located. This is a contested academic area, and the prevailing discussions and issues will be briefly reviewed here. Finally, I will take a closer look at the work and practice of biblical reception scholars who are particularly engaged in exploring the reception of the Bible in images.

Theory of Semiotics (London: Macmillan, 1977), 228; William J. T. Mitchell, *Iconology: Image, Text, Ideology* (Chicago: University of Chicago Press, 1986), 56.

This chapter is concerned with the left-hand stream of the diagram below (fig. 2.1), that which emerges from the field of hermeneutics. The following chapter will focus on the right-hand stream of the diagram, that which emerges from the field of semiotics.

2.1. The Influence of Hans-Georg Gadamer and Hans Robert Jauss

The contemporary study of the reception of the Bible finds its initial impulse in the foundational philosophical work of the two German theorists, Hans-Georg Gadamer (1900–2002) and Hans Robert Jauss (1921–1997). The influence of both is readily felt in the debates and endeavors of biblical exegetes working within this dynamic and burgeoning area of biblical reception history. Gadamer is renowned as a leading figure of influence in contemporary hermeneutics, an approach to the philosophy of understanding, meaning, and interpretation.[2] Traces of the study of hermeneutics can now be found across diverse fields and disciplines in the social sciences and humanities, ranging from anthropology to literary studies and including biblical studies.[3] Gadamer studied under both Edmund Husserl (1859–1938) and Martin Heidegger (1889–1976) and was influenced by the earlier work of Wilhelm Dilthey (1833–1911).[4] *Truth and Method* (*Wahrheit und Methode*), Gadamer's magnum opus, first published in 1960, has become important to a specific group of biblical scholars inter-

---

2. Hans-Georg Gadamer was born in Marburg, Germany, in 1900 and died in Heidelberg in 2002. He completed his doctoral dissertation on Plato, under Nicolai Hartmann and Paul Natorp at the University of Marburg. He moved to the University of Freiburg in 1923, where he studied under Husserl and Heidegger, who were more influential over his philosophical development. He lectured at many German universities, including Marburg, Kiel, Leipzig, Frankfurt, and Heidelberg. Following his retirement in 1968, he frequently traveled to lecture in the United States, where he maintained a long association with Boston College.

3. The significance of Gadamer's hermeneutics for the field of art is discussed by Dennis J. Schmidt, *Between Word and Image: Heidegger, Klee, and Gadamer on Gesture and Genesis* (Bloomington: Indiana University Press, 2013), 106–40. See also Nicholas Davey, "The Hermeneutics of Seeing," in *Interpreting Visual Culture: Explorations in the Hermeneutics of the Visual*, ed. Ian Heywood and Barry Sandywell (London: Routledge, 1999), 3–30.

4. Stanley E. Porter and Jason C. Robinson, *Hermeneutics: An Introduction to Interpretive Theory* (Grand Rapids: Eerdmans, 2011), 74.

ested in studying the nature of biblical interpretation.[5] Part of Gadamer's initial impetus was a refutation of the dominance of exclusively scientific and technological methods of arriving at a truth claim. "The experience of the sociohistorical world cannot be raised to a science by the inductive procedure of the natural sciences," he maintained.[6] Gadamer shifts the emphasis in studying interpretation away from the intention of the author, the dominant focus at the time, toward the actual reader-in-context in front of the text and the dialogical event of meaning that happens between the text and the reader. Arising from this is the term *Horizontverschmelzung*, or "fusion of horizons."[7] Understanding is, for Gadamer, a dialectical movement, whereupon one interacts with a text, responding to one's own tradition, while rethinking what was believed to be true as a result of what is encountered currently in the text. Understanding is not something one does but rather an event, an experience, something that occurs when a person engages with another person or object. This hermeneutical event is a linguistic "fusing of the objective and subjective that creates new horizons of possibility, i.e. new meanings and understandings."[8]

Gadamer views prejudice as a constitutive element of human existence; consequently, the prejudices people inherit are not necessarily either negative or positive in nature. The hermeneutical concept of prejudice, as used by Gadamer, comes from the German *Vorurteil* ("prejudgment"). Gadamer defined *Vorurteil* as the cognitive processes and ways of understanding the world that function in people's thinking at a preconceptual or prereflective level.[9] All people are formed within social and cultural traditions, some of which are considerably deeper than they may recognize

---

5. Dennis Schmidt highlights three critical texts of this year 1960 that sought to reexamine philosophical approaches to artworks, including Gadamer's *Truth and Method*—the others being the slightly revised reissue of Heidegger's previously published lecture "The Origin of the Work of Art" and Merleau-Ponty's essay "Eye and Mind." He posits German artist Paul Klee as being a pivotal influence, not only in his paintings but significantly also in his writings on these three philosophers—as well as Adorno, Foucault, Deleuze, Lyotard, and others (Schmidt, *Between Word and Image*, 106).

6. Hans-Georg Gadamer, *Truth and Method*, trans. Joel C. Weinsheimer and Donald G. Marshall (London: Bloomsbury, 2013), 4.

7. Gadamer, *Truth and Method*, 318.

8. Porter and Robinson, *Hermeneutics*, 86.

9. Gadamer, *Truth and Method*, 282. See David Paul Parris, *Reception Theory and Biblical Hermeneutics* (Eugene, OR: Pickwick, 2009), 3.

and from which they may not be able to extract themselves. These have an impact nonetheless on how people interpret the events around them. Gadamer's view of tradition, history, and prejudice informs his concept of *Wirkungsgeschichte*, the recognition that all interpretation is historically and linguistically situated. He contends, "The real meaning of a text, as it speaks to the interpreter, does not depend on the contingencies of the author and his original audience. It certainly is not identical with them, for it is always co-determined also by the historical situation of the interpreter and hence by the totality of the objective course of history."[10]

Gadamer's three primary concerns in *Truth and Method* are aesthetic experience, historical consciousness, and language. Martin O'Kane notes, however, "Since hermeneutics traditionally has placed so much importance on language, especially its written forms, his influence on biblical hermeneutics has generally been restricted to the aspect of language, while his application to biblical visual culture has remained largely unexplored."[11] Given his interest in the nature of understanding and his concern with the social-relational dimension of communication, Gadamer proves to be an important dialogical partner when considering the multimodal discourse put forth by Kress and van Leeuwen in their examination of the meaning-making potential of images.

Hans Robert Jauss, a student of Gadamer's, belonged to a small group of scholars who gathered in the German city of Konstanz in the second half of the last century and came to be known as the Konstanz school.[12] Jauss came to attention in 1967 with his inaugural address "Literary History

---

10. Gadamer, *Truth and Method*, 296.

11. Martin O'Kane, *Painting the Text: The Artist as Biblical Interpreter* (Sheffield: Sheffield Phoenix, 2007), 37–38. He acknowledges that "the application of Gadamer's hermeneutical esthetics to interpreting visual culture is central to current debates in other disciplines such as critical theory, post-modern philosophy, aesthetic theory, deconstruction and cultural studies."

12. Hans Robert Jauss was born in Württemberg, Germany, in 1921 and died in Konstanz in 1997. Jauss was a member of the SS during World War II and served on the Russian front. He was imprisoned after the war before completing his studies. From 1948–1954 he was at Heidelberg, where Heidegger and Gadamer were very influential in his philosophical development. He later taught at the universities of Münster and Gießen before joining the staff, in 1966, of the new University of Constance. This was a year before Jauss delivered his seminal inaugural address with a new vision for interdisciplinary research. He also traveled much and taught at the University of Zürich, the Freie Universität Berlin, Columbia, Yale, the Sorbonne, the

as a Challenge to Literary Theory," from which his reputation as a leading figure in reception theory arose.[13] He proposed seven theses in this seminal paper that have been taken up to varying degrees by recent biblical scholars. Appropriating Thomas Kuhn's thesis of paradigm shift, Jauss deliberately intended to shock, suggests Robert Holub, announcing a "'revolution' in the making, to proclaim the end of the *ancien régime* of literary scholarship."[14] Jauss engaged with two adverse methodologies, Marxism and formalism, rejecting Marxism as outmoded and crediting formalism with introducing aesthetic perception as a theoretical tool for exploring literary works. Having critiqued both schools as paying far too little attention to the "reader, listener, and spectator—in short, the factor of the audience," Jauss perceived himself as picking up where they left off.[15]

> My attempt to bridge the gap between literature and history, between historical and aesthetic approaches, begins at the point at which both schools stop. Their methods conceive the *literary fact* within the closed circle of an aesthetics of production and of representation. In doing so, they deprive literature of a dimension that inalienably belongs to its aesthetic character as well as to its social function: the dimension of its reception and influence.[16]

Rezeptionsästhetik, or the "aesthetics of reception," is the name Jauss gave to his theory in the late 1960s and early 1970s. Jauss developed Gadamer's analysis of horizons, adding the further dimension of a "horizon of expectation," or *Erwartungshorizont*. This horizon of expectation varies from one historical period to another: the same text can be valued in one period and rejected in another. The horizon of expectation is construed in both

---

University of Leuven, the University of California, Berkeley, Princeton, and the University of Wisconsin–Madison.

13. Hans Robert Jauss, *Toward an Aesthetic of Reception*, trans. Timothy Bahti (Minneapolis: University of Minnesota Press, 1982), 3–45. "Literary History as a Challenge to Literary Theory" features as chapter 1 of the volume.

14. Robert C. Holub, *Reception Theory: A Critical Introduction* (New York: Routledge, 1984), 54. Timothy Beal affirms, "The rise of the reception history of the Bible has indeed been revolutionary." See Beal, "Reception History and Beyond: Towards the Cultural History of the Scriptures," *BibInt* 19 (2011): 369. Kuhn's theory of "paradigm shift" can be found in Thomas Kuhn, *The Structure of Scientific Revolutions* (Chicago: University of Chicago Press, 1962).

15. Jauss, *Toward an Aesthetic*, 18.

16. Jauss, *Toward an Aesthetic*, 18.

the individual and the society, through the previous experiences of reading (or hearing) texts, with all the contingent exposures to different genres and forms, subject matter, and so forth, alongside the life experiences and memories of the readers within the cultural contexts of particular times and places. Jauss writes,

> A literary work is not an object that stands by itself and that offers the same view to each reader in each period. It is not a monument that monologically reveals its timeless essence. It is much more like an orchestration that strikes ever new resonances among its readers and that frees the text from the material of the words and brings it to a contemporary existence.[17]

Many aspects of Jauss's proposal overlap with aspects of Kress and van Leeuwen's social semiotics of the visual in significant and congruent ways, not least in these aspects of social context and this fluid approach to the meaning potential of the text. Jauss understood a work of literature as an event, not a fact, and believed that this moment of encounter between a text and a receiver of the text, the moment of meaningful relationship, must be historicized just as any earlier event, including the text's original creation.

Timothy Beal suggests that Jauss's aesthetics of reception are an "interruption" of Gadamer's notions of history and interpretation within the discourse of literary theory. Beal writes,

> Jauss essentially argued, in good Gadamerian fashion, that literary history is not a history of influence from an original text on its subsequent readers, but rather a history of hermeneutical fusions of horizons of pasts and presents, and that all of this history is part of the historical development and concretization of a work's meaning, thus transforming the canon itself over time within different "horizons of expectation" which are by no means individual but are constructed by one's culture, language, psychology, and so on (i.e., one's effective history).[18]

Robert Evans, in his monograph *Reception History, Tradition and Biblical Interpretation: Gadamer and Jauss in Current Practice*, takes an in-depth look at the reception of Gadamer and Jauss in contemporary biblical

---

17. Jauss, *Toward an Aesthetic*, 21.
18. Beal, "Reception History and Beyond," 363; Jauss, *Toward an Aesthetic*, 22.

studies and the differing approaches biblical scholars have taken in appropriating their philosophies and theories of interpretation. This study serves to provide a comprehensive overview of the current struggle concerning reception history in academic biblical studies and the breadth of work being undertaken. John Sawyer makes a similar undertaking in his discussion of the origins of interest in the reception history of the Hebrew Bible to a noticeable shift of emphasis in biblical studies in the 1990s, due mainly to the influence of feminist studies, liberation theology, and postmodernism.[19] Evans, in his volume, considers particularly the debates about the meanings of *Wirkungsgeschichte* and *Rezeptionsgeschichte*. He undertakes case studies of three different selections of Pauline texts, applying various methods drawn from the practices of other contemporary biblical scholars as a way of considering how Gadamerian and Jaussian approaches affect the interpretation of these texts. He notes that "the variety of method and different claims made for hermeneutical principles raise a number of questions, which some critics interpret as inadequate engagement with reception theory." He is at pains to insist that neither Gadamer nor Jauss supplies "a full methodological framework, nor objective criteria for 'validity' of interpretation of what a text can be held to 'mean.'"[20]

Having considered the overarching debate about the relationship between reception history and historical-critical exegesis, Evans also looks at the form of reception history itself, with a focus on the issue of which acts of reception are selected and valorized, and the role of tradition, prejudgments, and theology in relation to reception history. Throughout his monograph, he juxtaposes the work of biblical scholars from differing sectors and highlights their strengths and failings when held up against the hermeneutical principles laid out by Gadamer and Jauss. Evans argues that "neither Gadamer nor Jauss provides objective methodological criteria for constructing or valorizing a particular trajectory of interpretation in preference to another."[21] Christine Joynes suggests that Jauss transforms Gadamer's approach and treats reception history as a method that can be adopted, in contrast with Gadamer's own critique of empirical methodologies.[22]

---

19. John F. A. Sawyer, "A Critical Review of Recent Projects and Publications," *HBAI* 1 (2012): 298–329.

20. Evans, *Reception History*, 1, 23.

21. Evans, *Reception History*, 114.

22. Christine E. Joynes, "Changing Horizons: Reflections on a Decade at Oxford University's Center for Reception History of the Bible," *JBRec* 1 (2014): 163.

Evans is inclined to divide contemporary biblical scholars into two camps: as under the influence of either Gadamer or Jauss in their work.[23] However, as Anthony Thiselton has noted, one should be cautious of pigeonholing scholars in this way. Thiselton, who has focused predominantly on Gadamer's hermeneutics, has recently turned his attention to Jauss. This may have been prompted by Ormond Rush's thesis, in which he appropriates Jauss for theology (as distinct from biblical studies), drawing parallels between theology and the seven theses of Jauss.[24] Thiselton does something very similar drawing out direct parallels with biblical interpretation.[25] Jauss touched on biblical themes himself occasionally, for example in an article in the literary criticism journal *Comparative Literature*, "Job's Questions and Their Distant Reply: Goethe, Nietzsche, Heidegger."[26] There he analyzes the dialogue between Job and God and examines the literary interpretations of the questions and answers in the book of Job. He also produced an example of his theory practiced in "A Questioning Adam: On the History of the Functions of Question and Answer" in the volume *Question and Answer*.[27] The second volume of Jauss's work, *Aesthetic Experience and Literary Hermeneutics*, engages with the work of Theodor Adorno and aesthetic experience.[28] It touches briefly on the religious dimension of aesthetic experience.

With regard to the appropriation of the work of Gadamer and Jauss by biblical scholars, "Ulrich Luz is probably the most important New Testament scholar to have practiced reception history explicitly, in his three volume commentary on Matthew," maintains Thiselton.[29] Evans

---

23. Evans, *Reception History*, 13.

24. Ormond Rush, *The Reception of Doctrine: An Appropriation of Hans Robert Jauss' Reception Aesthetics and Literary Hermeneutics* (Rome: Gregorian & Biblical Press, 1997).

25. Anthony Thiselton, "Reception Theory, H. R. Jauss and the Formative Power of Scripture," *SJT* 65 (2012): 289–308.

26. Hans Robert Jauss and Sharon Larisch, "Job's Questions and Their Distant Reply: Goethe, Nietzsche, Heidegger," *CompLit* 34 (1982): 193–207.

27. Hans Robert Jauss, "Horizon Structure and Dialogicity," in *Question and Answer: Forms of Dialogic Understanding*, ed. and trans. Michael Hays, THL 68 (Minneapolis: University of Minnesota Press, 1989), 199–207.

28. Hans Robert Jauss, *Aesthetic Experience and Literary Hermeneutics* (Minneapolis: University of Minnesota Press, 2008).

29. Thiselton, "Reception Theory," 290. Finnish scholar Heikki Räisänen criticizes Luz for insufficient precision in the "destination" of *Auslegungsgeschichte* and

reiterates this assertion: "A key work that has promoted the practice of *Wirkungsgeschichte* in New Testament studies is Luz's commentary on Matthew (1985-2002) in the *Evangelisch-Katholischer Kommentar* series."[30] Luz has stirred up much debate around Gadamer's meaning of the term *Wirkungsgeschichte* and its appropriation by contemporary biblical scholars. He offers an image of the *Auslegungsgeschichte* ("history of interpretation") and the *Wirkungsgeschichte* ("history of influence") as being "related to each other like two concentric circles so that "history of influence" is inclusive of "history of interpretation." He makes a distinction between "the types of source material used, reflecting a convention that *Auslegungsgeschichte* usually or properly refers to the history of scholarship to be found in theological commentaries on the text. It is other parts of the legacy of the Church, hymns, prayers, art and confession, that can be called *Wirkungsgeschichte*."[31]

In making this distinction, Luz maintains that he is following his teacher Gerhard Ebeling, who defined church history as "the history of the exposition of Scripture," and the "exposition of Scripture," writes Luz, "was for him what we call 'reception history today,' including 'interpretations of the Bible in non-verbal media such as art, music, dancing, prayer' and also 'in political actions, wars, peace-making, suffering, institutions.'"[32] This reference by Luz to nonverbal media alludes to the multimodal dimension of reception of the Bible that is of particular relevance to this study, namely, iconic liturgical books used in the liturgies of gathered Christian communities.

Wirkungsgeschichte. See Räisänen, *Challenges to Biblical Interpretation* (Leiden: Brill, 2001), 271. Räisänen has in turn come in for criticism from both Evans and Markus Bockmuehl for his reading of Luz. Bockmuehl, however, agrees with Räisänen "that *Wirkungsgeschichte* is not to be restricted to mere legitimation of the *status quo*: 'The effective history of the Bible cannot be reduced to its effect on the formation of the traditions of creedal orthodoxy. Nor must it be seen as merely a way to legitimize certain conservative interpretations." See Bockmuehl, "A Commentator's Approach to the 'Effective History' of Philippians," *JSNT* 60 (1995): 57-88.

30. Evans, *Reception History*, 14.

31. Ulrich Luz, *Matthew 1-7: A Commentary*, trans. Wilhelm C. Linss (Edinburgh: T&T Clark, 1989), 95, 98; Luz, *Matthew 8-20: A Commentary*, trans. James E. Crouch (Minneapolis: Augsburg Fortress, 2001), 11.

32. Luz, *Matthew 1-7*, 95; Gerhard Ebeling, *The Word and Tradition: Historical Studies Interpreting the Divisions of Christianity*, trans. S. H. Hooke (Philadelphia: Fortress, 1968), 28.

The church is present as the community which shaped and formed the biblical texts, and which made the Bible its book par excellence by creating and handing down the canon. The church is present as the "home" that enabled our predecessors to undertake their interpretations, actualizations, reshaping and after-experiences of biblical texts, and directed them in their task. The church is present as the area of society which was primarily formed by the biblical texts and as the place where they are effective. The church is present when the Bible is read, as a space open to the past, and the place where the biblical texts of the past are proclaimed, read, interpreted or celebrated. The church is the "mother" of such reading, the "midwife" of understanding, or quite simply a point of reference without which the biblical texts—which are after all the church's canonical texts—cannot come into view at all.[33]

This study focuses on graphic designs made to illustrate lectionaries and missals. The whole concept of a lectionary, ancient as it may be, is about the curation of biblical texts. This is an extraordinary act of biblical reception. For each Sunday of the year, four biblical lections are chosen from the whole corpus of the Bible and brought together in a deliberate arrangement.[34] These include a lection and a psalm from the Hebrew Bible, a lection from the New Testament (apart from the Gospels), and a gospel reading. Wherever possible, the Hebrew Bible lection and gospel reading, most particularly, are understood to relate to each other in some meaningful way. Ideally, each lection and the psalm interact meaningfully with each other to draw out deeper meanings. The one will provide the hermeneutical key to the other, born from one tradition within ecclesial exegesis that perceives the New Testament to be anticipated in the Old Testament and the Old revealed as fulfilled in the New.[35] The lectionary, then, is a unique and profoundly rich site of the reception of Scripture within the context of the church. As will be discussed at greater length in chapter 4, the lectionaries in use today essentially emerged from the Second Vatican Council and quickly gained ecumenical acceptance and

---

33. Ulrich Luz, *Studies in Matthew*, trans. Rosemary Selle (Grand Rapids: Eerdmans, 2005), 350.

34. There is also a weekday lectionary that features three readings, most often a lection and a psalm from the HB and a gospel reading. During the season of Eastertide, readings from the Acts of the Apostles may replace the HB lection, in both Sunday and weekday lectionaries.

35. Pontifical Biblical Commission, *The Interpretation of the Bible in the Church* (Boston: Pauline Media, 1993), 91.

implementation through many denominations. This study focuses on a small but important area of such reception.

2.2. The Critical Debate concerning Reception History in Biblical Studies

Susan Gillingham, in a recent article, refers to an overheard remark about biblical reception studies that it is "Biblical Studies on holiday."[36] This aligns with a similar attitude that I have encountered where it is occasionally, condescendingly, referred to as "Biblical studies *lite*." These comments capture succinctly what is sometimes referred to as the crisis in academic biblical studies at this present juncture. The crisis is characterized by a conflict between the prevailing hegemonic paradigm of traditional historical-critical biblical studies, with its emphasis on ancient biblical languages and the historical context—archaeological, cultural, religious, and linguistic—within which the Scriptures were written and redacted, and newer emerging methodologies. This contest is by no means limited to biblical studies but is reflective of what can be seen far beyond the academy and is consistent with the prevailing, pervasive atmosphere of uncertainty fueled by the phenomenal level of change happening in every dimension of contemporary life. Disciplines such as biblical studies that have been built on sturdy theoretical and philosophical foundations have been destabilized by rapid cultural and technological changes.

Some of this uncertainty is reflected in critiques leveled at those doing biblical reception history, such as in the concerns that its methods seem unclear. The resistance against newer forms of biblical studies is sometimes characterized by a complaint that its methodologies do not conform to those within the historical-critical method.[37] The insistence that the only reliably academic approach to studying the Bible is through the traditional historical-critical method is perceived by reception history scholars as deeply problematic, as it consistently fails to consider the meaning of

---

36. Susan Gillingham, "Biblical Studies on Holiday? A Personal View of Reception History," in *Reception History and Biblical Studies: Theory and Practice*, ed. Emma England and William John Lyons (London: Bloomsbury, 2015), 17–30.

37. There are different branches with the historical-critical method, such as textual criticism, redaction criticism, and so forth. The online debate around biblical languages is well documented in various places, including in Larry Hurtado, "Tools of the Trade," Larry Hurtado's Blog, September 4, 2011, https://tinyurl.com/SBL6701d.

the Bible for later and contemporary readers and receivers of its message. New Testament scholar Bradley McLean maintains that biblical studies "in the present continues to be guided by the theoretical structure of the 19th century historicism, in the form of historical positivism."[38]

> The situation in which we find ourselves is all the more serious because with the discipline's ongoing fixation on historically based methodologies has come a corresponding dislocation with new developments in the closely related fields of study in the humanities and social sciences. For example, the impact on contemporary biblical studies of such movements as post-structuralism, psychotherapy, feminism, critical theory, neopragmatism, gender studies, New Historicism and post colonial criticism, to name but a few, has been modest in comparison with the continued hegemony of the discipline's traditional methodologies.[39]

Holub's rather narrow early critique of reception theory still finds an echo in some contemporary criticisms leveled at reception history in biblical studies:

> Reception theory has undoubtedly had a tremendous impact on the way in which literary studies are now conducted, but the paths it has explored have not always proved to be as open and productive as originally envisioned. Detours, dead ends, and circular trails have been frequently traveled. These become apparent when reception theory is confronted with the variety of positions associated with structuralist, poststructuralist, or other avant-garde directions in France and in the United States. For in these theories we likewise encounter a proliferation of discourses that challenge the dominant way of thinking about literature—and frequently in a more radical, if not always a more productive, fashion.[40]

Even those sympathetic to moving beyond historically based readings—including a focus on theoretical issues—have raised questions concerning reception history and method. Biblical scholars such as Roland Boer have been outrightly critical, while Stephen Moore and Yvonne Sherwood have called for clarity from reception history scholars about their methods, engagement with critical theory, appropriations

---

38. Bradley H. McLean, *Biblical Interpretation and Philosophical Hermeneutics* (Cambridge: Cambridge University Press, 2012), 3.
39. McLean, *Biblical Interpretation*, vii.
40. Holub, *Reception Theory*, 148.

of Gadamer and Jauss, and direction more generally.⁴¹ Mark Knight applauds the evident plurality of approaches in contrast with those others, such as Beal and Lamb, who are concerned to define terms more precisely in an effort to alleviate ongoing confusion.⁴² James Crossley openly acknowledges that there is, in some quarters, an "'anything goes' approach which has little concern for historical theology or 'correct interpretation.'"⁴³ However, he also points out that the precarious position of biblical studies in most universities means that "we cannot justify the importance of Biblical Studies by making the staple argument that the Bible is hugely important for people today and then keep studying the ancient contexts alone."⁴⁴ Biblical studies, then, is suspended in this fraught position between the historical positivism that "continues to serve a gate-keeping role within the discipline," which is severely under strain to justify its value, and continued existence in the modern secular university and beyond.⁴⁵

McLean pulls no punches in his critique of those gatekeepers who resist the development of the discipline, referring to the normalizing of "the outmoded epistemological framework of the Enlightenment with the result that other ways of knowing continue to be marginalized and excluded."⁴⁶ Brennan Breed, meanwhile, brings a quite different and interesting perspective to the debate, questioning the claimed boundaries between these two approaches and the understandings scholars maintain about what constitutes the original text and where reception begins.⁴⁷

---

41. Roland Boer, "Against 'Reception History,'" Bible and Interpretation, https://tinyurl.com/SBLPress6701d1; Stephen D. Moore and Yvonne Sherwood, *The Invention of the Biblical Scholar: A Critical Manifesto* (Minneapolis: Fortress, 2011), 101.

42. Mark Knight, "Wirkungsgeschichte, Reception History, Reception Theory," *JSNT* 33.2 (2010): 144–45; Beal, "Reception History and Beyond"; William R. S. Lamb, *The Catena in Marcum: A Byzantine Anthology of Early Commentary on Mark* (Leiden: Brill, 2012), 5.

43. James G. Crossley, *Reading the New Testament: Contemporary Approaches* (London: Routledge, 2010), 129.

44. James G. Crossley, "The End of Reception History, a Grand Narrative for Biblical Studies and the Neoliberal Bible," in England and Lyons, *Reception History and Biblical Studies*, 47.

45. McLean, *Biblical Interpretation*, 61.

46. McLean, *Biblical Interpretation*, 7.

47. Brennan W. Breed, *Nomadic Text: A Theory of Biblical Reception* (Bloomington: Indiana University Press, 2014), 3.

Due to discoveries in the Judaean desert, we now know that several biblical books existed in multiple, irreducible versions in antiquity, and that some textual differences presumed to be later corruptions or recensions are in fact alternative ancient versions, often composed in the "original" Hebrew. Textual critics are now shifting ever closer to the position that the Bible did not originate from pristine manuscripts, and neither was there one consistent line of authorship or editing that culminated in the communal authorization of a final, authoritative manuscript. Reception historians are in a position to ask some difficult questions about this original complexity, because if it is true that we study forms of texts and meanings in "later" periods, then we ascertain where the boundary lies between the original period and what we should be studying. Upon inspection, it appears that the history of a biblical text is a long process that often has indistinct beginnings, discontinuities and irreducibly different versions of the same text. What is the history of a text then, but a form of reception history.[48]

Further, Emma England and John Lyons are convinced, in their collaboration, that "there is no single methodology suitable for competent reception studies and the methodologies that do exist are still in their infancy."[49] Rather, a more measured and patient approach is required, and a willingness to allow for diversity within the development of new methodologies. It is important for scholars to resist the urge to appease critics by rushing to settle a methodology. One fixed methodology is neither suitable nor desirable, as reception history covers many different areas and ranges across a vast historical period, as the abovementioned recent contributions indicate. Nevertheless, methodological reflection should not be ignored, an issue to which I return in the following chapter.

Looking across to visual studies, it is pertinent to note that methodological shifts are not restricted to biblical studies but have been experienced there too. Barry Sandywell writes,

> Critical reflection within visual studies has moved from *inter*-disciplinary to *multi*-disciplinary and finally to *trans*-disciplinary—and perhaps *in*-disciplinary and *post*-disciplinary—research and theorizing. This questioning of disciplinary preconceptions and historical institutional

---

48. Brennan Breed, "What Can a Text Do? Reception History as an Ethology of the Biblical Text," in England and Lyons, *Reception History and Biblical Studies*, 97.

49. Emma England and William John Lyons, "Explorations in the Reception of the Bible," in England and Lyons, *Reception History and Biblical Studies*, 5.

boundaries is itself part of the larger social, economic and cultural processes that theorists express with the difficult concepts of *postmodernisation* and *globalization*.⁵⁰

Semiotician Gunther Kress reflects on this impact of globalization:

> The effects of this vastly diverse and complex phenomenon have led in very many places to the corrosion, fraying, dissolution, destruction and abandonment of older social relations, forms, structures, "givens." Globalization is not one "thing"; it is differently constituted in different places, as are its effects and impacts, interacting with the vastly varied cultural, social, economic and political conditions of any one specific locality. Yet the deep effects are constant and recognizable everywhere. They have brought a move from a *relative* stability of the social world over maybe the last two centuries (as in Western Europe) to an often radical instability over the last three decades or so. Stemming from that—and generated by it—are far reaching changes in the domain of meaning: in representation and in "semiotic production"; in dissemination and distribution of messages and meanings; in mediation and communication. All have profoundly changed. The semiotic effects are recognizable … most markedly … at the level of *semiotic production* in the shift from the dominance of the mode of *writing* to the mode of *image*. Academic interest in the characteristics of this new communicational world, the world of the screen and of multimodality, has been relatively belated, stumbling after the horse which had left the stable some while ago. Belated or not, there is a need to catch up and get back in the saddle.⁵¹

Kress's critique of academia's failure to deal with these changes wrought by postmodernity and globalization parallels McLean's perceived "tyranny of historicism" within biblical scholarship.⁵² Both are articulating similar failures in different academic fields of biblical studies and visual studies. Reception history is a constructive effort to catch up and get

---

50. Barry Sandywell and Ian Heywood, "Critical Approaches to the Study of Visual Culture: An Introduction to the Handbook," in *The Handbook of Visual Culture*, ed. Ian Heywood, Barry Sandywell, and Michael Gardiner (London: Bloomsbury, 2012), 4.

51. Gunther R. Kress, *Multimodality: A Social Semiotic Approach to Contemporary Communication* (New York: Routledge, 2009), 5–6, emphasis original.

52. McLean, *Biblical Interpretation*, 7.

back in the saddle, to grapple precisely with this new reality, with these "far reaching changes in the domain of meaning."[53]

2.3. Biblical Reception as an Emerging Area in Biblical Studies

Marcus Bockmuehl, writing in 1995, described the Bible's influence on culture as "very largely *terra incognita*, an unknown blank on the map of New Testament scholarship."[54] Evidently, this is no longer the case. The level of interest in reception history of the Bible is now reflected in the increasing quantity and range of publications being produced by academic publishers in the field. Much of this has happened since the turn of the millennium. Christopher Rowland, in his explication of the hermeneutical criteria informing the Blackwell Bible Commentary Series, writes, "The main difference about our commentary series is that the historical-critical exegesis is included as a part of *Wirkungsgeschichte* rather than as a primary datum to which matters of *Wirkungsgeschichte* can be added."[55] On the website, the editors make clear their purpose in this series: "'Reception history' combines the study of the *effects* of biblical materials on culture with the study of the *uses* to which people have put the Bible through the centuries."[56]

---

53. It is worth noting that those who study the semiotics of religion recognize the inauguration of printing (fifteenth century) on a large scale as a similar far-reaching change in the domain of meaning, as it facilitated a paradigm shift away from orality and image toward the authority and primacy of the printed word. See Robert A. Yelle, *The Semiotics of Religion: Signs of the Sacred in History* (London: Bloomsbury, 2013), 113–36. Elizabeth Eisenstein maintains, "Printing made it possible to dispense with the use of images for mnemonic purposes.... Printing fostered a movement from 'image culture to word culture.'" See Eisenstein, *The Printing Press as an Agent of Change: Communications and Cultural Transformations in Early-Modern Europe* (Cambridge: Cambridge University Press, 1980), 66–67.

54. Bockmuehl, "Commentator's Approach," 60.

55. Christopher Rowland, "A Pragmatic Approach to Wirkungsgeschichte: Reflections on the Blackwell Bible Commentary Series and on the Writing of Its Commentary on the Apocalypse" (paper presented at the Annual Meeting of the Society of Biblical Literature, San Antonio, Texas, November 2004), http://bbibcomm.info/?page_id=183.

56. "Reception History," Blackwell Bible Commentaries, https://tinyurl.com/SBL6701e. At present, this series has ten or eleven commentaries on individual books

German publisher Walter de Gruyter has established a four-part collection titled The Bible and Its Reception. This includes the projected thirty-volume *Encyclopedia of the Bible and Its Reception*—intended to serve as a comprehensive guide to the current state of knowledge on the background, origins, and development of the canonical texts of the Bible as they were accepted in Judaism and Christianity.[57] Expanding on the *Encyclopedia of the Bible and Its Reception*, de Gruyter is developing a series titled Handbooks of the Bible and Its Reception, offering "in-depth analyzes of selected issues found in *EBR*, focusing on particular themes, regions, figures, and historical contexts." Closely linked to these is a book series Studies of the Bible and Its Reception, which includes monographs and collected volumes that cover the broad field of reception history of the Bible in various religious traditions, historical periods, and cultural fields. Finally, de Gruyter has established a new *Journal of the Bible and Its Reception*. Published twice annually, this peer-reviewed journal began in 2014 and promises to establish itself as a leader in the field, as have de Gruyter's other journals *Zeitschrift für die alttestamentliche Wissenschaft* and *Zeitschrift für die neutestamentliche Wissenschaft*.

Another major reception history project in process is *The Bible and Women: An Encyclopedia of Exegesis and Cultural History*. This important series, of which each volume is published (almost simultaneously) in four languages, German, English, Spanish, and Italian, has a particular concentration on referencing women and gender issues. "The volumes in this encyclopedia study the Bible as 'The Book' of Western culture. They explore how religion has shaped gender identity and roles, stereotypes and relationships between men and women in Western culture."[58]

The Oxford Handbook of the Reception History of the Bible consciously allows for the interplay of the traditional and the new.

---

of the Bible, either published or in print. The series is edited by John Sawyer, Judith Kovacs, Christopher Rowland, David M. Gunn, and Rebecca Harkin.

57. Edited by Dale C. Allison Jr., Christine Helmer, Choon-Leong Seow, Hermann Spieckermann, Barry Dov Walfish, and Eric Ziolkowski.

58. Edited by Irmtraud Fischer, Mercedes Navarro Puerto, Christl M. Maier, Nuria Calduch-Benages, Marie-Theres Wacker, Kari Elisabeth Børresen, Adriana Valerio, Marinella Perroni, Elizabeth Schüssler Fiorenza, Eileen Schuller, Andrea Taschl-Erber, and others. See "The Bible and Women: An Encyclopaedia of Exegesis and Cultural History," Bible and Women, https://tinyurl.com/SBL6710f.

These case studies span two millennia of interpretation by readers with widely differing perspectives. Some are at the level of a group response (from Gnostic readings of Genesis, to Post-Holocaust Jewish interpretations of Job); others examine individual approaches to texts (such as Augustine and Pelagius on Romans, or Gandhi on the Sermon on the Mount). Several chapters examine historical moments, such as the 1860 debate over Genesis and evolution, while others look to wider themes such as non-violence or millenarianism. Further chapters study in detail the works of popular figures who have used the Bible to provide inspiration for their creativity, from Dante and Handel, to Bob Dylan and Dan Brown.[59]

Westminster John Knox has published *A Concise Dictionary of the Bible and Its Reception* that the publisher describes thus:[60]

This dictionary not only identifies terms and biblical figures but also examines them from the perspective of "reception history"—the history of the Bible's effect on its readers. Biblical books, passages, and characters certainly played important roles in the history of Judaism, Christianity, and Islam, but they also influenced other religious traditions, preachers, writers, poets, artists, and filmmakers. The study of such cultural effects of the Bible is an emerging field, and this work promises to open new avenues of exploration.[61]

Along with dedicated issues of journals exploring reception-related themes, of particular note is *Biblical Reception*, an annual, peer-reviewed journal devoted to these issues, originally published by Sheffield Phoenix Press, now Bloomsbury, edited by emeriti professors J. Cheryl Exum and David J. A. Clines.[62] This journal has a greater focus on the reception of

---

59. Jonathan Roberts, introduction to *The Oxford Handbook of the Reception History of the Bible*, ed. Michael Lieb et al. (Oxford: Oxford University Press, 2013), 5.

60. The editor in chief is John F. A. Sawyer. He also edited the *Blackwell Companion to the Bible and Culture*, published by Wiley Blackwell in July 2012. It engages with biblical reception as it "gives examples of how the Bible has influenced literature, art, music, history, religious studies, politics, ecology and sociology." See John F. A. Sawyer, ed., *A Concise Dictionary of the Bible and Its Reception* (Louisville: Westminster John Knox, 2009).

61. "A Concise Dictionary of the Bible and Its Reception (Paper)," Westminster John Knox Press, https://tinyurl.com/SBL6710g.

62. The third issue of the quarterly journal *Hebrew Bible and Ancient Israel*, which launched in early 2012, was devoted to reception history. It features an article

the Bible in the arts and popular culture than does the de Gruyter *Journal of the Bible and Its Reception*. The uptake among publishers is evidence of the rising level of interest in the work being produced in this field of biblical reception history. A further interesting development is the new Swiss offering *Die Bibel in der Kunst/Bible in the Arts*, a peer-reviewed, open-access, online journal.[63] I turn now to consider the particular area of the study of visual art as a mode of biblical reception.

2.4. Biblical Reception and the Visual Arts

The academic interest in the reception of the Bible in all forms of artistic endeavor, ranging through film, music, drama, and the visual arts, is a burgeoning and increasingly diverse area of scholarship.[64] It reflects a discernible trend in the wider cultural milieu. Within the visual arts the

---

on reception history and the visual arts by Martin O'Kane, "Interpreting the Bible Through the Visual Arts," *HBAI* 1 (2012): 388–409. The *Journal for the Study of the New Testament* also dedicated an entire issue to the subject of reception history. To this issue Martin O'Kane contributed an article titled "*Wirkungsgeschichte* and Visual Exegesis: the Contribution of Hans-Georg Gadamer," *JSNT* 33 (2010): 147–59.

63. *Die Bibel in der Kunst/Bible in the Arts* can be found at http://www.bibelwissenschaft.de/die-bibel-in-der-kunst/.

64. Apart from visual art, of these others areas film has received the greatest attention in recent years. A number of scholars have dealt with this topic, of which a few recent publications include David Tollerton, ed., *Biblical Reception*, vol. 4, *A New Hollywood Moses: On the Spectacle and Reception of Exodus: Gods and Kings* (London: Bloomsbury T&T Clark, 2018); Richard Walsh, ed., *T&T Clark Companion to the Bible and Film* (London: Bloomsbury T&T Clark, 2018); Rhonda Burnette-Bletsch and Jon Morgan, eds., *Noah as Antihero: Darren Aronofsky's Cinematic Deluge* (London: Routledge, 2017); Rhonda Burnette-Bletsch, *The Bible in Motion: A Handbook of the Bible and Its Reception in Film*, 2 vols (Berlin: de Gruyter, 2016); David J. Shepherd, ed., *The Silents of Jesus in the Cinema (1897–1927)* (London: Routledge, 2017); Shepherd, *The Bible on Silent Film: Spectacle, Story and Scripture in the Early Cinema* (Cambridge: Cambridge University Press, 2013). In the field of music, notable contributions have come from Siobhán Dowling Long and John F. A. Sawyer, *The Bible in Music: A Dictionary of Songs, Works, and More* (New York: Rowman & Littlefield, 2015); Siobhán Dowling Long, *The Sacrifice of Isaac: The Reception of a Biblical Story in Music* (Sheffield: Sheffield Phoenix, 2013). Drama and the work of playwrights has received less attention; however, notably, David J. Shepherd in collaboration with Nicholas Johnson coadapted Bertolt Brecht's *The David Fragments* for the stage in 2017. Shepherd will publish a monograph exploring Brecht's *The David Fragments*.

range is considerable; there is, for example, a renewed interest in traditional Byzantine iconography, often perceived as a "pure" form of biblical representation untainted by the personal ambition of the valorized artist.[65] Wendy Beckett, a contemplative nun, has had best-selling books and TV programs in which she offers reflections on artworks from a Christian faith perspective.[66] To mark the new millennium, the National Gallery in London curated *The Image of Christ* exhibition, anxiously awaiting an anticipated negative response in the media to the explicitly Christian-focused theme.[67] Much to everyone's surprise, the exhibition was a runaway success, attracting record numbers. The exhibition lent further impetus to this emerging area of scholarly research into the reception of the Bible in visual art, as it highlighted the public's desire to engage with religious imagery and exposed the gap in crossover expertise, with neither biblical scholars nor art historians having ventured too far into the other's domain.

Heidi Hornik, Barbara Baert, and John Harvey are notable exceptions from the discipline of art history. Hornik has written numerous articles and collaborated on three volumes on the reception of Luke's Gospel in Italian Renaissance art.[68] Baert, a specialist in the field of medieval art and

---

65. Martin O'Kane has looked at the representation of Elijah in classical iconography in his "The Biblical Elijah and His Visual Afterlives," in *Between the Text and the Canvas: The Bible and Art in Dialogue*, ed. J. Cheryl Exum and Ela Nutu (Sheffield: Sheffield Phoenix, 2007), 60–79. See also Andreas Andreopoulos, "Icons: The Silent Gospels," in *Imaging the Bible: An Introduction to Biblical Art*, ed. Martin O'Kane (London: SPCK, 2008), 83–100.

66. "Sister Wendy Beckett," Encyclopedia Britannica, 2015, https://tinyurl.com/SBLPress6701d2. Sister Wendy Beckett authored or coauthored thirty-nine books on the relationship among faith, spirituality, and art between 1998 and 2011. Some have explicitly biblical themes, such as *Sister Wendy Beckett Contemplates St Paul in Art* (London: St Pauls, 2008).

67. Gabriele Finaldi, "Seeing Salvation: The Image of Christ," *Pastoral Review* (June/July 2000). A catalog accompanying the exhibition has had three reprints (2003, 2005, 2011): Gabriele Finaldi, ed., *The Image of Christ* (London: National Gallery, 2000).

68. Heidi Hornik and Mikeal C. Parsons, *Illuminating Luke*, vol. 1, *The Infancy Narrative in Italian Renaissance Painting* (New York: Trinity Press International, 2003); Hornik and Parsons, *Illuminating Luke*, vol. 2, *The Public Ministry of Christ in Italian Renaissance and Baroque Painting* (New York: T&T Clark, 2005); Hornik and Parsons, *Illuminating Luke*, vol. 3, *The Passion and Resurrection Narratives in Italian Renaissance and Baroque Paintings* (New York: T&T Clark, 2008).

iconology, surveys the visual reception of the Bible in art from the Middle Ages.[69] John Harvey is a Welsh art historian who has given his attention to the relationship between works of art and the biblical texts that inspired them, focusing particularly on the Welsh nonconformist churches and the art and artifacts that have been emerged from within that tradition.[70] These scholars navigate the two disciplines responsibly and imaginatively, opening up new and fascinating areas of research and bringing fresh insight for the consideration of biblical scholars.

Historians, archeologists, and paleographers within biblical studies are increasingly aware of their need to develop a visual hermeneutics as they grapple with the visual artifacts and ephemera of the ancient world. Ryan Bonfiglio addresses this need for serious engagement with methodologies from the visual arts in his recent volume *Reading Images, Seeing Texts*.

> Whether they are classified as art or artifact, icon or idol, images are constituent components of human culture both in ancient and modern contexts. However ubiquitous images might be throughout history, it has only been in the closing decades of the twentieth century that the intellectual course of the humanities and social sciences has begun to shift more decisively towards questions about the place of images in cultural theory and the importance of visual data in historical research.[71]

Further evidence of scholarly recognition of the growing importance of methodological competencies for the interpretation of texts in relation to images—exemplified "in the increasing inclusion of visual material culture in interpretation of New Testament texts during the last two decades"—is

---

69. Barbara Baert, ed., *The Woman with the Blood Flow (Mark 5:24–34): Narrative, Iconic, and Anthropological Spaces* (Leuven: Peeters, 2014); Baert, *Interspaces between Word, Gaze and Touch: The Bible and the Visual Medium in the Middle Ages* (Leuven: Peeters, 2011).

70. John Harvey, *The Bible as Visual Culture: When Text Becomes Image* (Sheffield: Sheffield Phoenix, 2013); Harvey, "Framing the Word: Commentary, Context, and Composition," in *Bible, Art, Gallery*, ed. Martin O'Kane (Sheffield: Sheffield Phoenix, 2011), 27–54; Harvey, "Visual Typology and Pentecostal Theology: The Paintings of Nicholas Evans," in *Imaging the Bible: An Introduction to Biblical Art*, ed. Martin O'Kane (London: SPCK, 2009), 123–42; Harvey, *The Art of Piety: Visual Culture of Welsh Nonconformity* (Cardiff, UK: University of Wales Press, 1995).

71. Ryan P. Bonfiglio, *Reading Images, Seeing Texts: Towards a Visual Hermeneutics for Biblical Studies*, OBO 280 (Fribourg: Academic Press; Göttingen: Vandenhoeck & Ruprecht, 2016), 1.

found in *The Art of Visual Exegesis*.⁷² This fine volume focuses predominantly on two periods. It examines "the use of visual material culture of the Roman Mediterranean world during the emergence of early Christianity," and exegetical Christian paintings and prints "produced in France, Italy and the Low Countries from the fifteenth to seventeenth centuries."⁷³

Within the field of biblical reception history, the work of several scholars is worth noting. O'Kane is one of the preeminent biblical scholars in the field of the visual exegesis of biblical texts.⁷⁴ He has written extensively on this subject, with particular focus on the Hebrew Scriptures and European art of the fifteenth to seventeenth centuries. Throughout Europe and the United States, metropolitan art galleries own and display many large oil paintings of this period, and these may be the sole encounter some people have with biblical narratives. Exum and Ela Nutu note,

> Discussions of the Bible and art usually focus on easel paintings, mainly from the sixteenth century to the present, because it is primarily through painting, particularly of the sixteenth to nineteenth centuries, that certain ideas about the Bible have entered the public consciousness and influenced both cultural perception and scholarly interpretation of the Bible.⁷⁵

O'Kane writes,

> Visual images stir the imagination and we admire both the skill of the artists and the creative and original ways their artworks interpret and depict the narrative; yet there is a vital difference between the use of visual imagery to convey biblical stories to largely illiterate or semiliterate audiences, say in the period of the Middle Ages or the Renaissance, and the way we, as readers of the Bible today, can compare what the painting of a text visualizes with what the text itself actually says.⁷⁶

---

72. Vernon K. Robbins, Walter S. Melion, and Roy R. Jeal, eds., *The Art of Visual Exegesis: Rhetoric, Texts, Images* (Atlanta: SBL Press, 2017), 1.

73. Robbins, Melion, and Jeal, *Art of Visual Exegesis*.

74. O'Kane, *Painting the Text*; O'Kane, *Bible, Art, Gallery*; O'Kane, ed., *Biblical Art from Wales* (Sheffield: Sheffield Phoenix, 2010); O'Kane, *Imaging the Bible*; O'Kane, ed., *Borders, Boundaries and the Bible*, JSOTSup 313 (Sheffield: Continuum, 2002). O'Kane has contributed many articles to edited volumes and journals.

75. J. Cheryl Exum and Ela Nutu, eds., *Between the Text and the Canvas: The Bible and Art in Dialogue* (Sheffield: Sheffield Phoenix, 2007), 4.

76. O'Kane, *Painting the Text*, 1.

O'Kane highlights the anomaly at the heart of the interdisciplinary area, noting,

> Biblical commentators have explored "visual" themes relating to light and darkness or sight and blindness in their various literal and metaphorical permutations and many art historians have published compilations of "biblical" paintings; but very little interest has been shown by either group in exploring how the visual imagery contained in the narrative exercises the reader's imagination, or how the processes at work in the way a viewer sees and reacts to a biblical painting might serve as a paradigm or model for the way a reader should engage with highly visual texts.[77]

O'Kane engages both independently with the philosophy of Gadamer and with the work of contemporary philosopher and Gadamer specialist Nicholas Davey.[78] Davey, in turn, has made contributions to edited volumes by O'Kane, using a Gadamerian hermeneutic to explore various works of art.[79] Another scholar working in this area, David Jasper, suggests that it is crucial for the reader of a biblical text and the viewer of a biblical painting to try to reveal what lies hidden or undisclosed, to progress from the visible to what is unseen. "It is in [this] revealing of what cannot be seen that the painting enters into dialogue with the biblical text.... It is in the seeing what is not seen and imagining what is not written that a genuinely creative dialogue takes place (between a biblical text and painting)."[80]

Here Jasper refers to the fruitful collaboration between biblical scholar Philip Esler and artist Jane Boyd, and their project to bring the wealth of both disciplines to an academic study of the oil painting *Christ in the House of Martha and Mary* (1618) by Spanish artist Diego Velázquez.[81] Their work is a thorough exploration of this painting: taking into account

---

77. O'Kane, *Painting the Text*, 3.
78. O'Kane, *Painting the Text*, 38–40.
79. Nicholas Davey, "Hermeneutics, Aesthetics and Religious Experience," in O'Kane, *Bible, Art, Gallery*, 1–26; Davey, "Hermeneutics, Aesthetics and Transcendence," in O'Kane, *Imaging the Bible*, 191–211.
80. David Jasper, "Review of Jane Boyd and Philip F. Esler, *Visuality and the Biblical Text*," *ACE* 44 (2005): 8–9.
81. Jane Boyd and Philip F. Esler, *Visuality and the Biblical Text: Interpreting Velazquez—"Christ with Martha and Mary" as a Test Case* (Florence: Olschki, 2005).

the social context in which it was painted, seventeenth-century southern Spain, as well as the social context to which it refers, first-century Palestine of the Gospels. The bearing of the Council of Trent (1545–1563) and the Catholic Reformation on the creative works commissioned from artists such as Velázquez is considered as well as the social issue of lifelong servanthood, experienced by poorer people living in Seville, at that time. The worlds behind, of, and in front of the biblical text are dealt with in turn. Esler opens up the biblical text and its various possible interpretations—within this particular painting—which features five characters (not three). Boyd delves into the artistic preoccupations with perspective and spatial dynamics that exercised artists of this caliber in that period as well as fascinations with capturing in paint the textures of food and flesh in the domestic setting. She offers a technical explication of the use of mirrors as a tool for composing paintings. The value of the collaboration is clear to see in what both scholars bring to the artwork. Certain elements of the painting, such as the implications for interpretation of the framing of the biblical scene (in the background), are dealt with, but neither scholar explicitly employs semiotic analysis. This would have undoubtably added another layer of depth and interest to the study of the reception of the biblical text in this artwork.

Exum is a pioneering biblical scholar most associated with pursuing the visual dimension of biblical reception through the artistic afterlives of female biblical characters.[82] Joynes, Nutu, and Fiona Black are among others who have also followed this line of inquiry. In many ways, art and visual exegesis have served the feminist hermeneutical approach very well, precisely because the gender discrimination and sexism that is normative in the text has often been made explicit in image and may therefore be easier to expose in the familiar text. Art from periods of particular ecclesiastical power and prominence, of overbearing patriarchy in all facets of life—domestic, financial, religious, and political, such

---

82. J. Cheryl Exum, *Plotted, Shot, and Painted: Cultural Representations of Biblical Women*, 2nd ed. (Sheffield: Sheffield Phoenix, 2012); Exum, *Fragmented Women: Feminist (Sub)versions of Biblical Narratives* (London: Bloomsbury T&T Clark, 2016); Exum, "Second Thoughts about Secondary Characters," in *A Feminist Companion to Exodus to Deuteronomy*, ed. Athalya Brenner, Feminist Companion to the Bible (Sheffield: Sheffield Academic, 1994), 75–87; Exum, "Lethal Women 2: Reflections on Delilah and Her Incarnation as Liz Hurley," in O'Kane, *Borders, Boundaries and the Bible*, 254–73.

as the late Middle Ages, the Renaissance, and the Baroque—reinforce patriarchal interpretations of texts. This art has had a profound, lasting, and unquantifiable influence on the reception of female characters featured in biblical texts, in the Western world especially. Exum asks, "How is the gender ideology of the biblical text both reinscribed in and challenged by its cultural appropriations? How does what we think we know about biblical women, our preconceptions and assumptions shaped by our encounters with their visual personae, affect the way we read their stories?"[83] This reiterates O'Kane's assertion: "What is important for contemporary scholarship is not the doctrinal debates of the past but how we use the visual (in ways similar to literary approaches) as a way of bringing out the new and unexpected, the hidden and the silenced in the text."[84] Harvey, considering the role of the Bible in visual culture, writes:

> Biblical visual culture in general like blasphemous visual culture in particular provides an insight into, and an expression of, the religious imagination, and demonstrates that the content and influence of Scripture extends far beyond its primary condition as text. Visual culture illuminates the text not only as an illustrative adjunct but also as a means of commentary and exegesis every bit as nuanced, problematic, and insightful as textual criticism.[85]

As I will highlight in the following chapter, graphic design plays an important role in the history of visual design and imagery. Indeed, contemporary graphic designers working on projects involving biblical texts often understand themselves as inheritors of a rich tradition, much like members of a contemporary scriptorium of sorts. Through their work, often accompanying liturgical texts, they endeavor to produce illustrations that help "focus the senses and the mind and offer a mnemonic aid that gathers the worshipper's strongest and most fundamental ideas, emotions, and memories in an enriched present."[86] Craighead, Kacmarcik, Bethune, Gill, Moser, Corbin, Eichenberg, and Markell are all twentieth-century or contemporary designers who have grappled with this task in one form or another. However, very little and in some cases no critical engagement has

---

83. Exum, *Plotted, Shot and Painted*, 14.
84. O'Kane, *Painting the Text*, 9.
85. Harvey, *Bible as Visual Culture*, 200.
86. Margaret Miles, *Image as Insight: Visual Understanding in Western Christianity and Secular Culture* (Boston: Beacon, 1985), 9.

been undertaken with regard to their work. Daniel Kantor has written a book on *Graphic Design and Religion*, in which he laments this situation while sounding a clarion call for renewal:

> Much has been written on the importance of other art forms in religion and their roles as mediators in the human religious experience. Libraries are filled with books written about sacred music, painting and architecture. Yet while these art forms thrive within modern worship, the virtues of graphic design remain little celebrated. Rarely, if ever, has graphic design been formerly called out as an essential art form of contemporary religious expression.[87]

For this reason I am pursuing a critical scholarly engagement with the artwork of two particular contemporary graphic designers: Craighead and Markell. I believe that the "full box of analytical tools"[88] offered by semiotics (to be considered in the following chapter) provides a valuable method of analysis that, as yet, has not been applied to the twentieth-century designs for religious and liturgical literature illustrating biblical texts.

2.5. Conclusion

This literature review began with a brief overview of the work of Gadamer and Jauss. Both scholars address the impact of history and culture on the reception of texts by readers in different historical eras. The legacy of Gadamer and Jauss within biblical studies has resulted in a shift in the hermeneutical emphasis to the dialogical event of meaning that happens between the text and the reader. Their ideas have been enthusiastically embraced and have resulted in a new area within biblical studies: reception history. The term used within this discourse is *reception history*, including when it refers to the contemporary reception of the Bible, such as these graphic designs studied here. The proliferation of volumes—handbooks, journals, monographs, series, and dictionaries—now being published by leading academic publishers is a testament to the vitality of the field and expectation of its continued development.

---

87. Daniel Kantor, *Graphic Design and Religion: A Call for Renewal* (Chicago: GIA, 2007), 50.

88. Gillian Rose, *Visual Methodologies: An Introduction to Researching with Visual Materials*, 3rd ed. (London: Sage, 2012), 105.

One particular area of growth is that of scholars exploring the interpretative relationship between word and image. The Bible has always, even during and despite iconoclastic eras, found its way into the form of image.[89] From as early as the third century evidence of illustrated biblical passages and motifs has been discovered in diverse formats, mediums, and places, such as the walls of the catacombs and relief carvings around sarcophagi.[90] This visual dimension of the reception history of the Bible has received scant attention from biblical scholars until recently in the notable work of O'Kane and Exum, among others. Biblical scholars and art historians have tended to work independently, with different methods, exploring different aspects of works of art. Most biblical scholars' focus, however, has been the large oil-on-canvas paintings of the European Renaissance and Baroque periods. Contemporary graphic designs illustrating biblical texts have not yet been studied by scholars working within the field of reception history—making this an area of visual material ripe for exploration.

Reception history has come in for criticism in relation to the methodologies used within the field. Yet the scope of its remit is such that no one methodology can encompass the breadth of material and historical contexts it wishes to investigate. Nonetheless, methodological rigor is essential if reception history is to make a valuable contribution to biblical studies. A social semiotics of the visual as proposed by theorists Kress and van Leeuwen offers biblical reception history an as yet unexplored but

---

89. One example is the *Biblia pauperum*, or the "paupers' Bible." These were picture Bibles of the late Middle Ages, usually printed by wood block, initially on vellum and later on paper. The image dominated over the text, and what little text may have appeared on the page may have been placed as dialogue on a ribbon, near the character's face, in a way very similar to modern-day comic books.

90. See Jeffrey Spier, "The Earliest Christian Art: From Personal Salvation to Imperial Power," in *Picturing the Bible: The Earliest Christian Art*, ed. Jeffrey Spier (New Haven: Yale University Press, 2007), 12, fig. 7, "Sarcophagus with biblical scenes, Rome (?), c.300. Museo Civico, Velletri." Some of these artworks illustrating biblical passages predate the oldest known fragments of NT papyri available to us today. An example would be Papyrus 110 (Oxford University), containing, in fragments, Matt 10:13–15, 25–27. The manuscript has been paleographically dated to the early fourth century CE; however, papyrologist Philip Comfort dates the manuscript to the mid- to late third century CE. See Comfort, *Encountering the Manuscripts: An Introduction to New Testament Paleography and Textual Criticism* (Nashville: Broadman & Holman, 2005), 76.

viable and valuable methodology for considering how meaning is made in the realm of the visual arts. To this I now turn.

3
A Social Semiotics of the Visual

> Semiotics is centrally concerned with reception.
> —Mieke Bal, *On Meaning Making*

"Why do [people] behave as if pictures were alive, as if works of art had minds of their own, as if images had a power to influence human beings, demanding things from us, persuading, seducing, and leading us astray?" asks William J. T. Mitchell, pointing to the implicit recognition that images speak.[1] How can we begin to understand their language? I deliberately use the metaphor of verbal language here because it is so central to the debates, and new, shifting and expanding understandings, between linguists and semioticians in the past few decades. I suggest in what follows that semiotics is particularly well suited as a methodological approach for investigating how images work in the reception of the Bible, and in particular graphic designs that interpret biblical texts.

A broad definition offered by Umberto Eco to describe the theory of semiotics is this: "Semiotics is concerned with everything that can be taken as a sign."[2] These signs refer to anything that stands for something else and may take the form of words, images, sounds, gestures, and objects.[3] Greimasian scholar Ronald Schleifer describes semiotics as a "species of linguistics that takes all production of signification—linguistic as well non-linguistic—as its object."[4] While it is true that semiotics has always considered within its remit all signifying practices, linguistic as well as nonlinguistic,

---

1. William J. T. Mitchell, *What Do Pictures Want? The Lives and Loves of Images* (Chicago: University of Chicago Press, 2005), 7.
2. Eco, *Theory of Semiotics*, 7.
3. Daniel Chandler, *Semiotics: The Basics*, 2nd ed. (London: Routledge, 2007), 1.
4. Ronald Schleifer, *A. J. Greimas and the Nature of Meaning: Linguistics, Semiotics and Discourse Theory* (Lincoln: University of Nebraska Press, 1987), 85.

semiotics is no longer generally understood as a species of linguistics, even though it may be said to have originated in that domain. As seen in the fields of biblical studies and visual studies, the discipline of linguistics is undergoing a parallel revolution of sorts. Whereas until recently the field of semiotics was seen as belonging within the broad realm of linguistics, many semioticians, notably Halliday, argue that in fact that relationship, correctly perceived, is the other way around. They maintain that semiotics is the theoretical field within which linguistics may be found.[5] Verbal and written language are increasingly no longer viewed as necessarily being the primary vehicles of communication but rather two among many semiotic resources. This study explores the semiotic resource of the graphically designed image that illustrates the biblical text and the viability of semiotics as a method for analyzing how this semiotic resource functions.

This chapter briefly reviews the legacy of Ferdinand de Saussure and Charles Sanders Peirce on the field of semiotics as it has developed since the late nineteenth century. The influence of Halliday and his *Systemic Functional Grammar* is briefly explored, introducing the concepts of *metafunctions* and *multimodality*—foundational to Kress and van Leeuwen's theory of a social semiotics of the visual. The relationship between semiotics and graphic design is then considered. As I will show, semiotics has been appropriated by both academics and practitioners in the field of graphic design as the theory that best describes, analyzes, and critiques their practice. Graphic designers are concerned not only with generating meaning in multimodal forms but with understanding visual and other multimodal meaning-making events and practices as they occur. Kress and van Leeuwen have shown themselves to be theoretical forerunners—within emerging social semiotics—as they focus in their work on multimodal and visual semiotics in particular. Their work is reviewed in this chapter, with a view toward the usefulness of such analysis for the present project.

3.1. The Legacy of Saussure and Peirce

The "founding fathers" of semiotics are unanimously recognized as Ferdinand de Saussure (1857–1913) and Charles Sanders Peirce (1839–1914).

---

5. A thorough discussion of the paradigm shift in semiotics over the course of the late twentieth century can be found in Thomas A. Sebeok, *Global Semiotics* (Bloomington: Indiana University Press, 2001).

Saussure was a Swiss linguist and semiotician associated with structuralism.[6] His lectures about important principles of language description, delivered over three courses late in his career at the University of Geneva between 1907 and 1911, were collated and published by his pupils posthumously in the famous *Cours de linguistique générale* in 1916. Daniel Chandler writes,

> It is difficult to disentangle European semiotics from structuralism in its origins; major structuralists include not only Saussure but also Claude Lévi-Strauss in anthropology (who saw his subject as a branch of semiotics) and Jacques Lacan in psychoanalysis. Structuralism is an analytical method which has been employed by many semioticians and which is based on Saussure's linguistic model. Structuralists seek to describe the overall organization of sign systems as "language"—as with Lévi-Strauss and myth, kinship rules and totemism, Lacan and the unconscious and Barthes and Greimas and the "grammar" of narrative. They engage in a search for "deep structures" underlying the "surface features" of phenomena.[7]

In one of those strange but periodic occurrences of academic synchronicity, an American, Charles Sanders Peirce, developed similar theories to those of Saussure, independently and through his own interest in the philosophy of logic rather than the field of linguistics.[8] Peirce's semiotics

---

6. Ferdinand de Saussure was born in Geneva and began his early studies in Latin, Greek, and Sanskrit there before continuing at Leipzig and Berlin. He moved to Paris, where he began his illustrious career at the École pratique des hautes études before accepting an invitation to return and take up a professorship at the University of Geneva, where he spent the rest of his academic career. He died in Switzerland in 1913. In terms of publications, the key work containing Saussure's thought is *Course in General Linguistics*, his collated course notes published posthumously by his former students. See de Saussure, *Course in General Linguistics*, trans. W. Baskin (Glasgow: Collins, 1974).

7. Chandler, *Semiotics*, 1.

8. Charles Sanders Peirce was born in Cambridge, Massachusetts, into an academically oriented family—his father a lecturer at Harvard, where he later studied himself. He died in poverty in Milford, Pennsylvania, in 1914, after a long series of unfortunate events and unpleasant professional rivalries saw him denied academic posts and essentially excluded from a mainstream academic career despite his enormous intellectual capacity. His breadth of expertise ranged through mathematics, statistics, logic, and philosophy. In 1943, *Webster's Biographical Dictionary* claimed that Peirce was "now regarded as the most original thinker and greatest logician of his time." Interest

is distinctly triadic as opposed to Saussure's dyadic system. Peirce's main interest in language was as a mode of information and thought over and above social interaction. He believed that signification, or the consumption of signs, was essentially a mental process and that meaning resides in the mind, not in the objects themselves.[9] His concept of the process of signification privileges materiality in ways that Saussure's does not. Peirce was interested in the fundamental nature of signs and how they function in a concrete world. Unlike Saussure's signified/signifier relationship, in which meaning depends almost entirely on the position of the word within a linear text, Peirce's model considers the broader notion of context as influencing interpretation and the material nature of the sign as having consequences for our behavior. The duality of the sign, as both an object in the concrete world and as a mental artifact, is fundamental to Peirce's work.[10]

Saussure and Peirce are subsequently perceived as two pillars representing two divergent traditions in semiotics. The work of Louis Hjelmslev, Roland Barthes, Claude Lévi-Strauss, Julia Kristeva, Christian Metz, and Jean Baudrillard follows in the semiological tradition of Saussure, while that of Charles Morris, Ivor Richards, Charles Ogden, and Thomas Sebeok is in the semiotic tradition of Peirce.[11] Bridging these two traditions is the work of Umberto Eco.

---

in Peirce's work developed in the late 1940s and gathered momentum in the 1980s. "Currently, considerable interest is being taken in Peirce's ideas by researchers wholly outside the arena of academic philosophy. The interest comes from industry, business, technology, intelligence organizations, and the military; and it has resulted in the existence of a substantial number of agencies, institutes, businesses, and laboratories in which ongoing research into and development of Peircean concepts are being vigorously undertaken," claims Robert Burch. See Burch, "Charles Sanders Peirce," Stanford Encyclopedia of Philosophy, Fall 2010 ed., ed. Edward N. Zalta, https://tinyurl.com/SBL6710u. As with Saussure, the best-known of Peirce's writings are those collated and published posthumously. See Charles Sanders Peirce, *Collected Papers of Charles Sanders Peirce*, 6 vols, ed. Charles Hartshorne and Paul Weiss (Cambridge: Harvard University Press, 1931–1935), with a further two volumes added and edited by Arthur W. Burks just over two decades later (Cambridge: Harvard University Press, 1958).

9. James Liszka, *A General Introduction to the Semeiotic of Charles Sanders Peirce* (Bloomington: Indiana University Press, 1996), 18.

10. Mark Gottdiener, *Postmodern Semiotics: Material Culture and the Forms of Postmodern Life* (Oxford: Blackwell, 1995), 10.

11. A decision to employ universally the word *semiotics* was made in Paris in January 1969 by an international committee that brought into existence the International Association for Semiotic Studies (see Eco, *Theory of Semiotics*, 30).

Building on the foundational semiotics of Saussure and early adherents to his ideas, three schools of semiotics emerged in Europe, all approaching the analyses of nonlinguistic modes of communication with methods sourced from linguistics. The work of the Russian formalists was developed by the Prague school during the 1930s and early 1940s. The exploration of art (Jan Mukařovský), theater (Jindřich Honzl), cinema (Roman Jakobson), and costume (Petr Bogatyrev) as semiotic systems in their own right commenced. This was followed in the 1960s and 1970s by the Paris school, which applied Saussure's and other linguists' ideas to painting (Jean-Louis Schefer), photography (Roland Barthes, René Lindekens), fashion and advertising (Barthes), cinema (Christian Metz), music (Jean-Jacques Nattiez), and comic strips (Pierre Fresnault-Deruelle), among other media and creative forms.[12] Kress and van Leeuwen describe themselves as being among the harbingers of the third school to emerge in the late twentieth century:

> [The] third, still fledgling, movement in which insights from linguistics have been applied to other modes of representation has two sources, both drawing on the ideas of Michael Halliday, one growing out of the "Critical Linguistics" of a group of people working in the 1970s at the University of East Anglia, leading to the outline of a theory that might encompass other semiotic modes (Hodge and Kress), the other, in the later 1980s, as a development of Hallidayan systemic functional linguistics by a number of scholars in Australia, in semiotically oriented studies of literature (Threadgold, Thibault), visual semiotics (O'Toole, ourselves) and music (van Leeuwen).[13]

The prevailing critique of the Saussurean legacy, by these and other contemporary semioticians, is that it was too heavily reliant on and embedded within the theories pertaining to linguistics. Semiotics emerged from the mid-twentieth-century philosophies of linguistics and has now superseded linguistics, and it is argued that the relationship is reversed; linguistics may now be perceived to be a field within the broader realm of semiotics. Mieke Bal has noted her concerns: "it is right to wonder to what extent the 'expansion' proposed by a 'general' science of signs may in fact be an attempt at appropriation, the absorption of the visual domain into

---

12. Kress and van Leeuwen, *Reading Images*, 6.
13. Kress and van Leeuwen, *Reading Images*, 6. "Ourselves" here refers to Kress and van Leeuwen.

the empire of linguistics. For obviously there are a great number of aspects of visual art and visual experience that cannot be 'translated' into language at all."[14] Many scholars wonder whether a theory based on language has the scope to deal with the particularities of the visual.[15]

Halliday maintains that language is a semiotic system, "not in the sense of a system of signs, but a systemic resource for meaning."[16] In other words, the static, structuralist model of conceiving of language as a system of signs is too limited and does not allow for the vast array of ways in which people use language and the many ways in which language is both influenced by and influences other semiotic modes of communication. Moreover, the hegemony of language as *the* communicative system of signs, to which all other semiotic resources are subservient, is challenged by these scholars. Barry Sandywell echoes this in his call for images to be recognized as functioning as semiotic resources in their own distinct way that is often not directly comparable or translatable within a linguistic approach to understanding how language works. "The grammar of images needs to be analytically distinguished from the linguisticality of verbal communication. Visuality is not merely another department subsumed under the logic of signs."[17] Kress maintains that the dominance of the verbal has given way, in postmodernity, to the visual—and the categories of language conceived in a monomodal world "when the assumption was that 'language' did all the significant cultural semiotic work"—no longer serves the theories of semiotics. "'Language' isn't a big enough receptacle for all the semiotic stuff we felt sure we could pour into it." He adds, "In the monomodally conceived world, in other words, in a world regarded as operating with one kind of resource in a specific domain, reflection on the potential of that resource could not arise. 'Language' was all there was; and

---

14. Mieke Bal, *On Meaning Making: Essays in Semiotics* (Salem, OR: Polebridge, 1994), 175.

15. Margaret Iversen, "Saussure v. Peirce: Models for a Semiotics of Visual Art," in *The New Art History*, ed. Alan L. Rees and Frances Borzello (London: Camden, 1986), 85; Stuart Hall, "Encoding/Decoding," in *Culture, Media, Language: Working Papers in Cultural Studies*, ed. Stuart Hall et al. (London: Hutchinson, 1980), 132.

16. Michael A. K. Halliday, "Systemic Background," in *The Collected Works of M. A. K. Halliday*, ed. Jonathan J. Webster (London: Bloomsbury, 2004), 3:186.

17. Barry Sandywell, "Seven Theses on Visual Culture: Towards a Critical-Reflexive Paradigm for the New Visual Studies," in Heywood, Sandywell, and Gardiner, *Handbook of Visual Culture*, 661.

'language' was regarded as a means fully capable of dealing with all human (rational) meaning."[18]

Kress and van Leeuwen posit themselves in continuity with the stream of "Paris School semiotics generally taught in the Anglo-Saxon world."[19] They broadly outline their approach, now widely referred to as the Sydney school of social semiotics, thus:

> We see representation as a process in which the makers of signs, whether child or adult, seek to make a representation of some object or entity, whether physical or semiotic, and in which their interest in the object, at the point of making the representation is a complex one arising out of the cultural, social and psychological history of the sign-maker, and focused by the specific context in which the sign maker produces the sign. That "interest" is the source of the selection of what is seen as the criterial aspect of the object, and this criterial aspect is then regarded as adequately representative of the object in a given context. In other words, it is never the "whole object" but only ever its criterial aspects which are represented. These criterial aspects are represented in what seems to be to the sign-maker, at the moment of sign-making, the most apt and plausible representational mode (e.g. drawing, Lego blocks, painting, speech). Sign-makers thus "have" a meaning, the signified, which they wish to express, and then express it through the semiotic mode(s) that make(s) available the subjectively felt, most plausible, most apt form, as the signifier. This means that in social semiotics the sign is not the pre-existing conjunction of a signifier and a signified, a ready made sign to be recognized, chosen and used as it is, in the way that signs are usually thought to be "available for use" in "semiology." Rather we focus on the process of sign-making, in which the signifier (the form) and the signified (the meaning) are relatively independent of each other until they are brought together by the sign-maker in a newly made sign.[20]

The influence of Peirce is apparent in the work of Kress and van Leeuwen to the extent that Peirce's semiotics is about the transfer of meaning: the act of signifying. His understanding, contra Saussure, was not of a one-way process of signification with a fixed (yet arbitrary) meaning. Peirce understood the transfer of meaning to be an active process between the

---

18. Kress, *Multimodality*, 11, 15, 27–28.
19. Kress and van Leeuwen, *Reading Images*, 6.
20. Kress and van Leeuwen, *Reading Images*, 7–8.

sign and the reader of the sign, an exchange requiring negotiation and affected by the social and cultural background of the reader.[21]

3.2. Halliday's *Systemic Functional Grammar* and the Three Metafunctions

Halliday's early recognition that "there are many other modes of meaning, in any culture, which are outside the realm of language" set him up as a highly influential English linguist credited with reframing language as a social semiotic resource within the broader range of semiotics.[22] His model, originally presented as *An Introduction to Functional Grammar* in 1985, has been republished in revised editions three times (1994, 2004, 2014), the last two editions with the collaboration of Christian Matthiessen.[23] Kress and van Leeuwen's social semiotics of the visual, the theory central to this project, proceeds from Halliday's *Systemic Functional Grammar*, both theorists having collaborated closely with Halliday as part of his Sydney semiotics circle. This in time evolved into the Sydney school.

---

21. David Crow, *Visible Signs: An Introduction to Semiotics* (Lausanne: AVA, 2003), 36.

22. Michael A. K. Halliday, *Language as Social Semiotic: The Social Interpretation of Language and Meaning* (London: Arnold, 1978), 4. Halliday (1925–2018) spent a short period as a British counterintelligence operative in India before dividing his time between China and the UK, undertaking studies in Chinese linguistics. This was the subject of his PhD at Cambridge under another prominent linguist, J. R. Firth (who in turn had studied under the anthropologist Malinowski). Halliday taught in a number of British universities (Cambridge, Edinburgh, University College London, and Essex) as well as in the US (Indiana, Stanford, Illinois). He took up the position of professor of linguistics at the University of Sydney in 1976. Under his leadership the Sydney school of semiotics emerged out of the Sydney semiotics circle. Kress and van Leeuwen, along with other notable contemporary figures in social semiotics including Robert Hodge and Norman Fairclough (critical discourse analysis), were members of this group.

23. Halliday and Matthiessen, *Halliday's Introduction to Functional Grammar*. Christian Matthiessen (b. 1956) is a Swedish semiotician who went to work with Halliday in Sydney after a collaboration (on the Penman Project) in Los Angeles in the 1980s. Following that, he was "Halliday's closest associate and in collaboration with Halliday, he extended and revised Halliday's seminal *An Introduction to Functional Grammar*. Matthiessen's influence on this work, which for the last 30 years has functioned as a reference work for the systemic functional description of English, is clear in the third and fourth edition." See Thomas Hestbæk Andersen et al., *Social Semiotics: Key Figures, New Directions* (London: Routledge, 2015), 6.

A fundamental dimension of *Systemic Functional Grammar* that has been brought through into social semiotics by Kress and van Leeuwen is the concept of the three metafunctions. Halliday describes *metafunction* itself as a "rather unwieldy term," which he then explains thus:

> Systemic analysis shows that functionality is intrinsic to language: that is to say, the entire architecture of language, is arranged along functional lines. Language is as it is because of the functions in which it has evolved in the human species. The term *metafunction* was adopted to suggest that function was an integral component within the overall theory.[24]

Halliday defines the three metafunctions as, first, the *ideational*, which is distinguished into two components: the *experiential* and the *logical*. This is the function that "construes human experience"; it is representative. Further to this, beyond construing experience, "language is also always enacting: enacting our personal and social relationships with other people around us." This active dimension is called the *interpersonal* metafunction. These two metafunctions contain the notion that "every message is both about something and addressing someone," and these two motifs may be freely combined and do not restrain one another. There is a third component, "an enabling or facilitating function since both the others, construing experience and enacting interpersonal relations depend on being able to build up sequences of discourse, organizing the discursive flow, and creating cohesion and continuity as it moves along. This we call the *textual* metafunction."[25]

These three types of meaning, ideational, interpersonal, and textual, maintain a one-to-one correspondence with the metafunctional domains distinguished by Kress and van Leeuwen in their grammar of visual design to study the meaning potential of images in multimodal products. To elaborate briefly: The ideational metafunction is about representation, a key requirement of any semiotic mode; it must be able to represent aspects of the world as it is experienced by humans. In so doing semiotic modes offer an array of choices, of different ways in which objects and their relations to other objects and to processes can be represented.[26] This

---

24. Halliday and Matthiessen, *Halliday's Introduction to Functional Grammar*, 31.
25. Halliday and Matthiessen, *Halliday's Introduction to Functional Grammar*, 30–31.
26. Kress and van Leeuwen, *Reading Images*, 42.

may conventionally be broken down further into narrative and conceptual processes. Kress and van Leeuwen define the interpersonal metafunction: "Any semiotic mode has to be able to project the relations between the producer of a (complex) sign and the receiver/reproducer of that sign. That is, any mode, has to be able to represent a particular social relation between the producer, the viewer and the object represented." Different interpersonal relations are able to be represented through the choices of different modes. For example, a person may be shown addressing viewers directly, by looking straight at the camera, thereby conveying a sense of interaction, an engagement, between the depicted person and the viewer. Conversely, a depicted person may be shown as turned away from the viewer, conveying an absence of interaction. This allows the viewer to scrutinize the represented person as though they were a specimen on display.[27] Finally, the textual metafunction is that which brings all the modes at work into a meaningful, cohesive whole. In the visual realm this often has much to do with composition. These metafunctions will be developed much further in chapters 6 and 7, which analyze the graphic designs of Markell and Craighead.

Another aspect of the Sydney grammar (as *Systemic Functional Grammar* is sometimes referred to collegially among proponents of Halliday's theory) is the strong emphasis it places on the sociocultural factors. The social orientation of Halliday's grammar stems from the influence of the linguist John Rupert Firth and the anthropologist Bronisław Malinowski. Language cannot be studied separately from the function it fulfills in a specific context of communication and has essentially evolved to perform social functions. *Systemic Functional Grammar* is very much concerned with the relationships between language and the sociocultural context in which it is produced and understood. Linguist Christopher Butler emphasizes, "The social and cultural functions of communication are a major characteristic of Halliday's approach."[28] Of particular importance here is the transition made by Kress and van Leeuwen evolving *Systemic Functional Grammar* in the development of their social semiotics of the visual, a process that continues apace, as both scholars have assured me.[29]

---

27. Kress and van Leeuwen, *Reading Images*, 42–43.

28. Christopher S. Butler, *Structure and Function: A Guide to Three Major Structural-Functional Theories; Part 1: Approaches to the Simplex Clause; Part 2: From Clause to Discourse and Beyond* (Philadelphia: Benjamins, 2003), 44.

29. I have had the good fortune to meet and discuss briefly this project with both

We call this a "grammar" to draw attention to culturally produced regularity. More specifically, we have borrowed "semiotic orientations," features which we take to be general to all human meaning-making, irrespective of mode. We have taken Michael Halliday's social semiotic approach to language as a model, as a source for thinking about general social and semiotic processes, rather than as a mine for categories to apply in the description of images.

His model with its three functions is a starting point for our account of images, not because the model works well for language (which it does, to an extent), but because it works well as a source for thinking about all modes of representation.[30]

Kress and van Leeuwen posit that a *text* is a semiotic object in which various modes and resources of a verbal and nonverbal nature intervene in order to create meaning in a determined communicative context.[31] A *text* is "that phenomenon which is the result of the articulation in one or more semiotic modes of a discourse, or (we think, inevitably, always) a number of discourses." In other words, meaning making is necessarily always multimodal.

Another term that appears frequently in the social semiotic discourse—and is key to understanding the revolution in semiotics heralded by Halliday's *Systemic Functional Grammar* —is *semiotic resource*. Van Leeuwen describes a *semiotic resource* thus:

---

scholars: van Leeuwen at Semiofest in Paris, in June 2015, and Kress at the XXI Early Fall School of Semiotics in Sozopol, Bulgaria, in September 2016. Both insisted that their academic work around their theory continues to be very much a work in progress that they are continually modifying and revising in the face of new developments, further reflection, and in response to the work of other scholars using their approach. The third revised edition of their seminal *Reading Images: The Grammar of Visual Design* is in production.

30. Kress and van Leeuwen, *Reading Images*, 20.

31. Gunther Kress and Theo van Leeuwen, *Multimodal Discourse: The Modes and Media of Contemporary Communication* (London: Hodder, 2001), 40. Strictly speaking, in multimodal studies discourse, the semiotic artifact or event being considered is referred as a text. This would require speaking of the graphic designs as texts. Given that these image texts are being studied alongside biblical texts, it would add a layer of unnecessary confusion to refer to both the biblical text and the artworks as texts. In order to alleviate this double connotation to the term *text*, I will refer to biblical texts as texts, as is the convention in biblical studies, and the artworks shall simply be referred to as images, designs, or artworks, with the implicit understanding that these are multimodal texts.

> Semiotic resources are the actions, materials and artifacts we use for communicative purposes, whether produced physiologically —for example, with our vocal apparatus, the muscles we use to make facial expressions and gestures—or technologically—for example, with pen and ink, or computer hardware and software—together with the ways in which these resources can be organized. Semiotic resources have a meaning potential, based on their past uses, and a set of affordances based on their possible uses, and these will be actualized in concrete social contexts where their use is subject to some form of semiotic regime.[32]

He goes on to suggest that the preference for the term *resource* over *sign* in social semiotics illustrates the intention to move away from the idea of a preordained or given meaning in the sign.[33] Social semiotics, revealing its Peircean bias, is more fluid and appreciative of the change that naturally occurs in the use and reuse of *semiotic resources* in different contexts and by different users. This stands in contrast to the traditional understanding within semiotics of rules or codes that were fixed in meaning and resistant to change, the idea of a preexisting conjunction between the *signifier* and the *signified*, elements of a code that, once grasped, allowed people to make use of them within the confines of their preexisting meaning.[34] This notion of the sign in a coded system of semiotics placed people, users of the code, in a passive role in the production of meaning and implied that language and other semiotic modes were entirely stable, which they are not—as we see in the evolution of language constantly. Carey Jewitt develops the preference for *semiotic resource* further:

> In this perspective, signs are a product of a social process of sign-making.
> A person (sign-maker) "chooses" a semiotic resource from an available system of resources. They bring together a semiotic resource (a signifier) with the meaning (the signified) that they want to express. In other words, people express meanings through their selection from the

---

32. Theo van Leeuwen, *Introducing Social Semiotics: An Introductory Textbook* (London: Routledge, 2005), 285.

33. Van Leeuwen, *Introducing Social Semiotics*, 3.

34. Carey Jewitt, "An Introduction to Multimodality," in *The Routledge Handbook of Multimodal Analysis*, ed. Carey Jewitt (London: Routledge, 2009), 23. This is seen in Saussure's *Course in General Linguistics* and Roland Barthes, *Writing Degree Zero and Elements of Semiology* (London: Vintage Classics, 2010).

semiotic resources that are available to them in a particular moment: meaning is a choice from a system.[35]

This leads to the social aspect of social semiotics. The semiotic resources that people make use of are drawn from the social context. The "choice is always socially located and regulated, both with respect to what resources are made available to whom, and the discourses that regulate and shape how modes are used by people. Discourses of gender, social class, race, generation, institutional norms and other articulations of power shape and regulate people's use of semiotic resources."[36] These discourses may in certain instances be social rules of a type, but they are not unchanging codes; they are versatile and dynamic.

Liturgical books, such as lectionaries, missals, and the Evangelical Lutheran Worship *Worship* book (pew edition), are composite wholes in which the representation of reality (as understood by Christians) is expressed through both verbal and visual modes. In these books, words and images complement each other without necessarily offering the same information. They present a richer experience than the sum of their independent components. Thus, an appropriate approach to these books requires the adoption of a multimodal perspective that provides the tools to study their verbal and visual components, as well as the meaning that emanates from the combination of both semiotic modes (verbal and visual).

3.3. Multimodality

Jewitt in her *Routledge Handbook of Multimodal Analysis* identifies three main approaches to multimodality, including Kress and van Leeuwen's social semiotics of the visual.[37] Multimodality, she writes, "proceeds on the assumption that representation and communication always draw

---

35. Jewitt, "Introduction to Multimodality," 23.
36. Jewitt, "Introduction to Multimodality," 23.
37. Carey Jewitt, "Different Approaches to Multimodality," in Jewitt, *Routledge Handbook*, 28–39. These are Hallidayan social semiotics multimodal theory of communication, extended and elaborated by Kress and van Leeuwen; systemic functional grammar multimodal discourse analysis, associated with O'Toole, Baldry and Thibault, and O'Halloran; and multimodal interactional analysis as found in the works of Scollon and Norris.

on a multiplicity of modes, all of which have the potential to contribute equally to meaning." As such, language, whether as speech or as writing, is one of many representational and communicative modes through which meanings are made, distributed, received, interpreted, and remade in interpretation. Language is, as Jewitt explains, "only ever one mode nestled among a multimodal ensemble of modes."[38] Kress and van Leeuwen, along with others, therefore maintain that all interactions are multimodal. Sigrid Norris clarifies this, acknowledging that multimodality "steps away from the notion that language always plays a central role in interaction, without denying that it often does."[39] Significantly, language is not perceived as providing either the starting point or a prototypical model for all modes of communication.

> The second assumption central to multimodal research is that each mode in a multimodal ensemble is understood as realizing different communicative work. Multimodality assumes that all modes have, like language, been shaped through their cultural, historical and social uses to realize social functions. Multimodality takes all communicative acts to be constituted of and through the social. Image and other non-linguistic modes take on specific roles in a specific context and moment in time. The roles are not fixed but articulated and situated.[40]

Multimodality approaches representation, communication, and interaction as something more than language. It takes in the role of image, gesture, gaze, and posture as well as the use of space in representation and communication. Kress and van Leeuwen define multimodality as "the use of several semiotic modes in the design of a semiotic product or event."[41] Multimodality seeks to extend the social interpretation of language and its meanings to the entire range of representational and communicational modes or semiotic resources for making meaning that are available and employed in a culture.[42] Another member of the Sydney school, Kay O'Halloran, offers this definition:

---

38. Jewitt, "Introduction to Multimodality," 14–15.
39. Sigrid Norris, *Analysing Multimodal Interaction: A Methodological Framework* (London: Routledge, 2004), 3.
40. Jewitt, "Introduction to Multimodality," 15.
41. Kress and van Leeuwen, *Multimodal Discourse*, 20.
42. Carey Jewitt, introduction to Jewitt, *Routledge Handbook*, 1–8.

The multimodal social semiotic approach draws upon Michael Halliday's systemic function (SF) theory to provide frameworks for conceptualizing the complex array of semiotic resources which are used to create meaning (e.g. language, visual imagery, gesture, sound, music, three dimensional objects and architecture) and detailed practices for analyzing the meaning arising from the integrated use of those resources in communication artifacts (i.e. texts) and events.[43]

The iconic liturgical books wherein the graphic designs that I am analyzing are found are themselves multimodal artifacts, employing extensively the three modes of language, image, and color. These iconic liturgical books are profoundly rich semiotic objects—the products of people making creative use of the semiotic resources at their disposal. They are in turn semiotic resources for other dense multimodal semiotic events, the liturgical rituals in which these books are put to use. They are also books that, in this particular social context of the liturgy, perform semiotic acts. They iconize or sacralize the Scriptures. Moreover, and significantly, there is a direct semiotic correlation between the three modes—language, image, and color—that are put to use in the iconic books and those in use in the liturgies. The verbal text printed in the book is the same as that that will be read out aloud in the course of proclaiming the word of God (the liturgy of the word). The mode of language may be understood to appear in two modes: the printed verbal text and the corresponding spoken verbal text when it is read out aloud. This in turn will most likely be accompanied by other modes such as gesture. These gestures could potentially include the processing of the lectionary, raised aloft, through the congregation; the incensing of the book once placed on the ambo or lectern; the raising of the lectionary before and/or after the reading; a bowing toward the book; the kissing of the book; the marking of a sign of the cross over the gospel lection; and a gesture toward the congregation by the reader that gathers them into the reading of the Scriptures. In the case of *The Sunday Missal*, coherence exists between the text printed in the missal and that being read out aloud from a corresponding lectionary in the liturgy, as *The Sunday Missal* functions like a small, personal, handheld lectionary.

---

43. Kay L. O'Halloran, "Multimodal Analysis and Digital Technology," in *Interdisciplinary Perspectives on Multimodality: Theory and Practice; Proceedings of the Third International Conference on Multimodality*, ed. Anthony Baldry and Elena Montagna (Campobasso, Italy: Palladino, 2007), 2.

"The meanings in any mode are always interwoven with the meanings made with those of all other modes co-present and 'co-operating' in the communicative event. The interaction between modes is itself a part of the production of meaning," writes Jewitt.[44] This interaction between modes is particularly well evidenced in religious rituals. Christian liturgy is a pertinent and rich example of a multimodal semiotic event. Many of the graphic designs by Craighead and Markell make use of other graphic motifs that may find their echo in the church environment: in the form of stained-glass windows, banners, embroidered vestments, and other artifacts. Craighead's design *Christ, Yesterday and Today* (fig. 1.3) makes visual reference to the paschal candle. At the Easter Vigil a real paschal candle will be blessed, incised, and lit in front of the congregation, processed through the darkened church, raised and lowered into the baptismal waters, and prominently displayed until Pentecost. From this candle each person present will light a personal candle. The design is closely interwoven with the other modes and images unfolding before the viewer. The same may be said of the prominent colors of red and white in Markell's *Easter* design (fig. 1.1), and these feature in the vestments during Holy Week and Eastertide.

Multimodality, Jewitt continues,

> is built on the assumption that the meanings of signs fashioned from multimodal semiotic resources are, like speech, social. That is they are shaped by the norms and rules operating at the moment of sign making, influenced by the motivations and interests of a sign-maker in a specific context. That is, sign-makers select, adapt and refashion meanings through the process of reading/interpretation of the sign. These effect and shape the sign that is made.[45]

Christian liturgies are multimodal semiotic events, the influence of which may be clearly seen in the graphic designs in the liturgical books analyzed here. This study concentrates on the mode of image while also considering the mode of color and the intersemiosis of the modes of text and image.

---

44. Jewitt, "Introduction to Multimodality," 15.
45. Jewitt, "Introduction to Multimodality," 16.

3.4. Semiotics and Graphic Design

Graphic design is an academic anomaly. Open a history of graphic design, and one will invariably find oneself at the very beginning of recorded human visual communication, examining the cave paintings of Lascaux or southern Africa.[46] However, despite millennia of visual semiotic work and sign making, graphic design as an articulated academic discipline only appears in the mid-twentieth century.[47] The claim that graphic designers lay to the primordial hand stencils of Lascaux is rooted in the design's evident and implicit impulse to communicate to other human beings, to make a visual sign that may operate in a way similar to that which we unconsciously expect of verbal language. During the 1950s and 1960s, the influence of Saussure's semiotics is evident in Swiss graphic design, most notably in the area of typography, with the emergence of fonts such as Helvetica and Univers.[48] Over the last three decades, as semiotics itself has developed as a discipline, so too has its recognition and appropriation by graphic design theorists as the most viable theoretical system for explaining much of what graphic design is about.

Saussure, Peirce and Barthes are recognized as among the most influential semioticians in this field. Bal argues that Saussure had a rather static notion of how signs work and was uninterested in how meanings change and are changed in use, a point reiterated by Robert Hodge and Kress.[49]

---

46. Philip B. Meggs, *A History of Graphic Design* (London: Viking, 1983); Johanna Drucker and Emily McVarish, *Graphic Design History: A Critical Guide*, 2nd rev. ed. (Upper Saddle River, NJ: Pearson Prentice Hall, 2012); Patrick Cramsie, *The Story of Graphic Design: From the Invention of Writing to the Birth of Digital Design* (London: British Library, 2010).

47. The first recorded use of the term "graphic design" is attributed to William Addison Dwiggins in 1922. He uses the term in an inclusive way "to describe his various activities in printed communications, like book design, illustration, typography, lettering and calligraphy." The term gained general usage after World War II. See Alan Livingston and Isabella Livingston, *Dictionary of Graphic Design and Designers* (London: Thames and Hudson, 2012), 43.

48. Meredith Davis, *Graphic Design Theory* (London: Thames and Hudson, 2012), 118–19. By creating a neutral font, one so stripped of flourish and embellishment and reduced to the most elemental and purest form, the words themselves could be received free of prepackaged meaning.

49. Mieke Bal and Norman Bryson, *Looking In: The Art of Viewing* (London: Routledge, 2001), 174; Robert Hodge and Gunther Kress, *Social Semiotics* (Cambridge: Polity, 1988), 11.

David Crow, in his introduction to semiotics, *Visible Signs*, covers much of the same territory, introducing with graphic examples the many ways in which images function as signifiers in a culture. Crow is more influenced by the fluid and flexible Peircean semiotics than Saussurean semiotics. "What is distinct about Peirce's view of semiosis is that it is not a one way process with a fixed meaning. It is part of an active process between the sign and the reader of the sign. It is an exchange between the two which involves some negotiation. The meaning of the sign will be affected by the background of the reader."[50]

Semiotician Algirdas Greimas, popular with text-based scholars, including biblical scholars such as Daniel Patte and Gary Phillips, has not been taken up to the same extent as Pierce by graphic designers.[51] Meredith Davis writes,

> The earliest efforts to frame meaning making in graphic design in semiotic terms date to the early 1970s. Thomas Ockerse and Hans Van Dijk, professors of graphic design at Rhode Island School of Design (RISD), have dedicated much of their academic careers to building a semiotic theory of design that attempts to address not only the critical analysis of existing design but also generative approaches to making new work. Proponents of the ideas of Peirce, Ockerse and Van Dijk structured RISD's curricular experiences around Peirce's typology of signs and his notion of the *interpretant*, which they described as the context, condition or function of signs.[52]

Sean Hall notes that even though semiotics has seminal texts, established procedures, scholarly debate, publications, and an academic history,

---

50. Crow, *Visible Signs*, 36.

51. Daniel Patte, *The Religious Dimensions of Biblical Texts: Greimas's Structural Semiotics and Biblical Exegesis* (Atlanta: Society of Biblical Literature, 1990). Gary Phillips, along with Patte and others, translated Greimas and brought his ideas to biblical scholarship. See Algirdas J. Greimas and Julien Courtès, *Semiotics and Language: An Analytical Dictionary*, trans. Larry Crist et al. (Bloomington: Indiana University Press, 1981).

Brigitte Kahl is a biblical scholar working with Greimasian semiotics, including the semiotic square—and bringing this to the analysis of visual art (sculpture in particular) as well as texts. See Brigitte Kahl, *Galatians Re-imagined: Reading with the Eyes of the Vanquished* (Minneapolis: Fortress, 2010), 18, 86–89; Kahl, "The Galatian Suicide and the Transbinary Semiotics of Christ Crucified (Galatians 3:1): Critical Reimagination," in Robbins, Melion, and Jeal, *Art of Visual Exegesis*, 195–240.

52. Davis, *Graphic Design Theory*, 104.

it is still a diverse and eclectic subject. This diversity and eclecticism, particularly in terms of its methods, stems from the many different disciplines that it uses for inspiration, including linguistics, anthropology, psychology, philosophy, sociology, art history, communication studies, media studies, and material culture.

> The result of this is that the subject has both a weakness and a strength.
> The weakness is that there is no body of knowledge of which semiotics can be certain. Its strength is that the absence of such a body of knowledge gives it the freedom to explore new ways of thinking, avenues of interest and novel ways of exploring meaning. In other words, because it does not have the doctrinal quality of other intellectual disciplines, semiotics can be actively done rather than just simply decipher a coded meaning and leave it at that. Instead we are asked continually to reinterpret, reformat, rework, rethink and reinvigorate the meanings that we find around us.[53]

Others stress the "theoretical provenance" of semiotics (and its application to many sorts of visual materials) and hence its ability to critique those materials.[54] Within graphic design theory, semiotics is understood as being about the tools, processes, and contexts there are for creating, interpreting, and understanding meaning in a variety of different ways.[55] "Semiology offers a very full box of analytical tools for taking an image apart and tracing how it works in relation to broader systems of meaning. Semiology is also influential as an approach to interpreting the materials of visual culture because it draws on the work of several major theorists,"[56] says Gillian Rose, again situating semiotics academically for designers. It is, however, about much more than simply, as Margaret Iverson puts it, "laying bare the prejudices beneath the smooth surface of the beautiful."[57]

---

53. Sean Hall, *This Means This, This Means That: A User's Guide to Semiotics* (London: King, 2007), 173.

54. Rose, *Visual Methodologies*, 147. This "theoretical provenance" is found in the work of Saussure and Peirce.

55. Hall, *This Means This*, 5.

56. Rose, *Visual Methodologies*, 105. Rose's use of the term *semiology* interspersed interchangeably with *semiotics* is inconsistent with the contemporary theorists to whom she refers.

57. Iversen, "Saussure v. Peirce," 84.

Given this history, it is not surprising that the whole area of semiotics has come to be, as Davis says,

> of particular significance for graphic designers, whose work involves the combination of visual and verbal elements according to social and cultural conventions. This concern for meaning and how it is made and interpreted is as fundamental to graphic design practice as are the esthetics of form. Any text on design theory must therefore include explanations of how language and meaning-making work.[58]

Rose writes,

> The *sign* is the key term in semiology, which consists of a *signifier* and a *signified*; these are *semiotic resources*, which are often *multimodal*. The *referent* is what a *sign* refers to in the real world. The transfer of a sign's signifieds is structured through *codes*, which in turn give onto *dominant codes*. Codes and dominant codes encourage *preferred readings* of images by viewers.[59]

Throughout the theoretical works on graphic design one repeatedly encounters the many ways in which semiotic categories are applied to the interpretation of an image, for example in conceptual, binary structures: truth and falsity, sameness and difference, whole and parts. The foundational concepts of semiotics—signs and signification, signifier and the signified—continue to underlie and facilitate the *how* of the process of the transmission of meaning. Peircean terms such as *index, icon,* and *symbol* alongside Claude Shannon and Warren Weaver's categories of communication—*sender, receiver, intention, message, transmission, noise, receiver,* and *destination*—are all terms that undergird critical visual methodology.

3.5. The Social Semiotics of Kress and van Leeuwen

Kress and van Leeuwen are two academic semioticians who have collaborated over many years, often across continents, to develop the field of social semiotics emerging from the so-called Sydney school and Hal-

---

58. Davis, *Graphic Design Theory*, 104.
59. Rose, *Visual Methodologies*, 147, emphasis original.

lidayan *Systemic Functional Grammar*.⁶⁰ Although strongly inspired by the Paris school and Barthean semiotics, social semiotics has moved beyond structuralism. In social semiotics the focus has changed "from the 'sign' to the way people use semiotic 'resources' both to produce communicative artifacts and events and to interpret them—which is also a form of semiotic production—in the context of specific social situations and practices."⁶¹ While clearly aware of the slight resistance many semioticians feel toward the use of linguistic terminology to categorize semiotics, Kress and van Leeuwen use the metaphor of a grammar to elucidate their developing theory of a social semiotics of the visual.⁶²

> What is our "visual grammar" a grammar of? First of all we would say that it describes a social resource of a particular group, its explicit and implicit knowledge about this resource, and its uses in the practices of

---

60. Gunther Kress (1940–2019), MBE, until his recent sudden death, was professor of semiotics and education in the Department of Culture, Communication and Media at the Institute of Education of the University of London. He was one of the main developers of the subfield of social semiotics alongside van Leeuwen. He moved to Sydney in the 1980s, where his collaboration with van Leeuwen began. Theo van Leeuwen (b. 1947) worked as a film and television producer, scriptwriter, and director before becoming an academic. He is now professor emeritus of the Faculty of Arts and Social Sciences, University of Technology, Sydney.

61. Van Leeuwen, *Introducing Social Semiotics*, xi. He notes, "Although the approach to social semiotics presented here draws on a wide range of sources, the key impetus for its development was Halliday's social semiotic view of language (1978). In the second half of the 1980s and 1990s, it was elaborated by the work of the Sydney Semiotics Circle, whose members included, among others, Jim Martin, Terry Threadgold, Paul Thibault, Radan Martinec, Anne Cranny-Francis, Jennifer Biddle and above all, my long time collaborator Gunther Kress—as well as from a distance, Bob Hodge and Jay Lemke" (xi). He also cites the influence of members of the critical discourse analysis group, including Norman Fairclough, David Machin, and Carey Jewitt among numerous other influential colleagues and collaborators (xii).

62. Kress and van Leeuwen address critics who might mistakenly associate their work with a linguistic model thus: "We have not imported the theories and methodologies of linguistics directly into the domain of the visual, as has been done by others working in the field. We do not make a separation of syntax, semantics and pragmatics in the domain of the visual; we do not look for (the analogies of) sentences, clauses, nouns, verbs, and so on, in images. We take the view that language and visual communication can both be used to realize the 'same' fundamental systems of meaning that constitute our cultures, but that each does so by means of its own specific forms, does so differently and independently" (*Reading Images*, 19).

that group. Then, second, we would say that it is a quite general grammar, because we need a term that can encompass oil painting as well as magazine layout, the comic strip as well as the scientific diagram. Drawing these two points together, and bearing in mind our social definition of grammar, we would say that "our" grammar is a quite general grammar of contemporary visual design in "Western" cultures, an account of the explicit and implicit knowledge and practices around a resource, consisting of the elements and rules underlying a culture-specific form of visual communication.[63]

Van Leeuwen makes the important point that social semiotics is not "'pure' theory, not a self contained field. It comes into its own when it is applied to specific instances and specific problems, and it always requires immersing oneself not just in semiotic concepts and methods as such but also in some other field.... Interdisciplinarity is an absolutely essential feature of social semiotics."[64] For this reason, it is clear how such an approach is particularly well suited to the analyses of images designed to accompany biblical texts in the context of a communal, liturgical resource such as a lectionary, missal, or worship book. Social semiotics provides a powerful interdisciplinary bridge between text and image.

Kress outlines the fundamental assumptions underlying the social-semiotic understanding of the term *sign*, the central concept of semiotics. "In social semiotics theory, signs are made—not used—by a sign-maker who brings meaning into an *apt* conjunction with a form, a selection/choice shaped by the sign-maker's *interest*. In the process of representation sign makers remake concepts and 'knowledge' in a constant new shaping of the cultural resources for dealing with the social world."[65] He continues,

> Signs are always newly *made* in social interaction; signs are *motivated*, not *arbitrary* relations of meaning and form; the motivated relation of a *form* and a *meaning* is based on and arises out of the *interest* of the makers of signs; the forms/signifiers which are used in the making of signs are *made* in social interaction and become part of the semiotic resources of a culture.[66]

---

63. Kress and van Leeuwen, *Reading Images*, 3.
64. Van Leeuwen, *Introducing Social Semiotics*, 1.
65. Kress, *Multimodality*, 62.
66. Kress, *Multimodality*, 54.

The key term in social semiotics is "semiotic resource."[67] This is a progression of the term *sign*, fundamental to semiotics historically. "Semiotic resource" is both broader and sheds the sense of something pregiven, an accepted, static, conventional meaning. It allows for the fact that semiotic resources are affected and changed both by their use and their interpretation. Kress writes, "Resources are constantly remade; never willfully, arbitrarily, anarchically but precisely, in line with what I need, in response to some demand, some 'prompt' now—whether in conversation, in writing, in silent engagement with some framed aspect of the world, or in inner debate."[68] Closely linked to this is the acknowledgment of the semiotic potential of the semiotic resource. These resources are not restricted to speech, writing, and imaging but extend to almost everything we do or make.

> In social semiotics resources are signifiers, observable actions and objects that have been drawn into the domain of social communication and that have a *theoretical* semiotic potential constituted by all their past uses and all their potential uses and an *actual* semiotic potential constituted by those past uses that are known to and considered relevant by the users of the resource, and by such potential uses as might be uncovered by the users on the basis of their specific needs and interests. Such uses take place in social context and this context may either have rules or best practices that regulate how specific semiotic resources can be used, or leave the users relatively free in their use of the resource.[69]

Once an artifact, image, activity, or event is understood to constitute a semiotic resource, it becomes possible to describe its semiotic potential, its meaning-making potential. With regard to visual design, Kress and van Leeuwen maintain that a semiotic mode, such as the visual, fulfills three major functions. In order to function as a full system of communication, the visual, like all semiotic modes, has to serve several representational and communicational requirements. Expanding on the work of Halliday, Kress and van Leeuwen employ these three metafunctions, the *ideational*, the *interpersonal* and the *textual*.[70] Every semiotic resource fulfills an ideational function, a function of representing "the world inside and

---

67. Van Leeuwen, *Introducing Social Semiotics*, 3.
68. Kress, *Multimodality*, 8.
69. Van Leeuwen, *Introducing Social Semiotics*, 4.
70. Kress and van Leeuwen, *Reading Images*, 42.

around us," and an interpersonal function, a function of enacting social interactions as social relations. All message entities—texts—also attempt to present a coherent world, the world of the text, a world in which all elements cohere internally and which itself coheres with its relevant environment.[71] As such, the focus of social semiotics, for the purpose of this study, is on the description of these ideational, interpersonal, and textual resources as they are realized in the visual mode. Kress and van Leeuwen have developed and elaborated on a vast array of tools, some old and familiar to the work of image analysis, and some new and sourced from other disciplines, for conducting a thorough investigation into the meaning-making functions and potential of a semiotic resource.

3.6. Conclusion

The field of graphic design, concerned with both meaning-making events and practices as they occur and also with generating meaning in multimodal forms, recognizes semiotics as the theory that best describes, analyzes, and critiques its practice. In recent decades, Halliday's foundational *Systemic Functional Grammar* has fundamentally shifted the understanding about the relationship between language and other modes of communication. Semioticians Kress and van Leeuwen have expanded this theory to demonstrate how semiotics may provide a powerful method for exploring how images work to express meaning. They claim that the age of the hegemony of the densely printed page has come to an end and is being rapidly replaced by the emergent multimodal means of communication, and these are heavily reliant on visual components. The metaphorical semiotic toolkit is equipped with a vast array of comprehensive analytical tools that address every aspect of an image from composition through to color. This social semiotics of the visual, developed by Kress and van Leeuwen, offers an extensive and valuable approach to analyzing images. Moreover, it provides a dynamic avenue of investigation into the ways that images, inspired by biblical texts, have interpreted those texts and work to give meaning to them. Later chapters will endeavor to show, through detailed analysis of biblically inspired

---

71. Kress and van Leeuwen, *Reading Images*, 15. *Text* here refers to a "complex of signs which cohere both internally with each other and externally with the context in and for which they were produced" (43).

images, the value that a social semiotics of the visual holds out to the biblical reception project.

4
Liturgy and Lectionary in Biblical Reception History

> The liturgical assembly (the ecclesia in its primary sense) is the place where the Bible becomes the Bible.
> —Louis-Marie Chauvet, *Symbol and Sacrament*

The *Wirkungsgeschichte* of the Bible surely finds few more potent and profuse exemplars than the lectionary. So closely identified with the Bible is the lectionary in the context of the liturgies of many Christian churches that it is almost invisible in its own right as an extraordinarily rich and profound site of the reception of the Bible. Consistent with other areas of biblical studies and biblical theology, exegetical aids and commentaries abound, yet I have not encountered a study examining the lectionary as the pivotal site of the church's reception of the Bible. Even Gerhard Ebeling and Ulrich Luz, fine-tuned to the role of the church in the exposition of Scripture, extending their understanding of biblical reception to reaching out and embracing the "interpretations of the Bible in non-verbal media such as art, music, dancing, prayer" and "in political actions, wars, peacemaking, suffering, institutions," skip over the lectionary.[1] Here I seek to situate the lectionary as a primary site of the reception of the Bible. The lectionary is at once an iconic book, a hermeneutical approach, and a liturgical structure. This chapter endeavors to briefly chart the historical development of the lectionary as it has unfolded toward its contemporary role in the worship practice of Christians.

The general introduction to the Roman Catholic *Lectionary for Mass* sets out clear instructions about the handling, veneration, and display of the lectionary in the ritual of the Mass and context of the church:

---

1. Luz, *Matthew 1–7*, 95; Ebeling, *Word and Tradition*, 28.

The special prominence given to the gospel reading at the Sunday assembly has been expressed in a variety of ritual traditions, many dating back to the fourth and fifth centuries. For example, from the most ancient tradition to this day, only ordained ministers (bishops, priests, and deacons) proclaim the gospel. They also sign the book and themselves with the cross before, and kiss the gospel book after reading. The assembly greets the gospel reading with a sung acclamation and stands during the proclamation. Only the gospel reading is introduced with "The Lord be with you" and its response. On occasion, the proclaiming of the gospel is solemnized by a procession with candles and incensing of the book. Finally, in earlier centuries when there were separate Lectionaries for gospels (evangelaries) and for epistles (epistolaries), the more ornate was the gospel book, a practice encouraged today: In our times also, then, it is very desirable that cathedrals and at least the larger, more populous parishes and the churches with a larger attendance possess a beautifully designed Book of the Gospels, separate from the other book of readings.[2]

These instructions clearly point to the lectionary being understood as an iconic book according to indicators set out by scholars James Watts and Dorina Miller Parmenter, among others. Annabel Wharton describes an iconic book as one that "is an immediately recognizable symbol with connotations of admiration or veneration that has both social and psychological import."[3] George Aichele, writing about the semiotics of the Bible, notes: "The single physical volume—the biblical codex—connotes to many people that the Bible is a single book and that it consequently bears a single consistent message."[4] Parmenter notes that within the academic study of Christianity, the meaning and role of the Bible as a ritual object has been overlooked.[5] This is true to a far greater extent for the lectionary, the missal, and other liturgical books featuring Scripture passages that are

---

2. *General Introduction to the Lectionary for Mass (LM)*, *Ordo Lectionem Missae, Editio Typica Altera* (Rome: Libreria Editrice Vaticana, 1981), 36. It is pertinent to note the encouragement that the lectionary or book of the gospels be "beautifully designed."

3. Annabel Wharton, "Icon, Idol, Totem and Fetish," in *Icon and Word: The Power of Images in Byzantium*, ed. Anthony Eastmond and Liz James (Aldershot, UK: Ashgate, 2003), 4.

4. George Aichele, *Sign, Text, Scripture: Semiotics and the Bible* (Sheffield: Sheffield Academic, 1997), 132.

5. Dorina Miller Parmenter, "The Iconic Book: The Image of the Bible in Early Christian Rituals," in *Iconic Books and Texts*, ed. James W. Watts (Sheffield: Equinox, 2013), 66. This point has also been made by Colleen McDannell in her book *Material*

made use of in the context of liturgy. Moreover, not only has the iconicity of the lectionary not yet received due attention, but the hermeneutical significance of the lectionary also requires further exploration from biblical scholars. As liturgist Fritz West acutely observes: "What we have in lections are segments of the biblical narrative which when appropriated by the church, acquire a semantic autonomy, worlds of their own distinct from that of the Bible."[6] This appropriation is explicitly acknowledged by the church in its explanation of how the selection of lections is consciously oriented toward the formation of individual and collective Christian identity in the context of the worshiping community.[7]

Significantly for this study, the social-semiotic approach of Kress and van Leeuwen places an emphasis on the social dimension of meaning making. In the context of the Christian liturgy, the lectionary is not only a site and conduit for the reception of the Bible but a semiotic resource in itself. It is an iconic book that performs ritually in the proclamation of God's word, a word that is spoken directly into the lives of people, individually and collectively, chanted and preached, penetrating contexts personal, social, and political, and formative of those gathered. Liturgist Liam Tracey writes, "In this context the word is proclaimed and becomes the word for now. Not just a word from the past with information about the past, but a word for today which challenges, consoles and constructs a community, a worshiping assembly, participating in the prayer of Christ in the power of the Spirit, the inspiration of the word that has gathered them together."[8] The intention is that those gathered, the church, become "a living hermeneut of the word."[9]

As the graphic designs with which the present study is concerned are found in the context of the lectionary and missal, it is important to contextualize these books. In this chapter, then, I cover the history of the lectionary as it has developed over a lengthy trajectory originating in ancient Jewish practice and through much reform in recent decades.

Christianity: Religion and Popular Culture in America (New Haven: Yale University Press, 1995), 68.

6. Fritz West, *Scripture and Memory: The Ecumenical Hermeneutic of the Three-Year Lectionaries* (Collegeville, MN: Liturgical Press, 1997), 30.

7. *General Introduction to the Lectionary*.

8. Liam Tracey, "Word and Sacrament," in *The Study of Liturgy and Worship*, ed. Juliette Day and Benjamin Gordon-Taylor (London: SPCK, 2013), 60.

9. Thomas R. Whelan, "Eucharist and Word," *MS* 4 (2014): 117–18.

Following that, I will look at the current situation as it has emerged out of the liturgical reforms of the mid- to late twentieth century, with a particular focus on the Evangelical Lutheran Worship series, the lectionary and *Worship* pew edition, and the Roman Catholic *Lectionary for Sunday* and its accompanying *Sunday Missal*.

4.1. A Brief History of the Development of the Lectionary

The lectionary stems from a long tradition that reaches back beyond the early Christian churches into ancient Jewish practice. The earliest reference to the reading of the Scriptures in the context of the gathered community of believers comes from the history of Israel and the Jewish people. While archaeological evidence of synagogue buildings extends only to the second century BCE, many scholars believe that the Jewish tradition of assembling regularly for prayer and for the study of the sacred writings dates back to the time of the Babylonian exile (587–535 BCE). As Israel was deprived of its homeland, monarchy, and, most importantly, its temple, an important remaining collective focus for worship among the deported exiles and emerging diaspora was the Torah. The Talmud credits Ezra the scribe with instituting a communal practice of reading the Torah on Shabbat, and other days and occasions (b. B. Qam. 82a).

"It was probably in these circumstances that the Jewish people developed what could be called a 'Liturgy of the Word' for which they regularly gathered on the Sabbath."[10] There are specific readings associated with other festivals: Ruth at Shavuot, the Song of Songs at Passover, and Esther at Purim, for example, among others. This practice continued after the Jews returned to their homeland, rebuilt the temple, and restored the tradition of animal sacrifices in the temple. Both those Jews who remained in their adoptive lands and those resettled in Judah and Jerusalem continued to gather in synagogue and study their Scriptures together.[11] By the time of Jesus, the practice was already considered an ancient tradition, and a syna-

---

10. Normand Bonneau, *The Sunday Lectionary: Ritual Word, Paschal Shape* (Collegeville, MN: Liturgical Press, 1997), 7.

11. Shaye J. D. Cohen, *From the Maccabees to the Mishnah*, 2nd ed. (Louisville: Westminster John Knox, 2006), 106–8. Also see Stefan C. Reif, "The Early Liturgy of the Synagogue," in *The Cambridge Companion to Judaism*, vol. 3, *The Early Roman Period*, ed. William Horbury, William D. Davies, and John Sturdy (Cambridge: Cambridge University Press, 1999), 334.

gogue building was a standard feature in most Jewish communities both in Palestine and in the diaspora.[12] A regular system of Sabbath synagogue readings with a particular focus on the Torah is in evidence by the time of Jesus, and this tradition appears to have been widespread and firmly established. Indeed, James in his speech in the Acts (15:21) alludes to this: "For in every city, for generations past, Moses has had those who proclaim him, for he has been read aloud every Sabbath in the synagogues." Normand Bonneau suggests, "Chances are that the incident of Jesus reading from an excerpt from the prophet Isaiah in the synagogue at Nazareth (Luke 4:15–21) points to a system of *haftorah* readings." *Haftorah* were those secondary readings from the Prophets that followed the primary reading from the Torah—the most important reading—held especially sacred in the Jewish tradition.[13]

By the sixth century CE, there is strong evidence of a well-established Jewish ritual of using a lectionary system.[14] This involved "a sequential reading from the Torah, paired with a *haftorah* from the prophets, interrupted by special readings at the annual high feasts."[15] Two parallel traditions had evolved slowly from the time of the return from exile: "In Babylonia, the Torah was divided into fifty-four sections and the entire Torah was read through every year. In the land of Israel, the Torah was subdivided into more numerous sections and the cycle of readings was

---

12. Hanswulf Bloedhorn and Gil Hüttenmeister, "The Synagogue," in Horbury, Davies, and Sturdy, *Cambridge Companion to Judaism*, 3:270.

13. The Jewish tradition recognizes the Prophets as including the Former Prophets: Joshua, Judges, 1 and 2 Samuel, 1 and 2 Kings; and the Latter Prophets: Isaiah, Jeremiah, Ezekiel, and the twelve minor prophets.

14. Charles Perrot, "The Reading of the Bible in the Ancient Synagogue," in *Mikra: Text, Translation, Reading, and Interpretation of the Hebrew Bible in Ancient Judaism and Early Christianity*, ed. Martin J. Mulder (Philadelphia: Fortress, 1988), 137–59. It may seem anachronistic to speak of lectionaries in this context, yet this is a conventional term used by scholars in this area, e.g., Reif, "Early Liturgy," 335. It may be helpful in this context to think of lectionary as the concept of a collection of Scriptures (and possibly hymns) from which preselected lections may be read and sung, without that preselection necessarily being either a single book or as fixed as the contemporary term *lectionary* implies. See Cohen's description of the liturgical use of the Psalms as indicated by the Qumran scrolls in *From the Maccabees*, 65–66.

15. Bonneau, *Sunday Lectionary*, 7. The *haftorah* (Aramaic for "dismissal") "explained, amplified, or otherwise complemented the theme of the Torah excerpt of the day" (6).

completed every three or three and a half years."[16] The Babylonian tradition's one-year cycle, which prevailed, is the one used in synagogues today.[17] The structure of the three-year cycle that emerged from the reform of Vatican II and operates in the Roman Catholic *Lectionary for Mass* and the ecumenical *Revised Common Lectionary* can be detected in this early synagogue lectionary practice.

Many of the first Christians were, of course, also Jews and maintained their temple and synagogue attendance alongside their gathering together as Christians. There is no evidence to suggest that they brought the Jewish lectionary practice into their meetings when they came together to break bread in commemoration of Jesus. However, several Pauline epistles mention the nature of these gatherings as including the Jewish Scriptures, as the Christians are instructed to "sing psalms" and "hymns and spiritual songs" (Eph 5:18–20; Col 3:16). A more explicit reference to the reading of the Jewish Scriptures occurs in 1 Tim 4:13: "Until I arrive, give attention to the public reading of Scripture, to exhorting, to teaching." The practice of sharing and reading Paul's letters, not yet considered Scripture, began at his own behest: "I solemnly command you by the Lord that this letter be read to all [the brothers and sisters]" (1 Thess 5:27).[18] The author of the letter to the Colossians likewise promotes the sharing and reading aloud of letters (Col 4:16).[19]

> In addition to these exhortations to pray the Scriptures and to read the letters aloud to the assembled community, the many hymns, fragments of hymns, and canticles in the New Testament, all of them very much inspired by the Scriptures, point to an early Christian appropriation of the Scriptures for worship. Thus, even if no direct evidence of the pat-

---

16. Cohen, *From the Maccabees*, 64. Bonneau notes significantly that in both traditions these were sequential readings: "The Palestinian tradition read the Torah in 154 sequential segments over a three-year cycle of Sabbaths. The Babylonian tradition's one-year cycle, which prevailed, is the one used in synagogues today" (*Sunday Lectionary*, 6).

17. Perrot, "Reading of the Bible," 146. A detailed account of contemporary Jewish practice may be found in Ismar Elbogen, *Jewish Liturgy: A Comprehensive History*, trans. Raymond P. Scheindlin (Philadelphia: Jewish Publication Society, 1993), 129–56.

18. Frederick F. Bruce, *1 and 2 Thessalonians*, WBC 45 (Waco, TX: Word, 1982), 136.

19. Eduard Schweizer, *The Letter to the Colossians*, trans. Andrew Chester (London: SPCK, 1982), 210.

terned use of Scripture readings in the first decades of the Church exists, the New Testament books strongly suggest that the earliest communities enjoyed a rich liturgical life in which the Scriptures played a major role.[20]

4.2. The Christian Tradition of the Lectionary

Outside the New Testament, the earliest account of the Scriptures being read aloud in the Christian community comes from Justin Martyr around 150 CE:

> On the day which is dedicated to the sun, all those who live in the cities and who dwell in the countryside gather in a common meeting, and for as long as there is time the Memoirs of the Apostles or the writings of the prophets are read. Then, when the reader has finished, the president verbally gives a warning and appeal for the imitation of these good examples. Then we all rise together and offer prayers, and, as we said before, when our prayer is ended, bread is brought forward along with wine and water, and the president likewise thanks to the best of his ability, and the people call out their assent, saying the Amen. Then there is the distribution and the participation in the Eucharistic elements, which also are sent with the deacons to those who are absent.[21]

What is significant about Justin Martyr's account is that these early Christians were already pairing the gospels ("memoirs of the apostles" are understood to be what we now know as the gospels) with the "prophets" (probably by this time an amalgamation of the Torah and *haftorah*). If we accept the memoirs of the apostles to be what became in time the canonical New Testament gospels, Justin Martyr's account points out a significant development in the burgeoning ritual practice of the early Christians. They have placed the gospels in the position held by the Torah in the synagogue. They continue to read the "prophets," which scholars suggest should probably be understood to refer to the collection of Scriptures—Torah and prophets—inherited from the Jewish tradition.[22] While no formal canon of "New Testament" Scriptures existed in the first several centuries of the

---

20. Bonneau, *Sunday Lectionary*, 8–9. Bonneau lists as examples John 1:1–18; Phil 2:5–11; Col 1:15–20; Eph 1:3–14; 1 Tim 3:15; 2 Tim 2:11–13; Luke 1:46–55, 68–79; 2:29–32.
21. Justin Martyr, *1 Apol.* 67 (*ANF* 1:186).
22. Bonneau, *Sunday Lectionary*, 10.

Common Era, it is telling that these Christians believed their collection of writings to be of sufficient value and importance as to be paired with the Scriptures of their ancestors and read aloud in their worship ceremonies.[23] In this practice we see a kernel of that which persists to this day: "The reading of the gospels at the Sunday Eucharist was to become the most consistent practice of all later churches." Scholars suggest that this early habit of pairing implies that an Old Testament reading was paired to the gospel by way of illustrating how Jesus was the fulfillment of the promises made by God. In this sense the "Sunday Lectionary, then, continues the ancient trajectory launched by the New Testament."[24]

The legitimization of Christianity by Constantine and its emergence into the state religion during the fourth century saw the liturgy expand in ritual complexity, and the first elements of what would become Advent and Christmas appeared. This development in turn required an equally complete and rich lectionary. Evidence of prescribed and organized readings to celebrate the liturgical seasons dates from the fourth century, with patterns showing a mix of sequential and selected readings. There was a pattern in some churches of the following order of readings at the Sunday Eucharist: one from the Old Testament, one from the apostolic writings, and one from the gospel. The readers, in the main, still read directly from the full Bible codex.[25] It is only in the sixth and seventh centuries that actual books containing the texts to be read in their liturgical and calendrical order began to appear and proliferate. *Comites*, as they were named, were designed for greater ease of use and mobility for presiders to celebrate the Eucharist.

---

23. Aichele problematizes the concept of canon as it later developed in the Christian church, placing limits, as it did, on what came to be defined as Scripture. "The semiotics of canon and the theological importance of canon—the message conveyed by the canonical collection—are inseparably intertwined." They collude to constitute a "final signified" and confer an immutable, authoritative, and definitive status on the closed collection, thereby "effectively plac[ing] the selected texts in the past, a mythical past" as well as establishing "an illusion of continuity between the present community and the point of origin" and "an unchanging facade that nevertheless conceals many changes in belief and interpretation" (*Sign, Text, Scripture*, 129–39). He develops this further in George Aichele, *The Control of Biblical Meaning: Canon as Semiotic Mechanism* (Harrisburg, PA: Trinity Press International, 2001).

24. Bonneau, *Sunday Lectionary*, 10.

25. The Bibles used in liturgy had marginal markings indicating the beginning, called *incipit* and the end, *explicit*, of the excerpt to be read (Bonneau, *Sunday Lectionary*, 12).

The abandonment of Latin as the lingua franca after the fall of the Roman Empire and the embrace of vernacular languages precipitated an unfortunate impoverishment of the liturgy during the medieval period. The church's insisting on Latin as the liturgical language alienated many laypeople, for whom this was no longer a spoken language. The resulting absorption of the lectionary into the priest's missal saw many prescribed readings reassigned: "Traditional Sunday readings were relegated to weekdays; saint's day readings replaced Sunday readings; the practice of sequential readings fell away."[26] Along with the orientation of the priest away from the people, the inclusion of all the Scripture readings into the priest's missal saw an ever-increasing privatization of the liturgy in the power of an elevated clergy.[27]

The Council of Trent (1545–1563) made far-reaching reforms to the Roman Catholic liturgy. In 1570 Pope Pius V promulgated the *Missale Romanum* and imposed it as standard for the Roman Catholic liturgy the world over. This missal continued unchanged until the major reform of Vatican II and contained all the Scripture passages for every liturgy and for all possible occasions on which a Mass might be offered. It was a one-year cycle, and, strikingly, the Old Testament barely featured, being read on only three occasions during the year: Epiphany, Good Friday, and the Easter Vigil. There was little sequential reading of the books of the Bible, and all the readings were now to be found in the *Missale Romanum*. There was no longer a separate lectionary book, and all the readings were read in Latin by the priest from his missal. This situation prevailed for almost four hundred years until the reform of Vatican II.

In the decades preceding the Second Vatican Council, both liturgical and biblical studies enjoyed a renewed surge of interest among Catholic scholars. Kieran O'Mahony writes,

> The roots of the Liturgical Movement lay in the nineteenth century. There were several dimensions to this. In part, this was very scholarly:

---

26. Bonneau, *Sunday Lectionary*, 14. Until this period the priest's missal had functioned more as a book of rites, a sacramentary, containing the orders of services.

27. Laura Light expands on the thirteenth-century invention of a combined Bible and missal in one volume. Technical innovations such as thinner parchment made possible this practical solution to the problem of many books. In these Bible-missals, "The Missal appears either at the beginning, the end, or in the middle of the volume between the Psalms and Proverbs." See Light, "The Thirteenth Century Pandect: Bibles with Missals," in *Form and Function in the Late Medieval Bible*, ed. Eyal Poleg and Laura Light (Leiden: Brill, 2014), 192.

the recovery of plainchant (*Solesmes*) and of patristic texts with the publication of *Patrologia Graeca* and the *Patrologia Latina* (*Migne*). In part it was pastoral, with the founding of national institutes of pastoral liturgy and the promotion of pastoral theology as such. A great deal of this work was ecumenically inspired, and the Ecumenical Movement itself was part of the energy and vision. In the preparation period, the lectionaries of all churches of whatever tradition were inspected for inspiration and ideas. Finally, the Biblical Theology Movement was a reaction both to the Great War and to the failure of liberal Protestantism.[28]

4.3. The Reform of Vatican II

Turning their attention to the Sunday Eucharist and the Tridentine Lectionary (*Missale Romanum*), the council saw many deficiencies and expressed a desire for profound reform, especially the inclusion of a greater diversity of Scripture passages in the lectionary for the benefit of the faithful. The reforms of Vatican II saw a renewed emphasis on the Sunday Eucharist and primary feast days, with a corresponding purging of excessive alternative holy days and saints' feasts on Sundays. The reform of the lectionary was substantial and included a vastly expanded selection of texts from the full breadth of the Bible. Its aim was to adapt the lectionary to the modern era while still respecting the ancient tradition in which it stands: "that new forms grow in some way organically out of the forms already existing" (*SC* 23); "faithfully in accordance with the tradition" (*SC* 4). The task of reforming the lectionary (1964–1967) was undertaken by thirty-one biblical scholars, to which a further nine hundred biblical scholars, theologians, liturgists, catechists, and pastors gave consultation and evaluation. The three criteria for the reform of the lectionary were that it should (1) focus on Christ as (2) the center and fulfillment of salvation history (3) proclaimed for Christian life.[29] These criteria alert us to the hermeneutical focus of the lectionary.

The council's Coetus XI committee on lectionary reform set about its task and ultimately produced the *Lectionary for Mass*—a radical departure from the *Missale Romanum* to the extent that it included a far greater depth

---

28. Kieran O'Mahony, *Speaking from Within: Biblical Approaches for Effective Preaching* (Dublin: Veritas, 2016), 50.

29. These criteria are taken from *SC* 102, 5, 52, and 9, respectively.

and breadth of scriptural material.[30] Bonneau writes, "The first and most important characteristic of the Sunday and Feast Lectionary is its orientation to the paschal mystery of Jesus' death and resurrection." This provides the Christocentric orientation for the structure of this repertoire of biblical passages. As the context is the Eucharist—"liturgical principles take precedence over exegetical, catechetical, paraenetic or other principles in determining the selection and distribution of biblical passages"—the liturgy is concerned with the assembly here gathered, celebrating their common salvation history actualized in the present moment.[31] The liturgical year is seasonal: "The church unfolds the whole mystery of Christ over the cycle of the year, from his incarnation and birth to his return to heaven, to the day of Pentecost, and to our waiting for our hope of bliss and the return of the Lord" (*SC* 102). Precedents can be seen in a number of contemporary Protestant churches and the ancient Palestinian synagogue lectionary cycle, alongside very early Christian traditions in Milan, Rome, Byzantine, Spain, and Gaul, all of which influenced the reinstitution of an ancient three-year cycle. The committee's innovation was the ordering of these around the designation of a different synoptic gospel for each year of the cycle.

> In Year A the Lectionary offers Matthew's portrait of Jesus as teacher and preacher who announces the Good News of the Kingdom of Heaven; in Year B the Lectionary presents the Marcan Jesus as a man of God who confronts and overcomes the powers of illness, sin, and death; in Year C the Lectionary proposes the Lucan Jesus who, in his seeking out the poor and the outcast, reveals God's mercy and compassion.[32]

---

30. A thorough account of this work is given by Annibale Bugnini in *The Reform of the Liturgy 1948–1975*, trans. Matthew O'Connell (Collegeville, MN: Liturgical Press, 1990).

31. Bonneau, *Sunday Lectionary*, 31–32.

32. Bonneau, *Sunday Lectionary*, 37. A number of Irish scholars have written exegetical aids to accompany the lectionary and to assist lectors and preachers in their preparations. See, e.g., Sean Goan, *Let the Reader Understand: The Sunday Readings* (Dublin: Columba, 2007). Martin Hogan has a series: *Jesus Our Saviour: Reflections on the Sunday Readings for Luke's Year* (Dublin: Columba, 2006); *Jesus Our Teacher: Reflections on the Sunday Readings for Matthew's Year* (Dublin: Columba, 2007); *Jesus Our Servant: Reflections on the Sunday Readings for Mark's Year,* (Dublin: Columba, 2008). Martin McNamara has recently produced a volume for Year A: *Sunday Readings with Matthew: Interpretations and Reflections* (Dublin: Veritas, 2016).

John's Gospel is privileged during Lent, Holy Week, and Eastertide of every year, another hallowed ancient tradition. While each annual cycle has its own distinct flavor given by the synoptic gospel assigned to it, it retains a high degree of continuity from year to year, as it moves through the same pattern of feasts, seasons, and Sundays. A stable, recurring structure is patently discernible beneath the three-year cycle of readings.

In accordance with the council's desire to reintroduce the Old Testament readings at the Eucharist, a tradition that had fallen away and been neglected for almost a millennium, a first reading from the Old Testament was recovered.[33] It was decided that the Old Testament would be read, followed by a passage from the apostolic writings, culminating in the gospel passage of the day. "In this way each Sunday and Feast Day would find its focus in the paschal mystery—Jesus (the gospel passage) interpreted (the excerpt from the apostolic writing) as the fulfillment of salvation history (the Old Testament)."[34] Of the three readings the gospel is preeminent: "It is evident that among all the inspired writings, even those of the New Testament, the gospels rightly have the supreme place, because they form the primary testimony to the life and teaching of the incarnate Word, our saviour" (*DV* 18). As such, the gospel is proclaimed last, as the climax of the three readings, and it sets the tone and theme for the liturgy, most especially on major feasts such as Easter and Christmas. As Bonneau notes, "The gospel passages provide images and phrases which are often woven into the fabric of collects, prefaces, and blessings," and during the seasons of Ordinary Time, the gospel "determines the selection of the accompanying first reading from the Old Testament."[35]

The fruit of the council's deliberations was the *Lectionary for Mass*, promulgated by Pope Paul VI on 25 May 1969. It had an extraordinary and unforeseen impact and influenced a widespread renewal of interest in the use of the Bible in worship. "Within a decade of its appearance, a number of other church traditions in North America adopted the Roman Catholic *Lectionary for Mass*, and adapted it where necessary to meet the

---

33. The Roman Missal of 1570 contained in all a total of 138 passages of Scripture, while the revised lectionary offers a total of 529: 160 OT and 369 NT.
34. Bonneau, *Sunday Lectionary*, 37.
35. Bonneau, *Sunday Lectionary*, 37.

worship needs of their congregations."[36] This resulted in a number of different lectionaries, and in 1978 thirteen churches from Canada and the United States came together to consider the situation. In 1983, this group, the North American Committee on Calendar and Lectionary, proposed a *Common Lectionary*, which they sent forth to participating churches for their responses. The final outcome of their endeavors was the *Revised Common Lectionary*, published in 1992.[37]

There are a great many similarities between the *Revised Common Lectionary* and the *Lectionary for Mass*, most notably the emphasis on Sunday—the Lord's Day; the same annual calendar; the same three-year cycle of readings and nearly unanimous agreement on gospel selections throughout; three readings per Sunday, the first from the Hebrew Scriptures, the second from the Epistles, and the third from the gospels, with a responsorial psalm after the first reading.[38] There are also differences, and these arise largely in the section of Old Testament readings, where it deviates from the strict typological choice of Old Testament pericopes of the Roman Catholic selection, determined by the gospel. The *Revised Common Lectionary* also offers two tracks for the first reading to facilitate those churches that celebrate Eucharist monthly or quarterly.[39] The second of these tracks "favors a semicontinuous reading of more extensive narrative sequences over a number of Sundays."[40] The unexpected outcome of the work of the Coetus XI committee at Vatican II, "the most informed

---

36. Bonneau, *Sunday Lectionary*, 52. These traditions include Presbyterian Churches in the United States (1970), the Episcopal Church (1970), the Lutheran Church in the United States (1970), a consensus edition published by the ecumenical Consultation on Church Union representing nine Protestant Churches (1974), the Methodist Church in the United States (1976), and the Disciples of Christ (who adopted the Presbyterian edition in 1976). In Canada, both the United Church and the Anglican Church first adopted and adapted the Roman Catholic Sunday Lectionary in 1980.

37. Consultation on Common Texts, *Common Lectionary: The Lectionary Proposed by the Consultation on Common Texts* (New York: Church Hymnal, 1983); *The Revised Common Lectionary* (Nashville: Abingdon, 1992).

38. A full list of the lectionary readings, found in both the *Revised Common Lectionary* and the *Lectionary for Mass*, for the Easter season may be found in the appendix to this volume.

39. It is the *Revised Common Lectionary* that is the lectionary of the ELW *Worship* series of the Evangelical Lutheran Church in America.

40. Bonneau, *Sunday Lectionary*, 53.

and thorough Lectionary revision ever carried out in the church's history," resulted in great ecumenical advances, with previously unseen dialogue and collaboration on the subject of the Bible.[41]

These lectionaries are not without their detractors, of course. Gerard Sloyan pointed out drawbacks. He describes the process of a Christian community making choices of scriptural texts in the curating or composing of a lectionary thus: "It evaluates the selections it makes as potentially significant in the lives of hearers without declaring the omitted material nonsignificant; but surely less significant. The positive evaluation placed on the material chosen makes a Lectionary no less than a new canon."[42]

> The lectionaries now in use have many virtues, but they are badly flawed. If we assume that one of their major intents is to give Christian hearers a feel for the whole Bible, we must declare the plan a failure. The brevity of the readings selected from a very wide range sees to this. Another factor might be termed the overall absence of biblical robustness. Congregations are being protected from the insoluble mystery of God by a packaged providence, a packaged morality, even a packaged mystery of Christ. To record the latter view is painful, for the lectionaries show their greatest ingenuity in establishing the correspondence between the two testaments. But while rising to laudable heights, in ways that would have pleased the New Testament writers and church fathers, they also tend to reduce the Hebrew revelation to a matter of little consequence apart from the fact of Jesus Christ.[43]

In his observations, Sloyan clearly raises to the surface precisely why lectionaries are such extraordinary sites of reception of the Bible. As one of the images that I consider in this study is found in the lectionary used by the Evangelical Lutheran Church of America, it is important to note that the reform of the worship books of the three major branches of the Lutheran Church in North America that took place in the 1960s caused no small amount of conflict between these churches. Ralph Quere, secretary of the Liturgical Text Committee of the Inter-Lutheran Commission on Worship, chronicles much of the process in his monograph.[44]

---

41. Bonneau, *Sunday Lectionary*, 55.

42. Gerard S. Sloyan, "The Lectionary as a Context for Interpretation," *Int* 31 (1977): 131.

43. Sloyan, "Lectionary as a Context," 138.

44. Ralph Quere, *In the Context of Unity: A History of the Development of the Lutheran Book of Worship* (Minneapolis: Lutheran University Press, 2003). The three

4.4. The Lutheran Reforms of the Late Twentieth Century

Eugene Brand, a former director of the Inter-Lutheran Commission on Worship (ILCW), describes the parallel movements of reform that animated the Lutheran churches during the sixties:

> The ILCW began its work in 1966, just three years after the Second Vatican Council issued its *Constitution on the Sacred Liturgy*.
>
> It was a time when the Roman Catholic Church was working on a new Roman Missal and when most mainline churches in the English-speaking world were preparing new liturgical books. It was also a time when Lutherans were in the initial stages of ecumenical contact, setting up bilateral theological dialogues.[45]

The primary outcome of the committee's work was the *Lutheran Book of Worship*, which was not received with equal enthusiasm in every quarter, as is characteristic of liturgical reforms generally. However, in 2003, Brand maintained, "After 25 years the *LBW* has taken its place as a presence in Lutheran congregations and homes, including some Missouri Synod churches."[46] Since that significant milestone, a further development has evolved in the Evangelical Lutheran Worship series of lectionaries, sacramentaries, and *Worship* books (fig. 4.1): this Evangelical Lutheran Worship series has come about as a consequence of further collaboration, study, and reflection on the role of liturgy, Scripture, and sacrament. In 2005 the Evangelical Lutheran Church in America and the Evangelical Lutheran Church in Canada confirmed the completion of the Evangelical Lutheran Worship series and commended its use. The introduction to the *Worship* book, published by Augsburg Fortress in 2006, outlines the provenance for this development in line with the centuries-old Lutheran tradition:

---

major branches of the Lutheran Church mentioned are the American Lutheran Church (ALC), the Lutheran Church in America (LCA), and the Lutheran Church—Missouri Synod (LCMS).

45. Eugene L. Brand, "The Lutheran Book of Worship—Quarter Century Reckoning," *CurTM* 30.5 (2003): 327. "The *LBW* is also found in English-language congregations in various European cities as well as in other parts of the world where Lutherans desire to worship in English. One example is the Cathedral Church of Our Saviour in Bukoba, Tanzania, where a weekly Eucharist in English is celebrated."

46. Brand, "Lutheran Book of Worship," 327.

Fig. 4.1. Evangelical Lutheran Worship Lectionary, Year C, gold-foiled and stamped (leaf pattern) cover and title page.

At the beginning of the twenty-first century, Evangelical Lutheran Worship continues the renewal of worship that has taken place over the three centuries Lutherans have been on the North American continent and in the Caribbean region. During this time, renewal efforts have been marked by a movement from a variety of Lutheran immigrant traditions toward a greater similarity of liturgical forms and a more common repertoire of song. The liturgy set out in 1748 by Henry Melchior Muhlenberg and the Common Service of 1888 are two earlier milestones along this path. In the twentieth century, the consolidation of various immigrant Lutheran church bodies and those more established on this continent was reflected in the primary worship books used by mid-century, namely *Service Book and Hymnal* and *The Lutheran Hymnal*. In 1978 *Lutheran Book of Worship* was published, the fruit of an ambitious inter-Lutheran project that sought to unite most North American Lutherans in the use of a single worship book with shared liturgical forms and a common repertoire of hymnody.[47]

The hefty *Worship* pew edition (fig. 4.2), which "stands alongside a leaders edition and musical accompaniment editions,"[48] is intended for the

---

47. Introduction to *Evangelical Lutheran Worship* (Minneapolis: Augsburg Fortress, 2006), 7.
48. Introduction to *Evangelical Lutheran Worship*, 8. It is worth noting that the entire range of the ELW series of lectionaries, sacramentaries, *Worship* books, musical

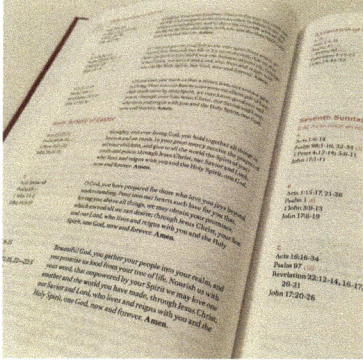

Fig. 4.2. The Evangelical Lutheran Worship *Worship* pew edition, and double-page spread detail showing lectionary readings.

worshiper in the pew, and while many bring their own copy, books may also often be found on the way into the Sunday service. The *Worship* book sets out the full mass as the normal Sunday service, with ten different Holy Communion settings, as well as the liturgies for various different occasions such as baptism, marriages, and funerals, among others. Much of the volume is given over to an extensive hymnal of almost nine hundred music settings. It also includes a complete Psalter. The liturgical calendar and list of the lectionary readings for the three-year Sunday cycle is found at the beginning of the book, but the full Scripture passages themselves are not included. For these, one must make recourse to the Evangelical Lutheran Worship lectionary (fig. 4.1), a separate volume for each year (A, B, and C) in the liturgical calendar, containing all the readings for each Sunday of the year and numerous other particular feast days (such as Easter and Christmas). The presumption is that the person in the pew shall listen actively to the proclaimed word or follow along in their own Bible, which they will have brought with them (having sourced the readings of the day from the list in the *Worship* book).

---

accompaniment volumes, etc., is referred to as the Worship series. The single-volume *Worship* pew edition pictured here (fig. 4.2) is also titled and referred to simply as *Worship*. The ELW *Worship* has a list of all the readings for the three-year cycle at the beginning of the book (fig. 4.2). This is followed by ten Holy Communion settings with music and settings for major feast and life passages. The majority of the book is composed of a Psalter and a hymnal (a staggering 893 pieces of music). Additional resources include a three-year daily lectionary listing at the back.

4.5. The Hermeneutics of the Lectionary

Lectionaries are books that contains lections (groupings of short Scripture passages, selected by the church from the Bible and reorganized according to the liturgical year), the calendar of liturgical seasons, and feasts celebrated throughout the year.[49] While the Bible is understood to have its own overarching narrative of God's enduring relationship with humanity and the world, from creation to the end of time, the lectionary revolves around the narrative of the salvific event of Jesus, the most significant moments of which are expressed liturgically in the feasts of the incarnation (Christmas) and the resurrection (Easter). These serve as axes in the calendar of the liturgical year. The hermeneutical orientation of the lectionary selections is deliberately Christocentric and serves the explicit purpose of the formation of the Christian community around the life, work, and person of Jesus Christ.[50] Fritz West writes,

> In creating a Lectionary, the church selects pericopes from the biblical narrative and organizes them into another one, the calendrical narrative of the liturgical year. It is a creative act of mnemonic composition, guided by the church's understanding of the salvation of God in Christ. In arranging the composition, the Church juxtaposes selections both diachronically and synchronically. Finally, the Lectionary system generates lections, sets of texts to be read in the liturgical assembly on specific occasions. Bible, Lectionary, and lection are all Scripture but distinct forms of it, irreducible one to the other.[51]

These Scripture passages, drawn from the Bible, are placed in a wholly different hermeneutical context. Bible and lectionary become distinctly different books in the process. West continues,

---

49. The liturgical year begins with the first Sunday of Advent, generally around the end of November, about a month before the short season of Christmas, and proceeds into the period known as Epiphany. Two periods of Ordinary Time occur: a short period between Epiphany and Lent, and a longer period between Pentecost and Advent. The most important liturgical seasons in the church's year are Christmas and Easter. In theological terms Easter is seen to be the most significant time of year for Christians.

50. Whelan gives a thorough account of the Roman Catholic understanding of the presence of Christ in the proclaimed word in the context of the mass ("Eucharist and Word").

51. West, *Scripture and Memory*, 27–28.

Whereas the Church included material in the Bible to offer a rule of faith (canon), it creates a Lectionary to proclaim that within the framework of the liturgical year. Whereas passages in the Bible contribute to the biblical narrative, sections of lectionaries serve the calendrical narrative. In the Bible the immediate context for the readings are the books in which they stand; in a Lectionary it is the Sundays, seasons, and segments of the liturgical year.[52]

4.6. The Overlooked Iconicity of Liturgical Books

Watts delineates three dimensions intrinsic to Scriptures that explain their cultural function and religious significance. These are the *semantic*, including the interpretation of what is written in commentary and homily; the *performative*, the ritualized forms of private and public reading, musical and artistic renditions; and the *iconic*, the attention paid to the physical form, the material artifact, its ritual manipulation and artistic representation.[53]

S. Brent Plate has added a fourth dimension, the *aesthetic*, the sensual aspect of sacred texts to this proposal.[54] Lectionaries are ritualized in all four of these dimensions, but attention here is on the third aspect, the iconic dimension, with a particular emphasis on the creativity and attention brought by artists to the lectionary (and missal) as a material artifact. Semiotically, lectionaries and missals are iconic in ways both similar and dissimilar to the Bible. The design of these books *and* their hermeneutical orientation toward a liturgical function collude to give them their own distinct qualities that in turn make them iconic books in their own right. There is a powerful social semiosis at work in every instance where these books are ritualized. They play a significant part in rich multimodal events where the Scriptures are simultaneously seen and read as verbal, printed text, heard as verbal text as lections are proclaimed aloud, repeated in homilies, and sung in hymns. They are further elaborated in image: in the designs found in lectionaries and missals, worship books and missalettes, banners, paintings and stained-glass windows.

---

52. West, *Scripture and Memory*, 26–27.

53. James W. Watts, "The Three Dimensions of Scriptures," in Watts, *Iconic Books and Texts*, 14–16.

54. S. Brent Plate, "What the Book Arts Can Teach Us about Sacred Texts: The Aesthetic Dimension of Scripture," in *Sensing Sacred Texts*, ed. James W. Watts (Sheffield: Equinox, 2018), 11.

At the center of this polyvalent multimodal event is the lectionary, an iconic book that has been designed to function as such, an instance of the church's reception of the Bible, replete in itself with rich intersemiosis of word and image. Design historian Patrick Cramsie notes, "From the end of antiquity, the iconographic traditions of the Bible progressively made their way into the different liturgical books."[55] The design of these contemporary books intended for the gathered community in the liturgical context—the Evangelical Lutheran Worship lectionary and *Worship* (pew edition), *The Sunday Missal* (fig. 4.3), and those of other congregations such as the Anglican Book of Common Prayer—aims to mimic this biblical iconicity in certain ways and thereby impart to these books a share in the iconic quality of the Bible. The designers consciously set out to create a visual connection, through the use of certain quality materials, typefaces, colors, and layouts, to the Bible. From a social-semiotic perspective, since the earliest *Comites*,[56] everything about these books—the superior quality of materials—be they pigments or parchments or paper, the use of gold leaf in illuminated manuscripts or gilding of page edges in modern mass-produced volumes, the languages in which they are written, the typefaces chosen (Roman or Gothic), the amount of white space on the page, the density of text, the number of columns, the use of particular colors (black, red, and white), the ratio of text to image, the placement and style of illuminations and illustrations, the use of colored ribbon placeholders—indicates the most apt choices being made from the semiotic

---

55. Cramsie, *Story of Graphic Design*, 47.

56. The oldest surviving Roman lectionary, the *Comes Romanus* of Würzburg, sometimes referred to as the *Comes of Würzburg* or the *Würzburg Lectionary* (composed between 600 and 650 CE), was written around 700 CE. "The *Comes of Würzburg* is of great importance because it is the oldest extant witness of the Roman lectionary system." See Cassian Folsom, "The Liturgical Books of the Roman Rite," in *Handbook for Liturgical Studies: Introduction to the Liturgy*, ed. Anscar J. Chupungo (Collegeville, MN: Liturgical Press, 1997), 1:258. The *Comes of Würzburg* may be found in the library of the University of Würzburg, where it bears the catalog number Mp th f 62 and is fully digitized and available to view online: http://vb.uni-wuerzburg.de/ub/permalink/mpthf62. "The place and date of writing are still the subject of disagreement. Three divisions can be recognized in the contents of this manuscript. No liturgical text is given, simply the day is indicated. Beginning with Christmas, the calendar follows the course of the church year in a manner similar to the sacramentaries and lectionaries of the eighth and ninth centuries." There are scholars who suggest a possible origin in the British Isles, among them Felice Lifshitz, "Gender Trouble in Paradise: The Problem of the Liturgical *Virgo*," in *Images of Medieval Sanctity: Essays in Honour of Gary Dickson*, ed. Debra Higgs Strickland (Leiden: Brill, 2007), 28.

Fig. 4.3. *The Sunday Missal* and internal double-page spread.

resources available at a particular time and place in order to make meaning among a particular community of people. Each of these visual elements of design contains its own range of affordances and meaning potentials that are further enhanced when they are brought together in a design. Watts writes: "Scriptures are icons. They are not just texts to be interpreted and performed. They are material objects that convey religious significance by their production, display, and ritual manipulation."[57]

This is evidently achieved in the relationship people have with these objects. Colleen McDannell notes, "Domestic religious objects may mirror ecclesiastical objects."[58] In the cases of the Roman Catholic *Sunday Missal* and the Evangelical Lutheran Worship *Worship*, they mirror to various degrees both the sacramentary and the lectionary—they may also physically travel frequently between the holy space and the domestic space, providing a further connection.[59] In the Catholic tradition *The Sunday Missal* often becomes the repository of other holy mementos: holy cards, bookmarks, and prayer cards for deceased family and friends; ordinations and professions; parish missions and pilgrimages; even little medals. This act in itself, of placing prayer cards and other objects between the pages, is a powerful personalizing of the book and linking of the believer's personal

---

57. Watts, "Three Dimensions of Scriptures," 11.
58. McDannell, *Material Christianity*, 23.
59. In format, the Roman Catholic *Sunday Missal* (fig. 4.4) is a version of the lectionary that is smaller in size and has at the beginning an order of service for the Mass.

Fig. 4.4. Detail from the Evangelical Lutheran Worship *Lectionary* cover showing gold-foil cross design.

life and prayer to the context of the church's liturgy and the communal life of faith. These books, like Bibles, may also be given as gifts for Christian coming-of-age rituals such as confirmation, often with personal dedications.[60] There has been a shift in recent years, however, in the Roman Catholic church away from the use of the personal *Sunday Missal* book in favor of weekly missalettes available in the pews.[61] In design terms, the

---

60. Augsburg Fortress offers an imprinting service where a silver imprint, words of the buyer's choice, can be placed in the gift edition of ELW pew edition.

61. Missalettes are usually an A3 page folded in half to A4 size. One side is printed in full color with a reflection (written by a theologian or biblical scholar), usually on

missalette is a considerable departure from the imitation of those material signifiers that lend themselves to the Bible's iconicity.[62] By contrast, Daniel Kantor, creative director of the graphic design of the Evangelical Lutheran Worship series, writes an almost poetic account of the designing of *Worship*, drawing parallels to the labor of medieval scribes and illuminators in terms of personal commitment, selection of materials, choice of colors, and dedication to the process, the self-conscious "sacred endeavor" of the modern designers involved.[63]

4.7. Conclusion

This chapter has illustrated the long passage, down through the religious history of both Jews and Christians, these scriptural texts have traveled to their position in these contemporary liturgical canons. They carry the weight and authority of the Bible into the communal arenas of Christian worship, themselves now iconic sacred books in their own right as they are displayed, incensed, blessed, kissed, venerated, thumbed, committed to memory, wept over, and prayed through.[64] As I will demonstrate in the

---

the gospel reading, and the order of Mass with the full three readings and psalm. The reverse is printed in the parish in black and white, and contains the parish notices. This same model is produced by various orders with publishing houses including (in Ireland) the Society of St Paul, the Dominicans, and the Redemptorists.

62. It would not be possible to describe the missalette as "iconic," nor to imagine it acquiring an iconic quality or status. The single-use and disposable nature of the missalette precludes this in itself. This is not to disparage the missalette, which is popular and clearly functions well. The full-color design and variety of fonts, including popular scripts, which can tend toward the gaudy on occasion; the lesser quality of the paper; the use of replicated religious art, including classics of Renaissance or Baroque art (occasionally distorted out of their original proportions) as illustrations, or royalty-free stock photography; and other design choices make the missalette a different type of religious artifact. Missalettes reflect many contemporary graphic design trends and biblical publishing trends, especially the look popularized in US Biblezines (*Becoming, Explore, Refuel*, to name a few), aimed at teenagers and young people. Timothy Beal considers many of these trends in Bible publishing in *The Rise and Fall of the Bible: The Unexpected History of an Accidental Book* (New York: First Mariner, 2012), especially in "Biblical Values," 41–69. These missalettes, with their thematic commentary and connected imagery exploring the topological theme in the Sunday lection, would make an interesting semiotic study in themselves.

63. Kantor, *Graphic Design and Religion*, 12–23.

64. Light notes in her discussion of two Bible missals that the crucifixion minia-

forthcoming chapters concerning the graphic designs of Craighead for the Roman Catholic *Sunday Missal* and Markell for the Evangelical Lutheran Worship *Worship* series, the Christocentric hermeneutical orientation of these liturgical books, in their Scripture lections, has profoundly influenced these designs.

---

tures "are now smudged from the practice of kissing the image of the Cross" ("Thirteenth Century Pandect," 202).

5
Color

Arguably, color itself is metafunctional.
—Gunther Kress and Theo van Leeuwen, "Color as a Semiotic Mode"

A veritable Holi festival of color has exploded in the public sphere in recent years.[1] The Natural History Museum in London made color the topic of a major summer and tourist-season exhibition.[2] The publishing sector has embraced color-focused material, and many fascinating books dedicated to color in general—or the histories and particularities of individual colors—now abound.[3] If one turns to art looking for creative indicators

---

1. Holi is a Hindu spring festival, also known as the festival of colors or the festival of love, during which participants play, chase, and color each other with dry colored powders and colored water. See "Holi," in *The New Oxford Dictionary of English* (Oxford: Oxford University Press, 1998), 874. This color festival has been appropriated into popular Western European and American music and color festivals far removed from the Hindu religious rituals from which they take their inspiration; see, e.g., https://www.holifestival.org.

2. Titled *Colour and Vision: Through the Eyes of Nature*, the exhibit ran from mid-July to November 2016 and explored the perception and role of color from a scientific and biological perspective. See "Colour and Vision," National History Museum, https://tinyurl.com/SBL6710i.

3. To consider very briefly just the color indigo, for example, and this may be replicated across other pigments and colors: Gösta Sandberg may have anticipated or influenced the interest in indigo with his monograph *Indigo Textiles: Technique and History* (London: Black, 1989). In the past decade three popular books on indigo have appeared and sold well. They include Jenny Balfour-Paul, *Indigo: Egyptian Mummies to Blue Jeans* (Buffalo, NY: Firefly, 2011); Catherine McKinley, *In Search of the Color That Seduced the World* (New York: Bloomsbury, 2011); and Catherine Legrand, *Indigo: The Colour That Changed the World* (London: Thames and Hudson, 2013). The Asian Art Museum in Seattle held an exhibition titled *Mood Indigo* from April to October 2016. A major exhibition *Indigo* was held at the Bibliothèque Forney (Paris)

for this, one could argue that the precedent is there throughout the second half of the twentieth century—anticipated in the color field paintings that emerged out of the abstract modernist movement—and characterized in the work of artists such as Piet Mondrian, Mark Rothko, Paul Klee, and Barnett Newman, among many others. It is also there in the bold pop art of Andy Warhol and Roy Lichtenstein.

No longer does color originate in organic pigments drawn from minerals, plants, or insects of the natural world and extracted through extremely costly, time-consuming, and labor-intensive practices. Science and technology have developed artificial pigments that can be cheaply reproduced in a plethora of readily available formats, for everyday use, from pens to paints.[4] Full-color printing, at the touch of a button, is now a norm in most workplaces and in many homes.[5] However, increasingly, most media that people deal with, not only what they read and view but what they produce themselves, for work or pleasure, is a digital file created and viewed via a screen. The digital realm facilitates the use of a staggering sixteen million different colors.[6] Color has

---

from January to May 2015. *Seas of Blue: Asian Indigo Dye* was one of three new exhibitions at the Charles B. Wang Center at Stony Book University in 2014.

4. In 1856, young chemist William Perkin, conducting experiments on coal-tar residue in a makeshift laboratory at his parents' home in East London, inadvertently discovered the first synthetic dye. "By the first decade of the twentieth century over 2000 colors had been isolated; by 1939 over 7,500 synthetic colors had been listed." See David Batchelor, *The Luminous and the Grey* (London: Reaction Books, 2014), 36. Anthropologist Michael Taussig has also taken up the subject of color. He maintains that color has a manifestly colonial history rooted in the West's discomfort with color, especially bright color, and its associations with the so-called primitive. He delves into Goethe's belief that Europeans were physically averse to vivid color while the "uncivilized" reveled in it, which prompts him to reconsider colonialism as a tension between chromophobes and chromophiles. He also recounts the strange story of coal, which, he argues, displaced colonial color by giving birth to synthetic colors, organic chemistry, and IG Farben, the giant chemical corporation behind the Third Reich. See Taussig, *What Color Is the Sacred?* (Chicago: University of Chicago Press, 2009).

5. The arrival of readily available color dyes did not thrill everyone. Aldous Huxley lamented the devaluing effect of these colors: "The fine point of seldom pleasure has been blunted. What was once a needle of visionary delight has now become a piece of discarded linoleum." See Huxley, *The Doors of Perception and Heaven and Hell* (London: Flamingo, 1994), 7. "For Huxley, science and industry had provided not a revival of or return to color but a corruption, as they rendered a rare wonder ersatz, cheap, commonplace and banal" (Batchelor, *Luminous*, 30).

6. Of these 140 colors have been assigned conventional names. Designers and architects Dixon and Moe provide online guides and tutorials in HTML color. "The

been put in the hands, or at the fingertips, of every person—whether they are printing a school project at home or selecting a color from a digital palette— in ways that were inconceivable half a century ago. As with other aspects of design, such as typography (the use of typefaces), the use of color is no longer the preserve of designers, artists, and printing technicians with specialist skills and access to expensive technologies. Color has been thoroughly democratized and placed within the domain of every person.

Semioticians recognize that something profound is happening in the social-semiotic use of this new and expanded possibility of expression through color. Van Leeuwen sums up:

> In the twentieth century, after a rather "monochrome" period, color began to extend its semiotic reach. Heralded by artists and thinkers, it soon began to play a more important role in the everyday expression of *ideational*, *interpersonal* and *textual* meanings, while all the time retaining its sensual attraction, so investing social communication with pleasure and sensuality.[7]

Greek Semiotician Evangelos Kourdis suggests that beyond sensuality, "color, as a carrier of meaning, is one of the dominant systems of nonverbal communication."[8]

---

most popular are Hex color codes; three byte hexadecimal numbers (meaning they consist of six digits), with each byte, or pair of characters in the Hex code, representing the intensity of red, green and blue in the color respectively.... With modern browsers supporting the full spectrum of 24-bit color, there are 16,777,216 different color possibilities." See Alex Dixon, "What Are HTML Color Codes?," https://tinyurl.com/SBL6710j.

7. Theo van Leeuwen, *Language of Colour: An Introduction* (London: Routledge, 2011), 12. An excellent visual demonstration of this transition from monochrome to color may be seen in the work of data artist Josh Begley in his one-minute visual timeline that scans through every front page of the *New York Times* since its first issue in September 1851. "The timelapse captures decades of text-only front pages before the newspaper began to incorporate illustrated maps and wood engravings. The liberal usage of black and white photography begins a century later and finally the first color photo appears in 1997." See Christopher Jobson, "The Rise of the Image: Every NY Times Front Page since 1852 in under a Minute," Colossal, February 22, 2017, https://tinyurl.com/SBL6710k.

8. Evangelos Kourdis, "Color as Intersemiotic Translation in Everyday Communication: A Sociosemiotic Approach," in *New Semiotics between Tradition and Innovation: Proceedings of the Twelfth World Congress of the International Association of Semiotic Studies (IASS/AIS)*, ed. Kristian Bankov (N.p.: NBU & IASS, 2017), 737, https://tinyurl.com/SBL6710l.

Apart from the chromatic delights of the illuminated manuscripts of the Middle Ages, the biblical text has conventionally been black text on a white substrate with red as the third color, denoting headlines, chapter and verse numbers, marginalia, notes, *incipits* and rubrics, and the spoken words of Jesus. This color triad of white, black, and red has been the prescribed color scheme for religious literature and many other secular forms, from legal documents to poetry, for millennia. It prevails robustly in contemporary liturgical books, as evidenced in the Evangelical Lutheran Worship series and *The Sunday Missal*. This chapter sets out to explore this color triad and its semiotic function within this context of lectionaries and missals. This color triad is formative of the iconicity of these books.

The intention of this chapter is to explore of the semiotic functioning of the three colors operative in the graphic designs created for the Evangelical Lutheran Worship *Lectionary* and *The Sunday Missal* through the social-semiotic method advanced by Kress and van Leeuwen. In the first part of this chapter each color—white, black, and red—will be analyzed individually in terms of the three metafunctions. This semiotic functionality will in turn be brought into dialogue with the two artworks and the biblical lections pertinent to these artworks. In both instances these are the readings of the Easter Triduum and Eastertide. This is a complex process that demands close attention, as there are three colors, three metafunctions, and three elements being considered (two different visual designs and verbal texts). In the second part of this chapter, I will likewise look at the color triad as a unit, through the model of the three metafunctions, and then how the triad functions in Markell's illustration *Easter* and the relevant Scripture passages from the lectionary. I have endeavored to avoid repetition but beg the reader's indulgence through the process of unpacking the polyvalent semiotic role color plays in these artworks.

5.1. Color and the Metafunctions

Social semiotics makes use of Michael A. K. Halliday's theory of metafunctions as a key heuristic in approaching images, and indeed color, as a semiotic resource. "In order to function as a full system of communication, the visual, like all semiotic modes, has to serve representational and communicational requirements." Van Leeuwen and Kress, the initiators of this social semiotics of visual images, refer to these three metafunctions: the *ideational*, the *interpersonal* and the *textual*.[9] They write,

> According to this theory, language simultaneously fulfills three functions: the *ideational function*, the function of constructing representations of the world; the *interpersonal function*, the function of enacting (or helping to enact) interactions characterized by specific social purposes and specific social relations; and the *textual function*, the function of marshaling communicative acts into larger wholes, into the communicative events or texts that realize specific social practices, such as conversations, lectures, reports, etc.[10]

Van Leeuwen has explored the workings of color in particular, as a semiotic mode, claiming that it is indeed possible to speak of a social semiotics of color through reference to these metafunctions.[11] The *ideational* metafunction is that dimension of the image—or color, in this instance— that works to *construe* an experience of the color for the viewer. This metafunction frames the experience of the color (or image or object), allowing it to be understood in terms of analogy and metaphor.[12] Color is also used to denote specific people, places, and things as well as classes of people, places, and things and more general ideas.[13] Graphic designers put considerable effort into choosing colors for logos and corporate identities of businesses and organizations. Combinations of colors, or "unique" colors, may even be copyrighted by corporations for their use alone.[14] We are

---

9. Kress and van Leeuwen, *Reading Images*, 41–43.

10. Gunther Kress and Theo van Leeuwen, "Color as a Semiotic Mode: Notes for a Grammar of Color," *VisCom* 1 (2002): 346.

11. Van Leeuwen, *Language of Color*, 1–12.

12. Halliday, *Language and Linguistics*, 16.

13. Kress and van Leeuwen, "Color as a Semiotic Mode," 347.

14. Kress and van Leeuwen give the example of car manufacturer BMW ensuring its dark blue is quite distinct from that of VW or Ford and legally prohibiting the other

also familiar with color being used to denote aspects of landscape, such as water or mountainous terrain on a map. In the London Underground, as a well-known and much replicated system, "green identifies the District Line and red the Central line, and both on Underground maps and in Underground stations many people look for those colors first, and speak of the 'green line' and the 'red line.'"[15] Increasingly, in this era of big data and the graphic representation of that data, often referred to as infographics, the use of color functioning in this ideational way, to denote classes of people, places, things, and other more general ideas, has become commonplace and even anticipated.

Any semiotic mode has to be able to project the relations between the producer of a (complex) sign and the receiver/reproducer of that sign.[16] The *interpersonal* metafunction is that aspect of the mode that is able to represent a particular social relation between the producer, the viewer, and the object represented. The interpersonal metafunction is about *enacting*: acting out the interpersonal encounters that are essential to our survival.[17] Halliday explains,

> These range all the way from the rapidly changing microencounters of daily life—most centrally, **semiotic** encounters, where we set up and maintain complex patterns of dialogue—to the more permanent institutionalized relationships that collectively constitute the social bond. This is language in its ***interpersonal*** functional, which includes those meanings that are more onesidely personal: expressions of attitude and appraisal, pleasure and displeasure, and other emotional states. Note that, while language can of course talk about these personal and interactional states and processes, its essential function in this area is to act them out.[18]

---

using "their" blue. Likewise universities, for example, have combinations of specific colors that are used across all their stationery, publications, and livery to mark out their identity. These colors are specific, numbered, and named colors within internationally recognized color systems such as Pantone and are indicated in their corporate identity "bibles" for use ("Color as a Semiotic Mode," 347).

15. Kress and van Leeuwen, "Color as a Semiotic Mode," 347.
16. Kress and van Leeuwen, *Reading Images*, 42.
17. Halliday, *On Language and Linguistics*, 16.
18. Halliday, *On Language and Linguistics*, 16, italics and boldface original.

Color is also used to convey *interpersonal* meaning. Just as language allows us to realize speech acts, so color allows us to realize color acts. Color can be used to do things to or for each other. Examples are people aiming to impress or intimidate through power dressing in black, or to warn against obstructions and other hazards by painting them yellow or orange, or even to subdue people.[19] Marie Louise Lacy documents an example whereby the Naval Correctional Center in Seattle found that "pink properly applied, relaxes hostile and aggressive individuals within 15 minutes."[20] Red is widely associated with physical energy and vigor and is often chosen as a color for sports teams.[21] According to research, red, when it forms the main color in the clothing of an athlete or sports team, enhanced their chances of winning. It has also been found that adding color to documents can increase readers' attention span significantly, and "an invoice that has the amount of money due in color is 30% more likely to be paid on time than a mono-color one."[22] Van Leeuwen maintains, "It is not color itself doing these things, it is people doing these things *with* color, using color to interact, albeit in a manipulative way, to energize or calm down—to express the values that go with such activities, to say as it were: 'I am exciting' or 'I am calm.'"[23]

Finally, the *textual* metafunction is that component of meaning that creates coherence with the actual text itself and within its context.[24] Again,

---

19. Kress and van Leeuwen, "Color as a Semiotic Mode," 348.

20. Marie Louise Lacy, *The Power of Colour to Heal the Environment* (London: Rainbow Bridge, 1996), 89.

21. A study conducted by anthropologists Russell Hill and Robert Barton asserts that when opponents of a game are equally matched, the team dressed in red is more likely to win. See Hill and Barton, "Red Enhances Human Performance in Contests," *Nature* 435 (2005): 293. They reached this conclusion by studying the outcomes of one-on-one boxing, tae kwon do, Greco-Roman wrestling, and freestyle wrestling matches at the 2004 Summer Olympics in Athens. This study was further developed looking at English football: Martin J. Attrill et al., "Red Shirt Color Is Associated with Long-Term Team Success in English Football," *JSportsSci* 26 (2008): 577–82. "A matched-pairs analysis of red and non-red wearing teams in eight English cities shows significantly better performance of red teams over a 55-year period. These effects on long-term success have consequences for color selection in team sports, confirm that wearing red enhances performance in a variety of competitive contexts, and provide further impetus for studies of the mechanisms underlying these effects."

22. *The Guardian's Office Hours Supplement*, 3 September 2001, 5, cited in Van Leeuwen, *Language of Color*, 11.

23. Van Leeuwen, *Language of Color*, 11.

24. Halliday, *Language and Linguistics*, 18.

referring to Kress and van Leeuwen: "Any semiotic mode has to have the capacity to form *texts*, complexes of signs which cohere both internally with each other and externally with the context in and for which they were produced."[25] In other words, "color can be used 'textually' to create coherence between the different elements of a larger whole and/or to distinguish between its different parts."[26]

The graphic designs illustrating biblical texts studied here are either created as black-and-white designs or as black, white, and red designs. In each of these cases, these color combinations are fundamental to the semiotic functioning of the illustrations. Building on this earlier exploration of the metafunctions, I will turn now to each of these colors and explore how these colors create meaning in the artworks individually, and then collectively as a color scheme.

5.2. White

In the Western world white is widely perceived as an inherently positive color. It is seen to represent purity, simplicity and clarity, air and space. It is also often connected with exclusivity and elegance. White is strongly associated with innocence, light, goodness, heaven, illumination, understanding, cleanliness, beginnings, transcendence, spirituality, potentiality, humility, sincerity, protection, softness, and perfection.

There are many examples of the ideational metafunction of white at work in the Bible. The simile "white as snow" is commonplace in modern English usage, and *snow* implies natural purity, something untouched, and the possibility of new beginnings. This simile appears in the Bible with two different connotations, one negative and one positive (Exod 4:6; Num 12:10; 2 Kgs 5:27; Dan 7:9; Matt 28:3; Rev 1:14). In a negative sense it refers explicitly to leprosy (Lev 13). Moses is able to make his skin leprous in order to make an impression on Pharaoh (Exod 4:6), and both Miriam (Num 12:10) and Gehazi (2 Kgs 5:27) are blighted with the white skin of leprosy. The positive incidences of white refer to an aspect, either the clothing or the head or hair, of a divine being: "an Ancient One" (Dan 7–9), or Christ in the transfiguration (Matt 28:3) and the vision recounted in Revelation (Rev 1:14).

---

25. Kress and van Leeuwen, *Reading Images*, 43.
26. Van Leeuwen, *Language of Color*, 11.

The most frequent use of white refers to the color of textiles, most often garments. In his instructions on the good life, the Teacher commands: "let your garments always be white" (Eccl 9:8a). White garments can connote royalty (Esth 2:40), glory (Dan 7:9), and faithfulness (2 Esd 2:40). Through a process of bleaching, all stains are removed, and hence the garment is a sign of moral purity (Rev 3:4–5). The color white is implicit in Isaiah's promise of a cleansing of sin: "though your sins are like scarlet, they shall be like snow ... (and) become like wool" (Isa 1:18). Whiteness indicates purity of character, as when the penitent pleads, "Purge me with hyssop and I shall be clean: wash me, and I shall be whiter than snow" (Ps 51:7 [Heb 51:9]).[27]

There are seven references to the color white in the Easter season readings in the *ELW Lectionary*. They include Matt 28:3; Mark 16:5; John 20:12; Acts 1:10; Rev 7:9, 13, 14.[28] The simile "white as snow" occurs in Matt 28:3, describing Jesus's appearance to his disciples: "His appearance was like lightening, and his clothing white as snow" (λευκὸν ὡσεὶ χιών).[29] The Catholic *Lectionary for Mass* shares all of these readings except John 20:12 (taken from the pericope of John 20:11–18, the appearance of Christ to Mary of Magdala), and verse 13 (with reference to those "robed in white") is omitted in the reading of Rev 7:9, 14–17 (fourth Sunday of Easter, year C).[30]

Acts 1:10 has "two men in white robes" (ἐσθῆτι λευκῇ) suddenly stand beside the disciples, who are gazing heavenward as Jesus ascends. Joseph Fitzmyer implies an ideational connection between their white robes and their identity as angels. "The 'white robes' signify their otherworldly nature. Thus the ascent of Christ is attended by heavenly figures, who act as apocalyptic *angeli interpretes*. Cf Acts 10:30; 2 Macc 3:26."[31] Craig

---

27. Mary Petrine Boyd, "White," *NIDB* 5:844.

28. This includes the Easter Vigil and continues through seven Sundays and includes the feast of Pentecost. There are twenty-three references to "light" in the Easter readings in the Evangelical Lutheran Worship lectionary cycle.

29. "Pertaining to being bright or shining, either of a source or of an object which is illuminated by a source—'bright, shining, radiant,' 'the bright morning star' Rev 22:16. 'his clothes became bright as light' Mt 17:2." See Johannes P. Louw and Eugene A. Nida, *Lexical Semantics of the Greek New Testament* (Atlanta: Society of Biblical Literature, 1992), 14.50.

30. John 20:11–18 is read on the Tuesday in the Octave of Easter.

31. Joseph A. Fitzmyer, *Acts of the Apostles* (New York: Doubleday, 1997), 210, emphasis original.

Keener also identifies them as angels and locates this within the context of the interpersonal function of white, being put to work in the social world of the first century and earlier.

> Their garb in white helps reinforce their identity as angels (cf. John 20:12; Rev 15:6). This color was not associated exclusively with angels. People wore white or linen for a variety of reasons. (Linen had long been the most common fabric for clothing in Egypt and elsewhere. Dyed garments were usually heavier woolen garments; white clothes could be of wool or linen, but linen was rarely dyed and could instead be bleached white.) People especially wore white or linen to enter or serve in sacred places, including the Jerusalem temple. Pythagoras's disciples used white and linen; some deities were portrayed wearing white, though those associated with death could be portrayed wearing black. Roman politicians also wore white to emphasize purity, and Romans wore white on other important occasions.[32]

The association of white with otherworldliness, purity, and sacred spaces is thus established in the broader cultural religious imagination and practice.[33] It is also borne out in the biblical text in the use of phrases such as "white as snow" and the white robes worn by the angels that they may be recognized as heavenly beings by the disciples. The white of their robes sets them apart and designates them as those who assist in the divine work; it signifies their heavenly character and therefore their authority, holiness, and trustworthiness as explicators of the event.

The ideational metafunction of white in Markell's *Easter* is to connote light—the sacred, *divine* light against which this silhouette of the risen *Christ* is seen. That divine light radiates through or from the figure of *Christ*

---

32. Craig S. Keener, *Acts: An Exegetical Commentary* (Grand Rapids, Baker Academic, 2012), 1:728–29.

33. Within the context of Christian liturgy the positive values of the color white, especially connotations of purity, are brought to the liturgical vestments generally (white albs echo the ancient practice of wearing white to preside in sacred settings) and emphasized for the major feasts of Christmas and Easter. Here, white is connected to ideas about the glory of God. All is made new in the incarnation of Jesus. Likewise, the glory of the resurrection is socially enacted in white garments. People are received into the church through baptism, conventionally clothed in white, indicating purity in the washing away of sin and the emergence of the new person in Christ. In all of these instances, white is being used semiotically in an interpersonally communicative way to enact a symbolic union with God through Christ.

and may be understood to radiate from his heart.[34] The color white functions similarly in Craighead's design. It is against the divine white light that the silhouetted *Christ* is seen, and this light reverberates through the intense black darkness. The wounds of *Christ* are depicted in white, linking them to the divine and signifying their sacred, redemptive significance.

It is possible to consider the color white as playing an interpersonal metafunctional role in Markell's piece in the white light radiating from the center of *Christ*. As I will develop in depth in chapter 7, this radiating light forms a vector that engages with the viewer in a direct way, and as such the color white may be said to function interpersonally, enacting an engagement with the viewer.

The textual metafunction of white within Christianity is its coherence in symbolic meaning, expressed across many different spheres, from scriptural references to the liturgical vestments and even in the use of white stone and marble in church architecture. The ideational metafunction of white, signifying purity, holiness, divine presence, glory, and light, resonates coherently across the many modes of meaning making found in the socially enacted worship practices of Christians. These reveal the textual metafunction of white within this context.

The ideational metafunction of the color white is closely wrapped up in the textual metafunction of these images. White, beyond being the background, is an integral third color of the artworks. Many of the composite scenes and design elements are formed in white against the red silhouette of the figure of Christ in *Easter* or the black of Craighead's *Christ, Yesterday and Today*. They are reversed out of the red or the black—because the white is not a printed third color but in fact the existing color of the substrate on which these designs are printed. In some ways, the white is the dominant color because it is that which exists first and on which the design sits visually—but this is not how Western viewers typically look at images. The white is often overlooked as incidental because it is the color of the paper and so is perceived as a noncolor. It is a given and therefore taken for granted. It may be thought of as neutral in value, transparent and invisible. Yet, paradoxically, it serves a textual function partly for this

---

34. The central position of the sunburst means it can be read as radiating from the heart. It is at the level of the physical heart and, much like the tradition of sacred heart iconography in Roman Catholic art, it is figured centrally. See David Morgan, *The Sacred Heart of Jesus: The Visual Evolution of a Devotion* (Amsterdam: Amsterdam University Press, 2008), 23.

reason. White creates coherence between the image and the page on which the image sits by virtue of this givenness. Beyond this, in both of these designs, it creates a further coherence and unity between the design and the vignettes therein and the narratives of the scriptural texts that appear in the following pages, to which these relate.

White operates in these graphic designs in much the same way that gold functions in classical iconography. It connotes sacred space and the presence of God. The divine white light signifies periods of liminality, both between the crucifixion and the resurrection and between the resurrection and the ascension. White is the color of transcendence. Japanese graphic designer Kenya Hara is finely attuned to the profound semiotic potential of white:

> White can be attained by blending all the colors of the spectrum together, or through the subtraction of ink and all other pigments. In short it is "all colors" and "no color" at the same time. This identity as a color that can "escape color" makes white very special. Not only does white's texture powerfully evoke the materiality of objects; white can also contain temporal and spatial principles like *ma* (an interval of space and time) and *yohaku* (empty margin), or abstract concepts such as nonexistence and zero.[35]

He goes on to describe the wonder of the invention of paper for human communication. "Paper's absence of color—its brilliant 'whiteness'—and its taut 'resilience' changed history. It was a breakthrough that evoked a primeval world of unblemished purity and calm, and an unprecedented sense of fulfillment. Its uniform thinness made it fragile and transient. Yet it preserved the intense 'blackness' of the inked words and images."[36]

Irish theologian Anne Thurston, writing beautifully about poetry, describes this compositional contribution that white makes in books of poems: "Poetry works with the paradox of knowing that words will not suffice and using words to tell us so, while also shaping its words in such a way that they are surrounded by the borders of silence, by the white spaces on the page honoring that mystery beyond words."[37] This thought-

---

35. Kenya Hara, *White* (Zurich: Müller, 2017), 008.
36. Hara, *White*, 015.
37. Anne Thurston, "Poetry as a Portal to Mystery" (unpublished paper presented

fully expressed insight into the role of the white spaces on the page as borders of silence that surround and shape the words illumines the textual metafunction of white as the substrate, the ground, in the context of the printed book. White holds everything together, from one page to the next; it unifies and binds the content to the material reality of the printed word or image.

5.3. Black

"In the beginning when God created the heavens and the earth, the earth was a formless void and darkness covered the face of the deep" (Gen 1:1–2). An allusion to primordial black exists in the very first line of the Hebrew Scriptures and yet, as Michel Pastoureau reminds us, "Neither the Bible nor astrophysics has a monopoly on this kind of image. Most mythologies evoke it to describe or explain the origin of the world. In the beginning was the night, the vast originary night, and it was by emerging from darkness that life took form." In many other ancient myths, especially those of Asia and Africa, this originary black is "often fertile and fecund, as the Egyptian black that symbolizes the silt deposited by the waters of the Nile."[38] Since time immemorial, black has also been associated with both death and power. In the artistic context it is associated with drawing. It is the originary first color in the sense of colors that were discovered and used by humans in their earliest mark making. Victoria Finlay explains,

> In 1994 an extraordinary discovery by three cave explorers in the Ardeche Valley in southern France revealed paintings that were at least twice as old as those in Lascaux or Altamira or anywhere else in Europe. They were the oldest cave paintings known to modern science, and the Panel of Horses represents one of the most astonishing uses of charcoal ever seen in prehistoric art.[39]

---

at Arts and Spirituality Ireland conference "The Artist as Seer," Dublin, 15 October 2015) (with kind permission of the author).

38. Michel Pastoureau, *Black: The History of a Color* (Princeton: Princeton University Press, 2008), 21.

39. Victoria Finlay, *Colour: Travels through the Paintbox* (London: Sceptre, 2002), 85.

The earliest blacks are associated with the aftermath or end products of fire: ashes, charcoal, and soot. "Charcoal can be found almost anywhere there has been a fire."[40] This reflects another understanding of black as that which is left after all the light has been spent or disappeared. Indeed, Craighead, as many artists, began her childhood experiments in drawing with charcoal, "the powdery mess of burnt earth."[41] She reminisces,

> I have become a painter, but as a youngster in the 1940s my first love was for charcoal. My father gave me a narrow gray box of six charcoal sticks. Knotty, crooked, still coated with the metallic sheen from the fire, messy. Black. My young soul had found the way to mark a surface significantly and see itself reflected. I had crossed a threshold and, from time to time, in the eternal round of my fifty-some years of creative work, I return to that naked place of the purity of black on white.[42]

The understanding of black as the complete negation of light or, conversely, the full absorption of all light waves or rays has occupied the science of color for centuries. These theories led to the notion, since abandoned, in the eighteenth and nineteenth centuries that black was not actually a color in its own right. In our era, in many ways similar to the color red, black connotes what may seem contradictory values. Black may be seen to be conservative, serious, and official, yet it is also sophisticated, sexy, and elegant. It remains symbolic of all those things associated with the absence of light: mystery, shadow, night, darkness, in both their positive and negative associations, in different cultural contexts.

Among congregations of believers within the Christian tradition the ideational metafunction of the color black continues to be associated, at the most immediate level, with the dichotomy of good and evil. There is no explicit reference to black in the lectionary cycles for Easter. Other references to black in the Bible include:

> The color black describes human hair (Lev 13:37; Sng 5:11; Matt 5:36), the color of goats (Gen. 30:32-40), horses (Zech 6:2; Rev 6:5), and ink (2 Cor 3:3; 2 John 12). Though occasionally employed metaphorically to

---

40. Finlay, *Color*, 86.
41. Craighead, "Lodestone," 1.
42. Craighead, "Lodestone," 1.

describe gloom or mourning (Job 3:5; Isa 50:3, Joel 2:2), black expresses a range from positive to negative sentiment.[43]

In Craighead's woodcut, the symbolic dualism of white is to black as life is to death is very much at work. Jesus is dead and in the realm of death. Here the blackness also connotes forcibly a quality of liminality, an abstract concept of suspended time and space. In Markell's design *Easter*, black is used for five discrete elements in the artwork: the *Cross*, the *Fish*, the boat on the Sea of *Tiberias*, *Waves/Net*, and a short sprig consisting of a black three-leafed *Sprouting Vine Shoot*. The most salient elements are the two dynamic curves of leaping fish on either side of the figure of *Christ* and the three vine leaves over his right shoulder. Black is used of that (organic) element, fish, which symbolize the miracle of abundance that takes place in the scene (John 21). The fish leap forth from the depicted waves, the central waves of which are black, signifying the depth of the waters. The ideational metafunction of black at work here, reaches back to that of black as fecund. What is black here has life and gives life.

Black creates an imposing and powerful presence. The interpersonal metafunction of black as a color signifying authority is often witnessed in black clothing, popularly described as power dressing. The gravitas of black is also associated with weight and solidity. "For automobiles, the advantage is that black cars are perceived to be solid and therefore safer. Conversely, commercial airliners avoid painting their aircraft black as people would perceive the aircraft as too heavy to fly."[44]

---

43. Rodney S. Sadler Jr., "Black," *NIDB* 1:475. It must be noted here that negative interpretations of the color black in the Bible, especially along the lines of ethnicity, have had negative consequences for nonwhite people. The racial implications are acutely discussed in Mukti Barton, "I Am Black and Beautiful," *BlTh* 2 (2004): 167–87. This has also been considered in the works of David M. Goldenberg, *The Curse of Ham: Race and Slavery in Early Judaism, Christianity and Islam* (Princeton: Princeton University Press, 2009); Renita J. Weems, "Song of Songs," in *The New Interpreter's Bible: Old Testament Survey* (Nashville: Abingdon, 2006), 262–69; Gerald West and Musa Dube, eds., *The Bible in Africa: Transactions, Trajectories, and Trends* (Leiden: Brill, 2000); Cain Felder, ed., *Stony the Road We Trod: African American Biblical Interpretation* (Minneapolis: Fortress, 1991); Hugh R. Page Jr., *The Africana Bible: Reading Israel's Scriptures from Africa and the African Diaspora* (Minneapolis: Fortress, 2010).

44. Gavin Ambrose and Paul Harris, *Basics Design 05: Colour* (Worthing, UK: AVA, 2007), 127.

Black is associated with weight and solidity, stability and authority. As with Torah scrolls, the textual metafunction of black within a Christian context is also revealed in its earliest written documents. The Codex Sinaiticus and Codex Vaticanus, for example, were written in black ink. These documents were in continuity with their predecessors in the form of the Torah. Indeed, the Qumran scrolls were written with a black ink. Ancient black inks were analyzed in several studies, and two types were detected and identified: carbon ink, based on lampblack or soot; and iron-gall ink, consisting of copperas treated with a decoction of oak-nut galls.[45]

In a general sense, the textual metafunction of black lies in its antiquity and its ubiquity. Black has been the default color for text for millennia.[46] Before printing emerged as the most suitable way to mass-produce documents, handwritten manuscripts were written in black ink. Even within the new multimodal media environments of webpages, word-processing applications, or PowerPoint presentations, for example, black remains the default color for both line and text before and until another color is chosen. The choice of another color for text has to be made deliberately and consciously. It is a decision to move away from black, to express something that black does not or cannot say or mean.

In Markell's design *Easter*, the horizontal shape of the boat in the *Tiberias* episode acts like a platform in the lower quarter of the illustration as it anchors the figures of the disciples and the figure of Christ. It creates visual weight in the design. Here the black in the artwork has a textual metafunction that relates to the black of the biblical text. In the design *Easter* red is the salient color, but throughout the rest of the lectionary, black is the salient color as the color of the printed text that dominates those other pages. The meaning of this black can be attached to the black of the actual text printed in this lectionary but also beyond that to the text of all Bibles, printed in black. The black serves to positively link the image into the broader context of the lectionary as a book of many pages of scriptural

---

45. Yoram Nir-El and Magen Broshi, "The Black Ink of the Qumran Scrolls," *DSD* 3 (1996): 157–67. The texts tested were 1QapGen (apocryphon Genesis); 1QH (Hodayot); 1QIsa^a (Isaiah^a); 2Q14 (Psalms); 4Q11 (Paleo-Hebrew Genesis–Exodus^1); 4Q17 (Exodus–Leviticus^f); 4Q26 (Leviticus^d); 4Q27 (Numbers^b); 4Q270 (Damascus Document^e); 4Q502 (papyrus Rituel du mariage); 11QT^a (Temple Scroll^a).

46. In Jewish religious practice strict laws pertain to the sourcing of the ingredients and the making of the kosher black ink that is used by the *soferim* to write a Torah.

text, printed in black. The black used in the illustration creates coherence between the illustration and the surrounding texts, not only visually but also in terms of complementarity of meaning. The text is scriptural, and the image is scriptural.

Importantly, it is perhaps in Craighead's design that the black extends its semiotic reach most profoundly, linking the artwork most explicitly to the scriptural lections that both precede and follow it. Black is the dominant color, covering most of the area of the design and almost covering the entire page to its very edges (figs. 5.1, 5.2). This verso page marks the transition between the Good Friday service and the Easter Vigil. There is no service on Holy Saturday (prior to the Easter Vigil traditionally beginning late, after dark). Holy Saturday symbolically and liturgically marks the time Christ spent in the tomb between the crucifixion of Good Friday afternoon and the resurrection, celebrated on Easter Sunday. It is a period of profound liminality and is marked in *The Sunday Missal* with this artwork. Instead of text, either liturgical or biblical, there is this remarkable graphic design illustrating a dead *Christ* suspended in time and space.

Maria Nikolajeva and Carole Scott have noted how the interaction between recto and verso pages creates temporality in a narrative.[47] The Easter Triduum is a chronological liturgical event commencing with the commemoration of the Last Supper on Holy Thursday and culminating in the celebration of the resurrection at the Easter Vigil. Craighead's design uses the tension between recto (Good Friday/crucifixion), verso (Holy Saturday/death), and recto (Easter Vigil/resurrection) pages to imply temporal and causal relations (figs 5.1 and 5.2). In other words, this visual design stands in for, holds the space of, this empty liturgical moment in place of verbal texts. The intense blackness of the page semiotically materializes the liminality of Holy Saturday between these two liturgies.

5.4. Red

Red is a good example of how "the same color can express many different meanings and the same meaning can be expressed by many different colors."[48] Red can mean romantic love and sexual passion, but it can also

---

47. Maria Nikolajeva and Carole Scott, *How Picturebooks Work* (New York: Routledge, 2006), 150–51.

48. Van Leeuwen, *Language of Color*, 14.

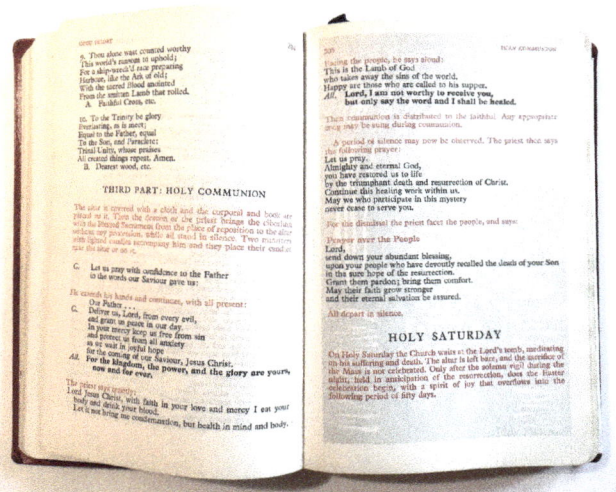

Figs. 5.1 and 5.2: Two sequential double-page spreads in *The Sunday Missal*, showing the final rubric of Good Friday when "All depart in silence" (recto), followed by a brief description of Holy Saturday, when no service takes place prior to the (over the page, recto) Easter Vigil during the night of Easter Sunday (usually after dark on Saturday night). On the verso page is the full-page design by Craighead, with *Christ* in the tomb, almost entirely black, in contrast with the white pages on either side of it. It holds the space of Holy Saturday in *The Sunday Missal*, and the intense black plays a significant role in that.

mean blood, death, violence, and hate. Its connotation as the color of blood alone holds within it, simultaneously, the possible positive meaning of vital lifeblood and the negative meaning of spilled blood and death. In one and the same society or period, different, contradictory systems can exist alongside each other, each covering one small domain of meaning.[49] Many of the ideational metafunctions of the color red are directly linked to the experience of red in the form of heat: the red of the setting sun, glowing coals in a fire, molten lava flowing from a volcano, and countless other examples. These are elemental encounters with red that all human beings experience, in some form or another, from early on in their lives. They serve to consolidate the social symbolism linking red with heat and energy and, in turn, to emotional states such as fear as well as passion and love. "Red-letter" is a catchphrase used to described a positively memorable occasion: "a red-letter day in my life." Festival days in the church calendar, known as red-letter days, are marked by red letters (rubrics) in the lectionary. There are also "Red-Letter Bibles" and "Red-Letter Christians."

Artists of the Middle Ages recognized two types of blood, also perceived as opposite. *Sanguis* was "sweet," referred to blood in the body, and was associated with fertility, whereas *cruor* was "corrupt," blood that had been shed and was associated with violence.[50] They were also interpreted as "good" female blood and "bad" male blood.[51] "Yet, since there are two types of blood, what is the red that sanctifies?" asks art historian Spike Bucklow. "Perhaps surprisingly, since it turns our gender stereotypes on their heads, Christ's saving blood was thought of by some devotional writers in the Middle Ages to be more like the 'flow of birthing than the flow of wounding.'"[52] Some of the earliest red dyes known to historians came from the Mount Ararat region of modern-day Turkey and ancient Phoenicia and Assyria, before 1000 BCE, from the blood of the cochineal, kermes, and other similar-scale insects.[53] Until the modern period

---

49. Van Leeuwen, *Language of Color*, 14.

50. Spike Bucklow, *Red: The Art and Science of a Colour* (London: Reaction Books, 2016), 163.

51. Caroline Walker Bynum, *Wonderful Blood: Theology and Practice in Late Medieval Northern Germany and Beyond* (Philadelphia: University of Pennsylvania Press, 2007), 17–18.

52. Bucklow, *Red*, 165, cites Bynum, *Wonderful Blood*, 256.

53. Bucklow, *Red*, 25–28.

of chemically produced colors red not only signified blood—it literally was the blood of insects.

In the Bible red first appears as the color describing the skin of Esau (Gen 25:25), and then later in the weeping face of Job (Job 16:16). It also describes food (red lentils, Gen 25:30), a heifer (Num 19:2), water (2 Kgs 3:22), wine (Prov 23:31), scarlet sins (Isa 1:18), robes (Isa 63:2, stained with blood or wine), shields (Nah 2:3), horses (Zech 1:8; 6:2; Rev 6:4), the sky (Matt 16:2–30), and a dragon (Rev 12:3).[54] The color red, used liturgically and artistically in the church, symbolizes foremostly the passion of Christ. Red is symbolic of the resurrection of Jesus (also often symbolized in white) in the sense of victory, of the life-giving triumph of this positive force or energy of divine love over inertia, destruction, evil, and death. Pentecost, the outpouring of the Holy Spirit manifested in tongues of fire, is symbolized using the color red. Martyrs are venerated on their feast days, and this is marked liturgically through the use of red vestments.

Ironically, there is only one reference to red in this Easter cycle of lections—and it does not refer to the color red literally. It occurs in Exod 15:4, "Pharaoh's chariots and his army he cast into the sea; his picked officers were sunk in the Red Sea."[55] There are, however, many references to blood: Deut 32:43; Ps 16:4; Jonah 1:14; Acts 2:19–20; 5:28, 1 John 1:7; 5:6, 1 Pet 1:19; Rev 1:5; 7:14. The red of the figure of *Christ* in the *Easter* artwork is meant to be understood in this context—the vital, salvific blood of the risen Christ.

In the artwork *Easter* by Markell, red is the most conspicuous color that gives the figure of the risen *Christ* dominance on the page (apart from the size of the figure). Red has the capacity to create the visual illusion of something advancing on the page, of bringing that which is colored red forward, and it certainly works in that manner here. Although there are figures in front of the *Christ* figure, lower down in the bottom third of the composition, the figure of *Christ* is given added visual salience through the use of this red. There is also a vibratory dimension to red when it is juxtaposed with another bright color, such as cyan (or light blues or greens). Here the juxtaposition happens in the center of the figure, with the white

---

54. Mary Petrine Boyd, "Red," *NIDB* 4:749.
55. The "Red" Sea does not use the Hebrew term אדם (*'ādōm*); see Reed Sea (Exod 10:19); Boyd, "Red," 749.

starburst, which has long, thin, sharply angled rays. The effect of the bright white within the red is the optical illusion of vibration or pulsation.[56]

Red is used in an interpersonal way in contemporary Western culture in almost all dimensions of social life. Gavin Ambrose writes, "Research indicates that seeing red releases epinephrine in the body, a chemical that causes you to breathe more rapidly, and your heartbeat, pulse rate and blood pressure to rise."[57] This type of research has also promoted red as a popular color for sports teams and entertainment activities. It is frequently chosen to form the primary color in the corporate identity of banks in the arena of business and economics (HSBC, Santander, Bank of America). "Bright reds are energizing and are good for offices in the banking or entertainment fields."[58] Red is the color of the ubiquitous seasonal sale signs used by retailers to grab the attention of passersby and entice them into the store. It also constitutes the brand identity of many famous food and beverage brands, such as Coca-Cola, Pizza Hut, KFC, Heinz, and Nestlé, used to signify the vitality of the product and, in turn, the potential benefit to the consumer. Red is used in an interpersonal metafunctional way to act on other people, with the intention of instigating an action response from them, in many both subtle and overt ways in culture.

The color red may be said to have an interpersonal metafunction in Markell's design *Easter*. That red is the color of health, vitality, and energy, and has an energetic impact visually, enhances the interpersonal meaning of the figure of the risen *Christ* in Markell's work. The red greatly increases the salience of the silhouette on the page so that it demands attention and response. The red heightens the interpersonal dimension of the demand of the silhouette (to be discussed at greater length in ch. 8).

Red, used for the rubrics in lectionaries and missals, signifies actions to be taken. These are the instructions for the reader about how one is expected to act at certain parts of the liturgy. This convention of red rubrics for the instructive texts distinguishes them from the black text, which is the content to be read, the lections or prayers. In chapter 4 I discussed this tradition in evidence in the earliest lectionaries, red marking out the *incipits* and *desinits*, where the reader was to start and stop a lection. Red is the color that implies an action to be taken by the reader, whereas the black text, while authoritative, is passive, there to be read and consumed.

---

56. Josef Albers, *Interaction of Colour*, rev. ed. (London: Routledge, 2006), 61.
57. Ambrose and Harris, *Color*, 108.
58. Cited in Kress and van Leeuwen, *Reading Images*, 229.

Red is used textually to create coherence, to lead the reader through the liturgical text.

5.5. The Color Triad Black, White, and Red as a Schema

Black, white, and red form a color triad, with a long history dating back to antiquity and Greek art in the sixth century BCE. Indeed, Aristotle proclaimed black, white, and red to be primary colors.[59] Pastoureau notes that during the high Middle Ages two systems seem to have coexisted for constructing the symbolic color base: a white-black axis, inherited from the Bible, and a black-white-red triad, originating in older and more distant sources.[60] This threefold system was not at all arbitrary nor exclusively religious. Pastoureau maintains,

> During the high Middle Ages three colors continued to play a more significant symbolic role than others: white, red and black. That was already the case in classic antiquity and would remain so until the great chromatic changes of the central Middle Ages, characterized by the remarkable promotion of blue in the transition in most codes and systems from three basic colors to six (white, red, black, green, yellow and blue). Before this time the ancient triad continued to dominate.

He continues,

> By about the year 1000 a certain number of customs were already common throughout all of Roman Christianity. These shared customs formed a system that all eleventh and twelfth-century liturgists would subsequently describe and comment upon, as would the future Pope Innocent III in 1195 (he was as yet only a Cardinal) in his famous treatise on the Mass. This system can be summarized thus: white, the symbol of purity, was used for all celebrations of Christ as well as for those of the angels, virgins, and confessors; red, which recalls the blood spilled by and for Christ, was used for celebrations of the apostles and the martyrs,

---

59. John Gage, *Colour and Culture: Practice and Meaning from Antiquity to Abstraction* (London: Thames and Hudson, 1995), 11–14.

60. Pastoureau, *Black*, 42. In contemporary culture, this triad is often found in the entertainment industry (black tie/red carpet/starched tablecloth) and the sports arena: Formula One racing, for example, where checkered flags and shiny red cars typify the high-octane energy and atmosphere of the racetrack.

the cross, and the Holy Spirit, notably Pentecost; as for black, it was used for times of waiting and penitence (Advent, Lent), as well as for the mass for the dead and for Holy Friday.[61]

Considering this color triad in the Markell piece, it is clear that white functions as the divine light that shines through the resurrected red silhouette of *Christ*. The black is a fertile black linked to organic matter. It is associated with the vital power of red, which signifies the salvific blood of *Christ*. Both the black and the red are inherently positive and linked to life-giving properties. Neither color is negative or destructive in this artwork. On the contrary, all three colors represent sources of life: earth, blood, and light, and their combination increases their value exponentially.[62] There is a charged fusion of new life breaking forth and irradiated in light. By contrast, in Craighead's piece the duality of black and white is very much at work.[63] *Christ* (God) is the light that dispels the darkness. Life is the antithesis of death, just as white is the antithesis of black. Medievalist John Carey makes a profound observation: "There can be no polarity in a triad and, although there is contrast, none of the colors is the opposite of either of the others. Life and death are states; but birth, dying and conception are processes, points of transition within a continuum."[64] When black, white, and red come together as a triad, the dynamic between these colors shifts profoundly from polarity to continuity, and, as seen in *Easter*, they collude semiotically to signify, enact, and accentuate different aspects of a life-giving transformation in the risen *Christ*.

A pertinent example of the interpersonal metafunction of red being put to work in the world of biblical publishing is the printing of the spoken words of Jesus, as they appear as quotations in the New Testament, in the color red.[65] For many Christians, a Bible without the spoken words of Jesus printed in red is now almost unthinkable. This development was

---

61. Pastoureau, *Black*, 39–40.
62. Pastoureau, *Black*, 22.
63. The triad white, black, and red is very much in evidence throughout the *Sunday Missal*. See figs. 5.1 and 5.2.
64. John Carey, "The Three Sails, the Twelve Winds, and the Question of Early Irish Colour Theory," *JWCI* 72 (2009): 224.
65. Red letters are especially useful in the KJV and in other translations where quotation marks are not used.

initiated by an enterprising German-immigrant journalist, Louis Klopsch (1852–1910), who had become a successful publisher.[66]

> This new adjunct to the New Testament of course had to include the words of Jesus quoted by others, in Acts and Revelation. It was decided to exclude anticipations of Christ ("Christophanies") in the Old Testament. An initial edition of 60,000 "Red Letter Testaments" was soon sold out. Accolades streamed in, including from the King of Sweden (a telegram) to President Theodore Roosevelt (a dinner invitation which Louis Klopsch accepted).[67]

One company unsuccessfully tried to print Christ's words in green. Some publishers use a pinkish red that is hard to read. Often the precise shade of red is left to the printer's discretion—or whim. Frank Couch, new products planner for Thomas Nelson Bibles, emphasizes that Nelson insists on a specific hue of brick red, distinctive yet easier to read.[68] Despite the changes in Bible publishing, the red-letter option seems to be a solid fixture welcomed and now expected by vast numbers of Bible readers. Around 1900 a red-letter edition of the King James Bible appeared and proved immensely popular.

"Red-letter" has also become the moniker for an emergent church movement.[69] Leader Shane Claiborne describes how the ideational value of those red letters, highlighting the words of Jesus, actively plays out for this movement in an interpersonal and textual way—framing a collective identity, motivating behavior, and giving coherence to their lifestyle and choices:

> The goal of Red Letter Christians is simple: To take Jesus seriously by endeavoring to live out His radical, counter-cultural teachings as set forth in Scripture, and especially embracing the lifestyle prescribed in the Sermon on the Mount. By calling ourselves Red Letter Christians, we refer to the fact that in many Bibles the words of Jesus are printed in red. What we are asserting, therefore, is that we have committed ourselves

---

66. I suggest that as an immigrant journalist with experience in publishing in Germany, Klopsch would no doubt have been familiar with rubricated liturgical texts. See Steve Eng, "The Story Behind: Red Letter Bible Editions," International Society of Bible Collectors, https://tinyurl.com/SBL6710m.
67. Eng, "Story Behind."
68. Eng, "Story Behind."
69. See Red Letter Christians, http://www.redletterchristians.org.

first and foremost to doing what Jesus said. The message of those red-lettered Bible verses is radical, to say the least.[70]

Another interpersonal function of red text that predates this practice is the convention of *rubricating* liturgical texts. The etymology of the word *rubric* is drawn from the Latin *rubrica*, meaning *red*. In the *Roman Missal*, since its inception, instructions for the presider explaining what he has to do during a liturgical service have been rubricated, printed in red, leaving the sections to be spoken aloud in black. There is an active dimension to rubrics; they imply actions to be taken or gestures to be made. With the arrival of printing, other typographic effects such as italic type, or using a bold or different size type, became used for emphasizing a section of text, and as printing in two colors is more expensive and time consuming, rubrics have tended to be reserved specifically for religious-service books, luxury editions, or books where design is emphasized.

Again, it is important to note that red ink is thought to have been one of the earliest invented and brought into use alongside black. The Dead Sea Scrolls, for example, were written in a black carbon ink but reveal evidence of the limited use of red ink. "On only four fragments, lines of writing in red ink were found and so the application of red ink on these manuscripts is very rare. Red ink was used in antiquity to write rubrics, that is, lines at the beginning of a chapter, lines at paragraph divisions, titles, or instructions for liturgical readings."[71]

The black-white-red triad brings coherence and unity to the social lives of Christians through its occurrence and repetition across two vitally important areas, the liturgy and the Scriptures. In the material, iconic artifact of the Evangelical Lutheran Worship *Worship* book (pew edition), this coherence is beautifully at work in the selection of a deep, rich red leatherette cover for a finely produced book with a high-quality finish. The tacticity of the embossed cover, the shimmer of the leatherette, and weight

---

70. "Mission and Values," Red Letter Christians, https://tinyurl.com/SBLPress6701d3.

71. Yoram Nir-El and Magen Broshi, "The Red Ink of the Dead Sea Scrolls," *Archaeometry* 38 (1996): 97. The red ink on four fragments of the Dead Sea Scrolls was analyzed by X-ray fluorescence and X-ray diffraction. "The red pigment was identified as mercury sulfide (HgS), cinnabar." Cinnabar is a mineral associated with recent volcanic activity and alkaline hot springs. It has been mined for thousands of years, as far back as the Neolithic era. See Jesus Martín-Gil et al., "The First Known Use of Vermillion," *Experientia* 51 (1995): 759–61.

of the book semiotize the esteem in which it is held, its place in the life of the congregation (locally and more broadly). Being handed a *Worship* book serves as an affirmation that one belongs to this worshiping community. The aesthetic quality of the book, in every aspect of its production, in turn is a gesture of respect, not only to God (in whose honor it has been designed) but also to every person who uses it.[72]

The seven occurrences of *white* in the lectionary readings for the season of Easter all relate to clothing: the clothing of Jesus (Matt 28:3), the young man (generally held to be an angel) in the tomb (Mark 16:5), the two angels (John 20:12), and the great multitude robed in white (Rev 7:9, 13–14). The clothing of Jesus is described in the simile "white as snow." White is therefore a marker not only for purity but also for divinity. It is the white of the angel's robes that signify them as heavenly beings. Finally, in Revelation, the great multitudes gathered before the white throne are robed in white: "These are they who have come through the great ordeal; they have washed their robes and made them white in the blood of the Lamb" (Rev 7:14).[73] There is a distinct transformation indicated in the progression to the color white. There is a purifying that takes place in the washing that is signified then in the color white. Interestingly, the color of the impurities washed to white is not explicitly mentioned. Yet, in contrast with the Christian association of sin with black (the darkness and death that is the opposite of the light and life of Christ), in the Hebrew Bible sin is often portrayed as red and is foremostly associated with the red violence of bloodshed. "There is bloodguilt on Saul and on his house" (2 Sam 21:1), while Isaiah cries out, "Your sins are like scarlet ... they are red like crimson" (Isa 1:18). At the end of the New Testament the great whore of Babylon in Revelation is clothed in scarlet and sits on a scarlet beast drunk with the "blood of the saints" (Rev 17:1–6). John Harvey writes, "The image of red stains runs through the Bible, now of sin, now of wine, now

---

72. Daniel Kantor, the art director (along with Lynn Joyce Hunter) of this Evangelical Lutheran Worship *Worship* project, writes about the theological motivations influencing designs of this nature in his volume *Graphic Design and Religion*, 167–201. See also Plate, "What the Book Arts"; Dorina Miller Parmenter, "How the Bible Feels: The Christian Bible as Effective and Affective Object," in Watts, *Sensing Sacred Texts*, 27–38, for a discussion of the esthetics of sacred books.

73. Rev 20:11 describes "a great white throne" (θρόνον ... λευκὸν). "*Throne* in Revelation represents God's sovereign rule and authority. A white throne contributes not only to the spectacle of Rev 20:11–15 but also speaks to the purity and righteousness of the judgment proceeding from it." See Gary Colledge, "White Throne," *NIDB* 5:845.

of blood, in changing equations.... Sin lives in a red triad of bloodshed, drunkenness and crimson fornication."[74] The concept of the stain of red sin that is washed white in the red "blood of the Lamb" (Rev 7:14) adds another particularly interesting dimension to this design—the transition from red sin to white purity through red purity (blood of the Lamb). Red is redeemed as the color of the full flourishing of humanity in Christ.

The description of the outcome of the washing, that the robes are made "white in the blood of the Lamb," is a poetic description that emphasizes the value of white as a signifier for ultimate purity. This intriguingly paradoxical image may be understood to be implied by the episode at the base of the *Easter* design, where the group of seven disciples is in the boat at *Tiberias*. They are white-and-red silhouettes set against the red of the Lamb, *Christ*. The black horizontal shape in front of them may be the boat of John 21 (as I suggest in ch. 7), or it may perceived as a kind of baptismal font, from which flows red and black, the red and black sins that are washed "white in the blood of the Lamb." The Revelation text is visually implied in this illustration that explicitly refers to John 21. The color triad lends a profound intertextuality to this episode in the design.

5.6. Conclusion

In a powerful way the colors white, black, and red collude, each strengthening the other to perform the semiotic functioning of the other. White holds the authority of the black letter and the dynamism of the red letter. The triad forms a triskele "of complementarity rather than negation, and of recurrence rather than closure."[75]

Francis Edeline, one of the founding members of the Belgian semiotic collective known as Groupe µ, divides color, in terms of its associations, into two categories: *sociochrome*, which evolves with society, its religious symbols, its trends, and has the resultant conventional associations; and *idiochrome*, which evolves based on personal experiences that commit to memory pleasant, warm, anxiety-ridden, frightening, and other situations that provide metonymic or synesthetic effect associations.[76] The white, black, and red color triad is a *sociochrome* that emerged from

---

74. John Harvey, *The Story of Black* (London: Reaktion, 2013), 68.
75. Carey, "Three Sails," 232.
76. Francis Edeline, "La Plasticité des Categories (2. Le Cas de la Coleur)," in

antiquity and persisted in the written and printed materials of religious communities to this present day—where it remains semiotically resonant in the liturgical books of the Christian community. Its potency as a semiotic resource is reflected in its embrace as a motivating identifier for an emergent, ecumenical movement, for whom the dynamic, instructive red letters set among the authoritative black letters (on the white substrate) resonate powerfully.

The color triad presents itself as a social-semiotic resource that has evolved out of a lengthy tradition and has functioned for diverse groups of Christian scribes, book designers, and readers from the Byzantine church to American millennials of the present. In the graphic designs considered here, color contains and brings together metaphor, symbol, and text, creating interactions and depths of meaning beyond the purely verbal text. Applying Kress and van Leeuwen's metafunctional approach reveals how these designs employ color in profound ways, within the context of the Scriptures surrounding them in the books within which they appear, to dramatically enhance their communicative potential. Color is a constitutive element formative of meaning. The color triad, black, red, and white is a semiotic mode in the iconic liturgical book.

La Sémiotique Visuelle: Nouveaux Paradigmes, ed. Michel Constantine (Paris: L'Harmattan, 2010), 218.

6
Silhouette

A silhouette suffices to express a physiognomy.[1]
—Attributed to French artist Edouard Dujardin

Throughout Christian history, artists and artisans in every era have made attempts to visually represent Jesus. These creative depictions of what Jesus looked like or how he might appear as member of a particular culture have been and remain a contested area.[2] They have tried the philosophical wits of the sharpest theologians of every age, warding off both iconoclasts and those of little artistic talent. Yet these creative efforts to image Christ have also produced art of sublime beauty and have at times been theologically prophetic. There is a touch of this prophetic nature in the artistic use of silhouette as a semiotic resource by the two designers featured in this study.

Two aspects of the visual representation of Jesus that have come in for particular attention in the past century have been his ethnicity and his gender. Throughout the history of Western Christendom, artists have taken the liberty of portraying Jesus as a (male) member of their own culture. In the postmodern, postcolonial era, these images have frequently been critiqued as Eurocentric and, occasionally, anti-Semitic, as they fail to recognize the Jewishness of Jesus. Parallel to this, an understanding

---

1. Physiognomy is the art of reading the facial features and countenance of a person as indicators of his or her character. It was popularized in the eighteenth century by Johann Kaspar Lavater and Johann Wolfgang von Goethe.
2. Joan E. Taylor offers an overview of this debate, the art it has spawned over two millennia, and indeed her own proposal in *What Did Jesus Look Like?* (London: Bloomsbury, 2018). David Morgan has also explored this topic. See *Visual Piety: A History and Theory of Popular Religious Images* (Berkeley: University of California Press, 1998).

developed that an authentic spirituality requires that every believer be able to imaginatively appropriate Jesus as a member of their own ethnic group. Indeed, Pope John Paul II in his address to the African Synod in 1980 in a far-reaching comment proclaimed, "Christ, in the members of his body is himself African."[3] Likewise, on the gender issue, feminist theologians have been at pains to point out that "theological tradition has virtually always maintained that the maleness of Jesus is theologically, christologically, soteriologically, and sacramentally irrelevant."[4] By making recourse to silhouette, Craighead and Markell have creatively and successfully navigated these two stumbling blocks for the reception of Jesus images in contemporary congregations. This chapter explores the use of silhouette as a semiotic resource by Craighead and Markell. I will begin by briefly charting the history of silhouette as a graphic device. Following that, I will look at metonymy as a concept in visual semiotics before turning to the designs featuring silhouette of the two artists central to this study.

---

3. Pope John Paul II, "Address to the Bishops of Kenya," Nairobi, 7 May 1980, https://tinyurl.com/SBL6710n. This idea is also found in Pope John Paul II, "Ekklesia in Africa," Yaoundé, Cameroon, September 14, 1995, §127, https://tinyurl.com/SBL6710o.

4. Sandra M. Schneiders, *Women and the Word: The Gender of God in the New Testament and the Spirituality of Women* (New York: Paulist, 1986), 3. This point is reiterated in the work of numerous feminist theologians such as Elizabeth A. Johnson and Elisabeth Schüssler Fiorenza, to mention but two. There are historical examples of artists who have represented Jesus as female. For a few examples from the late twentieth century and early twenty-first century, see Edwina Sandys, *Christa* (1975); Almuth Lutkenhaus-Lackey, *Crucified Woman* (1976); James M. Murphy, *Christine on the Cross* (1984); Margaret Argyle, *Bosnian Christa* (1993); Renée Cox, *Yo Mama's Last Supper* (1999); Emmanuel Garibay, *Emmaus* (2000); Janet McKenzie, *Jesus of the People* (1999) and *Woman Offered #5* (2003). Depictions of Christ crucified imaged as a women in other visual media and performance include the short film *Submission—Part One* by Ayaan Hirsi Ali and Theo van Gogh (2004), and Madonna, "Live to Tell" on the *Confessions on a Dance Floor* tour (2006). For discussions of some of these, see Anne-Marie Korte, "Madonna's Crucifixion and the Woman's Body in Feminist Theology," in *Doing Gender in Media, Art and Culture*, ed. Rosemarie Buikema and Iris van der Tuin (London: Routledge, 2009), 117–32; Julie Clague, "Divine Transgressions: The Female Christ-Form in Art," *CrQ* 47 (2005): 47–63.

6.1. A Brief History of Silhouette

The name *silhouette*, broadly given to the flat, monocolor (usually black), opaque, outline shape of a person or thing, arose during the latter half of the eighteenth century in Paris. It derives from the surname of "reforming" French finance minister Etienne de Silhouette (1709–1767). "His attacks on wealth and privilege soon made silhouette stand for anything miserly or cheese-paring, from trousers without pockets to impromptu paper portraits."[5] An amateur cutter himself, he promoted the making of paper cut-outs at home as an inexpensive yet creative and social hobby and means of acquiring a profile portrait of friends and family.[6] It caught on; various contraptions were even designed to facilitate this, somewhat defeating the democratic and frugal impulse that had animated Silhouette's initial promotion of the practice. The popularity of the silhouette spread throughout France, Germany, Austria, England, and to America. As a graphic device, it reached a high point in Parisian popular culture—a century later—in the last decade of the nineteenth century.[7]

Of course, prior to acquiring this moniker from a French finance minister in the eighteenth century, the silhouette had a much older genesis in art history and, indeed, philosophy. As art historian Darby English notes: "The silhouette participates in several elaborate dramas of origin."[8] It plays a central role in Pliny the Elder's classic account of the legendary origin

---

5. Anne M. Wagner, "Kara Walker: The Black White Relation," in *Kara Walker: Narratives of a Negress*, ed. Ian Berry (Cambridge, MA: Frances Young Tang Teaching Museum and Art Gallery at Skidmore College, 2003), 94. Walker is a contemporary artist, described as a "silhouettist," and known for creating room-size tableaux of black-and-white silhouettes that invoke themes of African American racial identity. See "Kara Walker," http://www.karawalkerstudio.com. Gérard Fromanger is a French artist who employs silhouettes in his art, most recently in political work about the fate of refugees in small boats trying to cross the Mediterranean. See his series *Série Le coeur fait ce qu'il veut* (*The heart does what it wants*), 2015, at "Gérard Fromanger," Artnet, https://tinyurl.com/SBL6710p.

6. A French print of about 1770, after a painting by Johann Schenau, *L'origine de la peinture; ou, les Portraits a la mode*, speaks to both the Pliny legend about the original portrait and the parlor games encouraged by Silhouette.

7. The theatre poster for the Moulin Rouge "La Goulue" by Toulouse Lautrec (1891) is one example among many of this decade to make use of silhouette. It was also incorporated into theater itself as a theatrical device.

8. Darby English, "This Is Not about the Past: Silhouettes in the Work of Kara Walker," in Berry, *Kara Walker*, 158.

of painting in his *Natural History*—in which the Corinthian maid, the daughter of Dibutades, traces onto a wall the shadow of a lover departing for battle. Finlay elaborates thus,

> Suddenly between impassioned embraces, she noticed his shadow on the wall, cast by the light of the candle. So, spontaneously, she reached out for a piece of charcoal from the fire and filled in the pattern. I imagine her kissing the image and thinking that in this way something of his physical presence would be fixed close to her while his beloved body was away in the distant Mediterranean.[9]

Pliny's description of the origin of the silhouette is potent. The silhouette not only captures the likeness of the lover but is able to hold or contain something of the essence of the presence of the absent lover. However, some twenty-four hundred years ago, long before Pliny the Elder, the philosopher Plato had narrated his enduring account of the shadows cast on the back wall of a cave. Plato's cave, one of the founding narratives of Western philosophy, is of a journey away from the shadowy world of ignorance toward enlightenment, from darkness to light, from ideology toward knowledge, from appearance to substance.[10] The moral value and play of dark and light, firelight and sunlight, is pivotal to this didactic myth. Thirty thousand years before Plato, in the Chauvet cave in France, cave dwellers had illustrated their knowledge of their world on their walls. Using charcoal, they drew the outline shapes of people and animals in profile, by firelight. While the descriptor *silhouette* only came into play some 250 years ago, the making of silhouettes is primordial in human image-making

---

9. Finlay, *Color*, 78. Scottish artist David Allan painted a version of this legend in 1775 (at a time when silhouettes were very popular), as have many others, titled *The Origin of Painting*. See "David Allan: The Origin of Painting ('The Maid of Corinth')," National Galleries Scotland, https://tinyurl.com/SBL6710q.

10. Contemporary artist William Kentridge offers an interesting critique of Plato's cave, suggesting that the light does not have a monopoly on truth, that the cave dwellers might have also had something to say about the truth, might have learned something in the cave. "My interest in Plato is twofold. For his prescient description of our world of cinema—his description of a world of people bound to reality as mediated through a screen feels very contemporary—but more particularly, in defense of shadows, and what they can teach us about enlightenment." See William Kentridge, "In Praise of Shadows," in *In Praise of Shadows*, ed. Paulo Colombo (Milan: Charta, 2009), 17–18.

practice. A silhouette is more than a sign or an infographic; it has an archetypal quality to its simplicity that enables profound and rich semiosis.

6.2. Silhouette and Essence

Johann Caspar Lavater was a Swiss poet, pastor, physiognomist, and theologian who popularized the idea that the silhouette held the very essence of a person. Between 1775 and 1778 he published a work of importance in the history of silhouette that greatly influenced its ascent in the popular culture of Europe, and France especially, for over a century. That work was *Physiognomische fragments zur Beförderung der Menschenkenntniss und Menschenliebe*.[11] Lavater's book on physiognomy included an elaborate ninefold division of the silhouetted profile, and he made and analyzed the profiles of many famous people of the period, including Moses Mendelssohn and Nikolai Karamzin. Nancy Forgione writes, "Lavater's endorsement of the silhouette as 'the truest representation that can be given of man' again invokes its power to reveal an underlying essence not available from a surface description." The ensuing valorization of shadow implied a new aim—to impart the truth behind appearances. Silhouette was credited with the ability to externalize the intrinsic essence of things. Shadow and silhouette constituted a crucial pictorial strategy for making visible notions of duration and essence.[12]

6.3. Metonymy

> The word *metonymy* comes from Greek *metonomasia* (Latin *metonymia*), "a change of name," and the action it designates involves moving or extending a name from one referent to another: "Sail" is extended to the referent of "ship." The relations of metonymy are various modes of contiguity and association: between whole and part, container and contained, sign and thing signified, material and thing made, cause and effect, genus and species.[13]

---

11. It is available in English, titled *Essays on Physiognomy; Calculated to Extend the Knowledge and Love of Mankind*.

12. Nancy Forgione, "'The Shadow Only': Shadow and Silhouette in Late Nineteenth-Century Paris," *ArtB* 81 (1999): 493.

13. Harry Berger Jr., *Figures of a Changing World: Metaphor and the Emergence of Modern Culture* (New York: Fordham University Press, 2015), 11.

Visual metonyms are the stock-in-trade for graphic designers. The communicative task facing designers requires that sometimes "where we want to signify reality in some way then we are forced to choose one piece of that reality to represent it," designer David Crow explains.[14] A metonym works in a similar way to a metaphor except that it is used to represent a totality. In metonymy one entity is used to refer to another that is related to it. In speech, the whole is sometimes used when only referring to a part. One might say "He's in *dance*," where *dance* stands for the whole dancing profession. Or, "The *Times* has not yet arrived at the press conference," meaning the reporter from the *Times*.[15] The whole is being used to refer to a part. Within metonymy there exists another special case referred to by rhetoricians as *synecdoche*, which reverses this and where the part stands for the whole. Familiar tourist advertising shows a spectacular photograph of the Cliffs of Moher, for instance, where this scenery (part) stands in for the entire west coast of Ireland or possibly all of Ireland (whole). Similar things might be done with a *bodhrán* (part) standing in for a *céilí* festival or Irish music (whole). George Lakoff and Mark Johnson elucidate the difference between metaphor and metonym thus:

> Metaphor and metonym are different *kinds* of processes. Metaphor is principally a way of conceiving of one thing in terms of another, and its primary function is understanding. Metonymy, on the other hand, has primarily a referential function, that is it allows us to use one entity to *stand for* another. But metonymy is not merely a referential device. It also serves to provide understanding. For example, in the case of the metonymy THE PART FOR THE WHOLE there are many parts that can stand for the whole. Which part we pick out determines which aspect of the whole we are focussing on.[16]

Other representative examples of metonymy include the producer for the product ("I'd love to own a *Van Gogh* one day"), the object used for

---

14. Crow, *Visual Signs*, 44.
15. George Lakoff and Mark Johnson, *Metaphors We Live By* (Chicago: University of Chicago Press, 1980), 36–37. "We are using 'The *Times*' not merely to refer to some reporter or other but also to suggest the importance of the institution the reporter represents. So 'The *Times* has not yet arrived at the press conference' means something different from 'Steve Roberts has not yet arrived at the press conference,' even though Steve Roberts may be the *Times* reporter in question."
16. Lakoff and Johnson, *Metaphors We Live By*, 36.

user ("The *buses* are on strike"), the controller for controlled ("*Churchill* attacked Dresden"), the institution for people responsible ("The *Health Service Executive* issued a statement"), the place for the institution ("*Rome* held a synod"), the place for the event ("*Hiroshima* is commemorated with a memorial cherry tree").[17] Metonyms use indexical relationships to create meanings.[18] A significant aspect of metonymy, as Raymond Gibbs explicates further, is that it "involves only one conceptual domain, in that the mapping or connection between two things is within the same domain."[19] The conceptual domain for the designs of Markell and Craighead is the biblical narrative presented in the lectionary and the praxis of the worshiping community in liturgy. Lakoff and Johnson remind us,

> The conceptual systems of cultures and religions are metaphorical in nature. Symbolic metonymies are critical links between everyday experience and the coherent metaphorical systems that characterize religions and cultures. Symbolic metonymies that are grounded in our physical experience provide an essential means of comprehending religious and cultural concepts.[20]

Silhouette is clearly a part-for-whole synecdochal metonym. Both Markell and Craighead in their designs make use of silhouette consistently to represent three different categories of person: the character of Jesus Christ (the deity and central focus of the Scripture readings and the liturgies), the disciples and other biblical characters (the woman at the well, King David, etc.), and contemporary believers participating in the rituals of the church. One of the significant benefits of the use of silhouette for all is to stress commonality between all these characters. There is no visual differentiation between the first-century disciples around Jesus and the contemporary believers being baptized or anointed in a sacramental ritual. The *part*, the silhouette, stands in for the *whole*, the person of Jesus and the

---

17. Lakoff and Johnson, *Metaphors We Live By*, 38–39. Examples given are my own.

18. Hall, *This Means This*, 40. Hall provides a good example of a familiar technique in graphic design that demonstrates a visual synecdochal metonym—the simple depiction of different iconic hairstyles of Elvis Presley, with nothing else (no facial features or shape at all) to immediately signify Elvis (41–42).

19. Raymond W. Gibbs Jr., *The Poetics of Mind: Figurative Thought, Language and Understanding* (Cambridge: Cambridge University Press, 1994), 322.

20. Lakoff and Johnson, *Metaphors We Live By*, 40.

community of believers, past and present, biblical and contemporary, who gather around him in faith.

Semiotician Charles Forceville makes the point that "the stylistic form in which a metonym occurs affects its construal and interpretation. Aspects of the specific form of the metonymic source can add to, or intensify the connotations made salient in the target."[21] There are two ways in which this works. First, the silhouettes serve as great levelers or flatteners to make salient the fundamental equality of all before God, the equanimity that should ideally characterize all human social life (and most especially the Christian community if it is to be true to its theology). As difference is minimized, aspects of race, gender, class, or ethnicity are no longer apparent or significant. This radical new unity is the ideal gaze or disposition of the Christian community as proposed in many Pauline texts especially, such as 1 Cor 12:13; Gal 3:28; Eph 2:15; and Col 3:11, among others. Second, there is a mimetic quality in the silhouetted Christ, and the depiction of the follower of Jesus in silhouette infers imitation of Christ, or the desire to align oneself to Christ. There is a visual likeness between the Christ figure and the disciple figure. This underscores the shared humanity of Christ as reflected in many Pauline texts.[22]

Turning to the two works considered primarily in this study, I suggest aspects of the silhouette of Christ can add to or intensify the connotations made salient in the resurrection. Primary among these is the bodily dimension of the resurrection. It is not a spiritual resurrection alone but an embodied resurrection that takes place, from the tomb in the garden, and is witnessed to by the disciples. Both designers use of full-body silhouettes to make salient the physical bodily transformation of the resurrection.

---

21. Charles Forceville, "Metonymy in Visual and Audiovisual Discourse," in *The World Told and the World Shown: Multisemiotic Issues*, ed. Eija Ventola and Arsenio Jesús Moya Guijjaro (London: Palgrave Macmillan, 2009), 70.

22. For further discussions on these themes, see James D. G. Dunn, *A Commentary on the Epistle to the Galatians*, BNTC (London: Black, 1993), 205–8; Michael Tilly, "Social Equality and Christian Life in Paul's First Letter to the Corinthians," *AcT* supplement 23 (2016): 225–37; Bruce Hansen, *All of You Are One: The Social Vision of Galatians 3:28, 1 Corinthians 12:13 and Colossians 3:11*, LNTS 409 (London: T&T Clark, 2010); Beverly Roberts Gaventa, *Our Mother Saint Paul* (Louisville: Westminster John Knox, 2007); Andrew T. Lincoln, *Ephesians*, WBC 42 (Nashville: Nelson, 1990), 123–65; Richard N. Longenecker, *Galatians*, WBC 41 (Dallas: Word, 1990), 150–59; Schweizer, *Colossians*, 55–88.

Another connotation central to the gospel narratives concerning the resurrection is the presence of Christ among his followers. Markell's *Easter* silhouette illustrates this dimension most forcefully. Behind the postcrucifixion confusion or disillusion of the disciples, elaborated in the dialogues of those on the road to *Emmaus* (Luke 24:13–24) and in the boat at *Tiberias* (John 21:1–14), looms large the *presence* of Christ, able to manifest physically in their daily lives at any moment, as in other accounts (Matt 28:9, 16–20; Mark 16:9, 12, 14; Luke 24:36–51; John 20:19–28). The graphic device of the silhouette serves powerfully the synecdochal metonymical value of allowing a simple part to stand for the whole, the risen *Christ*, however individual believers or congregations appropriate that biblical and theological concept imaginatively for themselves.

Fig. 6.1. Meinrad Craighead, *Christ, Image of God* (Col 1:15). © Meinrad Craighead. All Rights Reserved.

Fig. 6.2. Meinrad Craighead, *Give Witness* (1 John 5:8). Note the small figure between the rays in the center. © Meinrad Craighead. All Rights Reserved.

Fig. 6.3. Meinrad Craighead, *Bread of Life* (Matt 6:11). © Meinrad Craighead. All Rights Reserved.

Fig. 6.4. Meinrad Craighead, *Bread and Wine* (Heb 4:16). © Meinrad Craighead. All Rights Reserved.

6.4. Meinrad Craighead's Use of Silhouette in *The Sunday Missal*

Craighead makes use of silhouette throughout her woodcuts for the Roman Catholic *Sunday Missal*.[23] These designs may be accurately described as multimodal synecdochal metonyms, as they also contain lettering and so directly reference the verbal text. In some instances that included text is a short biblical lection in its own right (figs. 6.1–2), and in others it is a liturgical text (fig. 6.5) that is in turn itself paraphrased from biblical texts.

Of all the silhouetted figures throughout the series, the figure of *Christ* is the least defined (figs. 1.3, 6.1–2, 6.6). Craighead's figures are expressive. Where those figures are not *Christ*, they most frequently hold a gesture of having their arms and hands raised in line with or above their heads (figs. 6.3–6). This is a joyous celebratory gesture, and it sits well within busy and dense designs replete with birds and flowers and other elements of the natural world. In figures 6.4 and 6.5 the silhouetted figure is clearly intended to represent the presiding celebrant at the Eucharist at the altar. In both instances the pose adopted is that of *orans*, the ancient standing posture of prayer.[24] Interestingly, other figures that accompany these priestly figures are also in the *orans* position—this is seen most demonstrably in figure 6.3 (also fig. 6.5 and to a limited degree fig. 6.4). In this circular design with the large chalice in the center and the bread equally distributed around the table before each participant, it is hard to definitively claim any one of these figures as the presider. There is a cross pattern created by the four bulkier figures at the cardinal points, with four shorter figures in between—these could represent children. I suggest that, as this missal

---

23. Craighead created seventeen different woodcut designs that appear throughout the *Sunday Missal*. Some are repeated, as they appear at the appointed position in each of the three years of the lectionary cycle.

24. The *orans* position, with arms raised, elbows at the side, and hands facing up, is a classic position of prayer inherited by the earliest Christians from the Jews and the classical world. It is depicted in the earliest Christian art found in the catacombs, including that believed to be evidence of a female deacon of the first centuries. This particular fresco, known as the *Donna Velata* (veiled lady), is found in the Catacomb of Priscilla, Rome, fourth century. For an image, see Mary Charles-Murray, "The Emergence of Christian Art," in *Picturing the Bible: The Earliest Christian Art*, ed. Jeffrey Spier (New Haven: Yale University Press in Association with the Kimbell Art Museum, 2007), 53. In Byzantine iconography the Virgin Mary is often depicted in the *orans* position.

was the first lay missal issued after the liturgical reforms of Vatican II and documents such as *Gaudium et Spes*, it strives to visually articulate some of the progressive reimagining of the role of laypeople in the church and in the liturgy. Scriptural passages such as "a royal priesthood, a people set apart" (1 Pet 2:9) as inspirational proclamations for a new model of church resonate as possible underlying or intended reference points for an illustration such as this. Each figure could conceivably be the presider at the table. In effect all the figures actively participate around the circular table in the blessing of the bread and wine. A circular table itself speaks powerfully of a fundamental equality. The use of silhouette, then, serves to visually reinforce this egalitarianism.

There are three similar silhouettes of *Christ* in figures 6.1 and 6.6 and the Holy Saturday design (fig. 1.3) that is the main design explored here. In these images *Christ* is suspended in a circle, whether the womb of Mary (fig. 6.6), an abstract shape (fig. 6.1), or the tomb (fig. 1.3). The circular shape with the figure suspended within echoes something of Leonardo da Vinci's *Vitruvian Man* drawing, an archetypal figure of vitality and perfection, an everyman figure of classic proportions. This would resonate with the scriptural text illustrated therein and the understanding of Vatican II as expressed in *Gaudium et Spes*, "He Who is 'the image of the invisible God' (Col. 1:15), is Himself the perfect man" (§22). Yet Craighead's *Christ* figures subtly resist perfect proportionality—they are fluid and organic, and may even be slumped in posture (fig. 1.3). Nonetheless, the notion of an original, a divine archetype, is there in these rudimentary forms suspended in light.

There are no other biblical characters, with the exception of Mary (fig. 6.6), in Craighead's series of woodcuts. The human figures may be understood as Jesus's disciples (figs. 6.3–6.5) or more conceivably received as contemporary believers actively engaged in the liturgy of the church.[25] The

---

25. The active participation of the laity is clearly enunciated in SC §14. "Mother Church earnestly desires that all the faithful should be led to that fully conscious, and active participation in liturgical celebrations which is demanded by the very nature of the liturgy. Such participation by the Christian people as "a chosen race, a royal priesthood, a holy nation, a redeemed people (1 Pet. 2:9; cf. 2:4–5), is their right and duty by reason of their baptism. In the restoration and promotion of the sacred liturgy, this full and active participation by all the people is the aim to be considered before all else; for it is the primary and indispensable source from which the faithful are to derive the true Christian spirit; and therefore pastors of souls must zealously strive to achieve it, by means of the necessary instruction, in all their pastoral work."

Fig. 6.5. Meinrad Craighead, *Through Him and with Him* (Eucharistic Prayer 3). © Meinrad Craighead. All Rights Reserved.

Fig. 6.6. Meinrad Craighead, *Hail Mary* (Luke 1:26–38). © Meinrad Craighead. All Rights Reserved.

Eucharist is a clear focus in the designs. There are many visual references to the natural environment: waves and water, palm trees, plants and birds abound, as do the cosmic elements of stars, suns, and moons. The human figures are not perfectly formed but are chunky and expressive, heavy, solid, organic, and rooted to the earth. The medium of woodcut lends itself to this and may be understood in the carving out of figures from soft wood to visually and metaphorically imply the fashioning of human beings from clay (Gen 2:7). The earthy figures of Craighead's Eden are also "a chosen race, a royal priesthood, a holy nation, God's own people"

(1 Pet 2:9), gathered around the table of the Lord. It seems plausible that the ground-breaking document on the liturgy, *Sacrosanctum Concilium*, that issued forth from the Second Vatican Council and was the motivation behind the reformed liturgy of *The Sunday Missal* was itself a major influence in Craighead's artworks.

6.5. Nicholas Markell's Use of Silhouette in the Evangelical Lutheran Worship *Worship* Books

Throughout the Evangelical Lutheran Worship series of liturgical books, featuring his designs, Markell makes use of the graphic device of silhouette.[26] Where those designs illustrate gospel vignettes (fig. 6.7), the Christ figure is always depicted in red. Markell has developed a unique and visually striking way of dealing with silhouette to maximize the effect. By reversing out in white an arm or hand here and there, greater expression and emphasis is added to the gestures. Likewise, a simple flowing line through the figure indicating something about a garment or hair, for example, lends a poetic dimension to the shapes and is visually pleasing. It adds to the movement and gesture depicted and lifts the silhouette, preventing it from becoming too static. It is far more difficult to achieve a highly communicative simple design than a complex design. Yet at a glance each of these four episodes, in the four quadrants around the cross, is immediately recognizable to even a less knowledgeable viewer as to which gospel narrative is being illustrated.[27] This is achieved through color difference at one level, indicating the figure of *Christ* in red consistently and setting him off from the character with whom he interacts. However, beyond color, posture and gesture are the essential signifiers in the designs. The gestures have a multimodal effect in that, despite the lack of verbal content, the

---

26. Markell designed 113 different designs illustrating biblical lections for particular seasons or feasts in the liturgical calendar, and ministries and activities within the life of the church. These can be sourced on a CD-ROM titled *Evangelical Lutheran Worship Graphics* (Minneapolis: Augsburg Fortress, 2011).

27. Clockwise from top left: (1) the anointing of Jesus by Mary, John 12:1–8, read on the fifth Sunday of Lent, year C; (2) the cure of the man born blind, John 9:1–41, read on the fourth Sunday of Lent, year A; (3) the encounter between Jesus and the Samaritan woman at the well, John 4:5–42, read on the third Sunday of Lent, year A; (4) the raising of Lazarus, John 11:1–45, read on the fifth Sunday of Lent, year A.

viewer's imagination is stimulated to call forth from memory something of the signified gospel texts as they have heard or read them themselves in the past. In other words, one might hear in one's mind's ear (if you will indulge a clunky metaphor) a phrase of dialogue from the encounter, for example: "How is it that you, a Jew, ask a drink of me, a woman of Samaria?" (John 4:9). The gestures encourage the imagination to fill in the anticipated dialogue.

Other biblical characters such as Moses (fig. 6.8) are also given graphic treatment. Here, again, with beautiful simplicity Moses is portrayed in two key moments in his relationship with God, the encounter at the burning bush (Exod 3:1–4:17) and the receiving of the Ten Commandments (Exod 24:12–31:18; 34:1–34:28). Other designs feature major feasts in the liturgical calendar, such as the Easter Vigil (fig. 6.9). In these designs, where the characters depicted are intended to be understood as the contemporary gathered community, they continue to be shown in either black or white, and the symbolic christological dimension is illustrated in red. The paschal fire is red, and the flames of the paschal candle and those candles lit from it are likewise in red. The church is gathered around the paschal fire, in a space illuminated by that fire, after dark under the night sky. Typically, the interior of the church is also in darkness, as the people process in with their candles behind the paschal candle and listen to the first reading from the Scriptures, Gen 1:1–2:4a, the creation of the world.

The sacraments of the church are a further focus, and the example of baptism (fig. 6.10) displays again how the thoughtful use of color and gesture with the silhouettes can lend profound theological value to a simple design, enabling it to function simultaneously at different and profoundly symbolic levels of meaning. The figures in black on the outside the baptismal pool may be taken to be a minister on the left and a catechumen on the right. In white in the center is another risen *Christ* motif. The church's theological understanding is that Christ is present in the sacraments, so that when a minister baptizes it is really Christ himself who baptizes. Baptism is understood to be baptism into the life, death, and resurrection of Christ and so this *Christ* figure receives the person seeking baptism into this new life in Christ. The design might also be understood temporally, and the figure in the center may be a newly baptized Christian, washed in the blood of the cross. Markell's silhouettes are perceptive and evocative, enabling wonderfully satisfying little eureka moments for the viewer as connections are made between specific biblical texts and liturgical actions that overlap in the multimodal context of the liturgy.

Fig. 6.7. Nicholas Markell, *Lent*. © 2011 Evangelical Lutheran Church in America, admin. Augsburg Fortress. All rights reserved.

Fig. 6.8. Nicholas Markell, *Moses*. © 2011 Evangelical Lutheran Church in America, admin. Augsburg Fortress. All rights reserved.

Fig. 6.9. Nicholas Markell, *Easter Vigil*. © 2011 Evangelical Lutheran Church in America, admin. Augsburg Fortress. All rights reserved.

6.6. Conclusion

An anticipatory gesture, the Corinthian potter's daughter traces a shadow, draws a silhouette, before her lover has left, preparing herself for the time to come when all she will have is her memory. An aid to memory, a mnemonic device, the silhouette she traces does not give her a fully realized image, a replacement, or a simulacrum of her lover. Instead, it gives her an outline, a marker, a designated space in which to remember.[28]

The silhouette's deep origins in bodily absence and memory make it a powerful visual metonym for the Christian community. There is an interesting paradox at the heart of the silhouette of the risen *Christ* especially. On one hand, silhouette is about simplicity, about reducing something to its most basic and essential shape for an immediate apprehension of its significance. Yet, on the other hand, silhouettes are opaque, dense, and

---

28. Lisa Saltzman, "Faraway, So Close: Mythic Origins, Contemporary Art: The Case of Kara Walker," in *Contemporary Art and Classical Myth*, ed. Isabelle Wallace and Jennie Hirsch (Surrey, UK: Ashgate, 2011), 35.

Fig. 6.10. Nicholas Markell, *Holy Baptism*. © 2011 Evangelical Lutheran Church in America, admin. Augsburg Fortress. All rights reserved.

impenetrable. While acknowledging that the resurrection is received in faith and remains a mystery, unfathomable in concrete terms, silhouette in its simplicity resists complex abstract or philosophical dogma. Paradoxically, while silhouettes are simple outlines and shapes, they are also containers. They are able to contain and carry narratives. A silhouette may be a site of reception for the projections laid on it. The shape, the contour of the outline, becomes profoundly significant as it delineates the boundaries of what may or may not be conceivably projected on it.

The Christian Bible gives no account of what Jesus actually physically looked like, and so the creative visual imaging of Jesus has always been fraught with challenges as differing interpretations and theologies have sought to be definitive, reaching right back into biblical injunctions against making and worshiping a graven image (Exod 20:4) and other, later iconoclastic controversies. The ethnicity and gender of Jesus as a Near Eastern Jewish male are delineated in the biblical text, yet both have been and remain sites of struggle for many contemporary believers and nonbelievers. Gender, in portrayals of Jesus in art, is a site of much contention and resistance, and this will continue to be the case in the future.[29]

Craighead's poignant *corpus Christi* suspended in a tomb or womb of divine white light, at the heart of her Holy Saturday woodcut (fig. 1.3), is full of pathos and liminality. It is the physical body of *Christ* in transformation. It is the unfolding of the resurrection before his bodily appearances to his followers. The long flowing hair suggested by Markell's *Easter* (fig. 1.1) silhouette may be argued as being historically consistent with the hairstyles of Jewish men in the ancient Near East and with often culturally accepted images of Jesus through the ages. However, it may also be read as implying a more gender-neutral representation of Jesus. Silhouette serves to camouflage both the ethnic and gender identities of these Jesus figures. Both Craighead and Markell have used silhouette as a semiotic resource to subvert these contentious issues of difference by refusing to delineate either race or gender and thereby placing the mystical body of Christ at the center. This is a highly inclusive act. The silhouette allows for the visual embodiment of Paul's invocation of an inclusive body of Christ: "There is no longer Jew or Greek, there is no longer slave or free, there is no longer male and female; for all of you are one in Christ Jesus" (Gal 3:28). A shift in both Christology and ecclesiology is marked by the use of silhouette in this context.

---

29. US artist Janet McKenzie was awarded the first prize in an international art competition that was run by the American journal *National Catholic Reporter* to mark the year 2000. The theme was an image of Jesus for the new millennium. The competition received thousands of entries and was judged by respected art critic Sister Wendy Beckett. McKenzie's model for her painting was an African American woman. McKenzie's painting *Jesus of the People* won the competition and was both widely, enthusiastically applauded and also reviled, to the point of death threats to the artist. See "Jesus of the People," Janet McKenzie, https://tinyurl.com/SBL6710r. Elizabeth A. Johnson, in her reflection on the painting, describes McKenzie's Jesus as "an unexpected figure … androgynous, mulatto, framed by symbols of indigenous and Eastern religions." See Johnson, "Jesus of the People," in *Holiness and the Feminine Spirit: The Art of Janet McKenzie*, ed. Susan Perry (Maryknoll, NY: Orbis, 2009), 69.

7
A Semiotic Analysis of the Graphic Design *Easter* by Nicholas Markell

The iconic image is catechizing, transforming, enlivening.
—Nicholas Markell

Easter is the title of a graphic illustration designed by contemporary American artist Nicholas Markell for a series of liturgical books of the Evangelical Lutheran Church of America (fig. 7.1).[1] This series of publications, known as Evangelical Lutheran Worship, includes a range of books used in the liturgy of the church: a sacramentary, lectionaries and hymnals, and the pew edition *Worship* book. Markell was commissioned by the Evangelical Lutheran Church in America to design a series of graphic illustrations for application across the range of Evangelical Lutheran Worship books and associated materials. The books were published in 2006 by Augsburg Fortress Press in Minneapolis and are used internationally by the wider Lutheran church for their English-language liturgies.[2] The design titled *Easter* appears in the lectionary on the right-hand page (recto) of a double-page spread at the beginning of the section containing the Easter readings.[3] It serves as a marker for a new section in the lectionary. The word *Easter* appears in large italics in the top right corner. It

---

1. These liturgical books are also recommended as the primary worship resource for the Evangelical Lutheran Church in Canada. They are used further afield, too—including in Ireland.

2. On a visit to the Lutheran Church in Dublin, one can expect to be greeted and handed a copy of the ELW *Worship* book at the door. The sacramentary from this series is also used by the presider. The lectionaries from this ELW series are not used in Ireland, as this church follows the German lectionary cycle, which is slightly different.

3. The Easter readings include those beginning with Maundy Thursday of Holy Week and continue to Pentecost.

Fig. 7.1. Nicholas Markell, *Easter*. © 2011 Evangelical Lutheran Church in America, admin. Augsburg Fortress. All rights reserved.

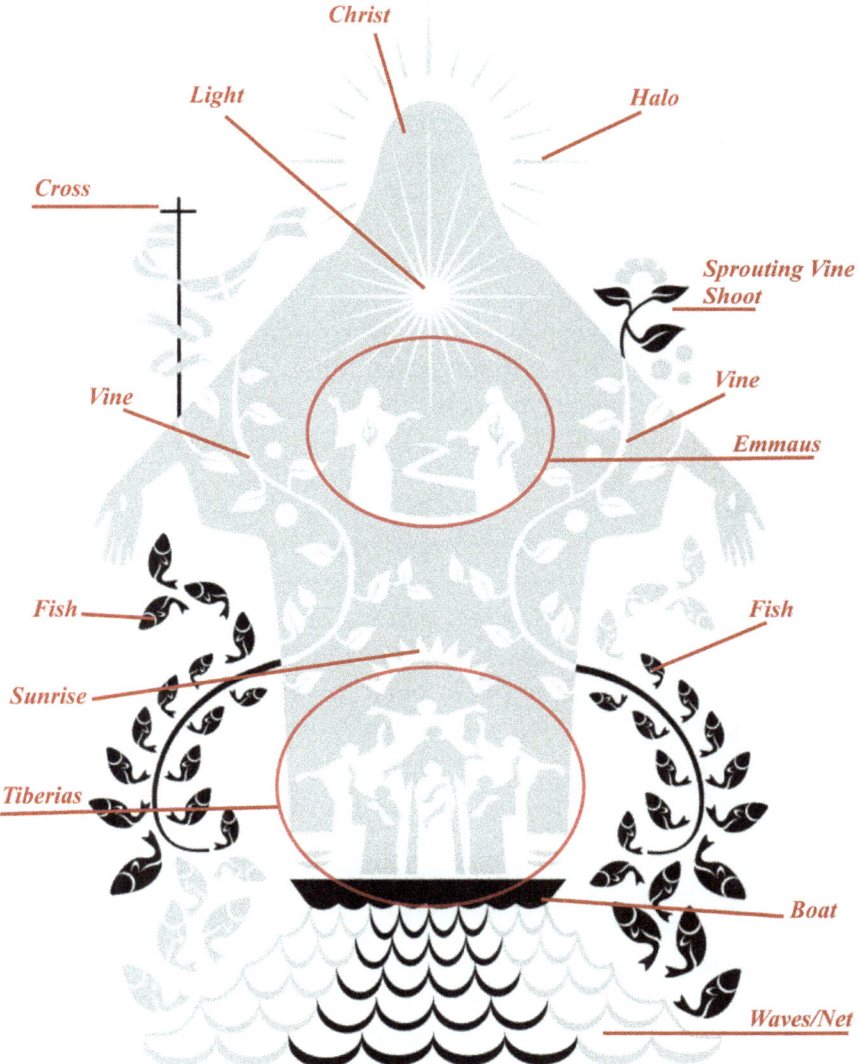

Fig. 7.2. *Easter* with labels as detailed sections are referred to throughout the chapter.

signals the beginning of the Easter season in liturgical time in the liturgical calendar of the church's year. The lectionary is a hefty volume, weighing over a kilogram, and produced to a beautiful, high-quality finish including an embossed leatherette cover.

Markell, the designer, was presented in the introduction, as was the design *Easter*. Chapter 5 considered the mode of color, and chapter 6 looked at the semiotic functioning of silhouette in this artwork. This chapter will expand on these explorations and provide a technical, in-depth analysis of Markell's *Easter* design using the social semiotics of the visual methodology developed by Kress and Van Leeuwen. This is a multimodal text; the modes in use are image, color, and silhouette. Using the three metafunctional categories, ideational, interpersonal, and textual, outlined in previous chapters and brought to the task of analyzing images, I will open up the semiotic functioning of this design. Alongside this, I bring into the discussion the many biblical texts that are proclaimed in the Easter liturgies and that appear printed in the pages following this artwork in the Evangelical Lutheran Worship lectionary.[4] A small number of these Scripture readings are given prominence in this design. These principal texts that have operated as primary resources for this artwork will be considered here. It obviously would not be possible to include in a design a visual reference to every lection read during the Easter season. This is a composite image that has chosen and features some of the many resurrection motifs and metaphors found in the gospels. While there is a strong Lukan episode in the center of the design, it has a predominantly Johannine flavor.

7.1. The Ideational Metafunction in *Easter*

The ideational function is usually the first to be described when conducting a technical analysis of a semiotic production, such as an image, and concerns the representation to the viewer of ideas about people, places, and things and their relation to one another. Kress and van Leeuwen maintain that images may be seen as potentially involving three aspects of experience: participants (who or what is depicted), processes (depicted

---

4. There are 132 different biblical texts read during the Paschal Triduum and over the seven Sundays of the Easter season, 54 from the HB and 78 from the NT (some of these may be read more than once).

actions or relations), and circumstances (where, when, how, with what)—elements that together make up what Halliday and Matthiessen refer to as ideational figures.⁵ Jewitt, elaborating on Halliday, writes,

> People, Halliday theorized, construct representations of "what goes on in the world" and their experience of the world through the *ideational resources of a mode*. (*Ideational* meaning is also referred to as presentational meaning, and sometimes called experiential meaning or logical meaning). In language this may be achieved in a number of ways including the words chosen to represent people, places, and things in the world; or the creation of different kinds of relationships between these "participants" by positioning them as active, passive, or reactive.⁶

The ideational function considers how an image works to convey to the viewer basic information about the character, social status, actions, and position of each individual. It would also include details of species, size, and material qualities of inanimate objects. "We 'read' these characteristics of the people from the same kind of clues by which we know people in everyday life: facial features and expression, stance, gesture, typical actions, and clothing."⁷ Building on this brief introduction, I will introduce a few foundational terms that will appear consistently and form the framework for this analysis.

Fig. 7.3. A simple diagram of a *vector*. A represents the *actor* and B the *goal*.

7.1.1. Participants and Vectors

Two key terms of visual social semiotics are *participants* and *vectors*. Instead of objects or elements or volumes, social semiotics refers to *represented participants*. This has two advantages: it points to the relational

---

5. Clare Painter, J. R. Martin, and Len Unsworth, *Reading Visual Narratives: Image Analysis of Children's Picture Books* (Sheffield: Equinox, 2014), 55.
6. Jewitt, "Multimodality," 24.
7. Michael O'Toole, *The Language of Displayed Art*, 2nd ed. (London: Routledge, 2011), 17.

characteristic of participant in something, and it draws attention to the fact that there are two types of participant involved in every semiotic act: the *represented participant* and the *interactive participant*.[8]

Vectors are an essential element of this design. Almost every represented participant in this design in fact operates as a vector. The *Cross* is a vector, as are the banners that fly from it. The three sun designs, *Halo*, *Light*, and *Sunrise*, all comprise radiating vectors. The *Emmaus* road is a vector. The arm gestures of all the disciples form vectors. Vectors are one way in which two represented participants may be represented visually as being in a process of interaction (fig. 7.3). Vectors are processes. Vectors are lines that have direction, that point to something, that interact with something. It is important to reiterate that vectors are always indicative of a narrative process. "When participants are connected by a vector, they are represented as doing something to or for each other."[9] These vectoral patterns are called *narrative*. Whole objects or represented participants may constitute vectors, or they may carry vectors (e.g., swords, guns, the cross). The participant from which or whom the vector emanates is known as the *actor*, and the participant at which or whom the vector is directed is referred to as the *goal*.

> The hallmark of a narrative visual proposition is the presence of a vector: narrative structures always have one, conceptual structures never do. In pictures, these vectors are formed by depicted elements that form an oblique line, often a quite strong, diagonal line.... Vectors may be formed by bodies or limbs or tools "in action," but there are many ways to turn represented elements into diagonal lines of action. In abstract images such as diagrams, narrative processes are realized by abstract graphic elements—for instance, lines with an explicit indicator of directionality must always be present if the structure is to realize a narrative representation.[10]

---

8. Kress and van Leeuwen, *Reading Images*, 47–48. Interactive participants "are those in the act of communication—the participants who speak and listen or write and read, make images or view them, whereas the *represented participants* are the participants who constitute the subject matter of the communication; that is, the people, places and things (including abstract 'things') represented in and by speech or writing or image, the participants about whom or which we are speaking or writing or producing images."

9. Kress and van Leeuwen, *Reading Images*, 59.

10. Kress and van Leeuwen, *Reading Images*, 59.

Different kinds of narrative processes can be distinguished on the basis of the kinds of vectors and the number and kind of participants involved.[11]

> The *Actor* is the participant from which the vector emanates, or which itself, in whole or in part, forms the vector. In images they are often also the most salient participants, through size, place in the composition, contrast against background, color saturation or conspicuousness, sharpness of focus, and through the "psychological salience" which certain participants have for viewers.[12]

Christ, from whom the two primary vectors, his outstretched arms, emanate, is not only the most perceptually salient or conspicuous represented participant in the image; he also plays the most crucial role in the grammatical structure that constitutes the meaning of the image. A *transactional* relation between *Christ* and the disciples (of both *Emmaus* and *Tiberias* episodes) is realized by the vectors that link them, namely, the oblique lines formed by both their gazes and gestures of their outstretched arms. *Christ* has the role of actor, and the disciples have the role of goal in a structure that represents their relation as a *transaction*, as something done by an actor to a goal.[13] The disciples in their gestures respond to *Christ*.

The shape of *Christ*, the silhouette of his figure, itself forms a distinct and powerfully salient vector in the shape of a vertical, upwardly pointing arrow (fig. 7.4). The head of *Christ* is the head of an arrow. The triangle is formed by his outstretched arms and the sleeves of his garment, while his body forms the vertical shaft of the arrow. At the base of the silhouette, one does not find the feet of *Christ*—which may be understood to be obscured by the group of disciples. However, in the white space between the horizontal hem of his garment and the horizontal of the black boat, there are a pair of shallow, upward-facing half-ellipses. These are symmetrically repeated on either side of the disciples. My own interpretation is to understand these as suggestive of oars, given their contextual proximity to the disciples in the boat on the water. Their slight vibration, similar to that of the *Light* rays, the visual frisson of red and white acting against each other, creates movement under *Christ*. Without being flippant, they

---

11. Kress and van Leeuwen, *Reading Images*, 63.
12. Kress and van Leeuwen, *Reading Images*, 63, emphasis added.
13. Kress and van Leeuwen, *Reading Images*, 50. I will pick up again on the gaze as vector in the following section on the *interpersonal* metafunction.

function visually to literally propel *Christ*, the vertical arrow, upward, as they imply imminent ascent. They give liftoff to *Christ* as a vertical vector. In this sense they subtly allude to the ascension narratives of Mark 16:19; Luke 24:51; and Acts 1:2, 11, 22.[14]

Fig. 7.4. Diagram demonstrating how the figure of *Christ* may be read as a vector.

The upward vertical thrust is reiterated throughout the design through the use of other vertical vectors: within the *Halo* (the thin wedge pointing directly north above the head of *Christ*); the central, vertical ray of the *Light*; the curved road of the *Emmaus* episode; the rays of the *Sunrise*; the

---

14. Lections including Luke 24:51 and Acts 1:2, 11 feature on the feast of the ascension every year in the ELW lectionary, but this Markan verse is not read.

vertical bodies of the individual disciples; the *Cross*; the *Sprouting Vine Shoot*; the curved line of the joined *Vine/Fish* flourish; and the connected points of the upward-facing curves of the *Waves/Net*.

It is important to take notice of the quality of line throughout this design. As has been noted before, there is a crispness to the edge of the shapes. Yet, it is significant that there are very few completely straight lines in this artwork. The lower hem of the *Christ* silhouette is straight, as are a few of the lines framing the hands. Apart from these, all the lines are slightly, gently, and almost imperceptibly curved. The corner angles, significantly those of his garment, have been rounded off to give a softer appearance.

> Circles and curved forms generally are the elements we associate with an organic and natural order, with the world of organic nature—and such mystical meanings as may be associated with them derive from this. The world of organic nature is not of our making, and will always retain an element of mystery. Curved forms are therefore the dominant choice of people who think in terms of organic growth rather than mechanical construction, in terms of what is natural rather than in terms of what is artificial.[15]

The most elaborate curves in this design are those of the *Vine* tendril extending vertically up either side of *Christ* from the *Fish* line. The line alternates from a black line to a reversed-out white line as it forms a continuous thread that links the *Fish* and the *Vine*. In terms of salience in the design, it may be argued that these two episodes, drawn from the natural world, carry the same weight as the two episodes featuring the disciples in the center. The *Fish* appear to leap out of the water toward the hands of *Christ*. There is great movement and energy suggested in the surge of flying or leaping fish. They spin and turn. There is a propulsion of movement created from the larger fish at the base to those further up. The *Vine* leaves sprout in all directions and bear the fruit of grapes. This natural world flourishes in the presence of *Christ*. Not only, as the dominant represented participant in the image, does he have power over it, but it is oriented toward him, responds to him, and is animated by him. There is an interaction between the actor, *Christ*, and the goal, the *Vine/Fish* episodes, conjoined here to represent the natural world: plant and animal, that which lives on the land and that which lives in the sea.

---

15. Kress and van Leeuwen, *Reading Images*, 55.

The extraordinary sophistication of this design enables it to subtly hold and convey, simultaneously, two apparently opposite qualities: stability and dynamism. The visual weight, the salience of the bold silhouette, makes *Christ* an anchor on the page. He is portrayed as the eternal Christ: "the Alpha and the Omega, the first and the last, the beginning and the end" (Rev 22:13), who promises to be with the viewer always (Matt 28:20).[16] Yet, he is also the dynamic living Christ, risen and rising, who will imminently ascend to the Father (Mark 16:19; Luke 24:51; Acts 1:2, 11, 22).

7.1.1.1. The Vine and the Fish

The grapevine is an ancient symbol of abundance and life. "In the earliest times, the supreme ideogram of life was the vine leaf."[17] Many religions have held the grapevine as a sacred plant with manifold meanings. The people of Israel are described as a vine planted by God. The image of the vine is used to speak both negatively (Jer 2:21; Ezek 19:12–14) and positively (Isa 27:2–6; Ezek 19:10–11; Ps 80:8–9; 2 Bar 39.7) of Israel.[18] The grapevine is also the "Tree of the Messiah."[19] God is the vinedresser, while Jesus equates himself with the true grapevine that, as a living root, bears the faithful as its branches (John 15:1–11). "The Father cares for the fruitful branch on the vine, pruning it so that it will become more fruitful, and he destroys the branch that bears no fruit by separating it from the vine (v.2). Jesus is the life-giving vine but it is the Father who promotes growth."[20] The vine here represents Jesus's assertion: "I am the true vine" (Ἐγώ εἰμι ἡ ἄμπελος ἡ ἀληθινή), one of the defining "I am" statements of Jesus's revelation to his disciples (John 15:1a).[21] Jesus claims that he is the unique source of life and fruitfulness, and offers it to those who take up

---

16. All three scriptural references to the "Alpha and the Omega" (Rev 1:8; 21:6; 22:13) are read during Eastertide in year C on the second, fifth, and seventh Sundays, respectively. Matthew 28:20 is heard on Holy Trinity Sunday (the Sunday after Pentecost).

17. Juan E. Cirlot, *A Dictionary of Symbols*, 2nd ed., trans. Jack Sage (London: Routledge & Kegan Paul, 1971), 360.

18. Francis J. Moloney, *The Gospel of John*, SP (Collegeville, MN: Liturgical Press, 1988) 4:422.

19. Udo Becker, *The Element Encyclopedia of Symbols*, trans. Lance W. Garner (Dorset: Element, 1994), 132.

20. Moloney, *Gospel of John*, 420.

21. This reading, John 15:1–8, occurs on the fifth Sunday of Easter in year B.

his invitation to abide in him. "Abide in me, and I in you. As the branch cannot bear fruit by itself unless it abides in the vine, neither can you unless you abide in me. I am the vine, you are the branches" (15:4–5a). And this invitation comes with a promise: "Those who abide in me and I in them bear much fruit" (15:5b).

Fig. 7.5. Detail of the *Vine* and the *Fish*.

Of John 15:1–11, Thomas Brodie writes, "The word 'abide' is used ten times, a frequency not matched elsewhere in the NT. The image in question, the vine and its branches, is particularly effective in suggesting unity, for unlike other trees where one may distinguish clearly between trunk and branches, such a distinction is not clear. The vine consists of its branches; all flow together into one."[22] The placing of the *Vine* within the silhouette quite literally illustrates this invitation to abide *in* him, and its lively movement, characterized by the curving vine with pert spring leaves and bearing grapes, is suggestive of flourishing and fruitful life. The bold red further enhances the energized environment, in Christ, of life-giving love (15:9–11). As Dorothy Lee notes, "The vine is a vibrant image of fecundity and growth, the flourishing of human life in relationship with God."[23]

---

22. Thomas L. Brodie, *The Gospel according to John: A Literary and Theological Commentary* (Oxford: Oxford University Press, 1993), 479.

23. Dorothy Lee, *Flesh and Glory: Symbolism, Gender and Theology in the Gospel of John* (New York: Crossroad, 2002), 95.

This invitation to "abide in me" is made through Jesus's extended arms and outward-facing palms. The inward curves of the *Vine* and pointing leaves gesture into the center, the vital stem, to join the *Emmaus* and *Tiberias* disciples, who literally abide in him. The *Sprouting Vine Shoot* is the fullest realization of life abiding in Christ and the transformation of the unavoidable element of suffering, the *Cross*, that also pertains to human life. The *Cross* is linked to the *Vine*. The invitation to abide in this life-giving bond comes with the promise of love and joy: "Abide in my love. If you keep my commandments you will abide in my love, just as I have kept my Father's commandments and abide in his love. These things I have spoken to you that my joy may be in you, and that your joy may be complete" (15:9b–11).

The natural elements, the *Vine* and the *Fish*, constitute vectors (fig. 7.5). Not only are the shapes of the fish and the leaves almost identical, but each shape is also an arrowhead; it points, it interacts.[24] The thoroughly dynamic curved shapes of the fish and the leaf are vectors, and each is further animated by internal lines: the arc of the gills and the fins, the lateral line of the fish, and the stem of the leaf. Each fish is a vector. Each leaf is a vector. The line to which they are attached is a further, dominant vector curving up the sides of *Christ*, spiraling in an upward thrust—realized on the left in the *Cross* and on the right in the *Sprouting Vine Shoot* episodes. Most of the *Fish* point in an upward fashion: three fish on either side deviate from this pattern.[25] Likewise with the leaves; most of the leaves point upward, inwardly toward the *Emmaus* episode and outwardly toward the hands of *Christ* and his gesture. A few leaves (four) point down into the

---

24. The similarity of the shapes of the *Vine* leave and the *Fish* might remind one of the morphing shapes in an M. C. Escher design.

25. In the *Tiberias* pericope there is a special mention of 153 fish (John 21:11), and commentators have given varying explanations for this odd and precise number. In this design there are twenty fish on either side, making a total of forty: a symbolic number in the Bible. It is the number for expectation, preparation, penitence, fasting, and punishment. The waters of the flood flowed for forty days and forty nights; Moses waited forty days and nights on Mount Sinai before he received the tablets of law; the city of Nineveh did penance for forty days to escape God's punishment; the Israelites were forty years in the wilderness; Jesus fasted for forty days in the wilderness; after the resurrection Jesus appeared to his disciples during a period of forty days. With reference to Jesus's fast, the church practices a forty-day fast (Lent) before Easter, hence its relevance as a symbolic number in this illustration even if it does not directly concur with the amount of 153 described in John 21:11.

center of the composition. Four leaves, again matched symmetrical pairs, point vertically upward, to the *Cross* and the *Sprouting Vine Shoot* episodes, respectively.

Fish are a symbol of life and fertility. The fish was also a secret symbol of Christ in the earliest Christian communities, where the church was persecuted.[26] Early baptized Christians saw themselves as fish who had been reborn in the baptismal waters—indeed, Tertullian spoke of how "We, little fishes, after the example of our *ichthus* Jesus Christ, are born in water."[27] At a symbolic level one might see these fish as representing the many baptized Christians who are the fruit of the vine. "As an embodiment of Christ, the fish also symbolizes spiritual nourishment and, especially when pictured along with bread, the eucharist."[28] This arises from the accounts of meals the disciples shared with Jesus that involved fish and bread. In broad terms, the fish is a psychic being, in the world of psychology and spirituality. The fish is the mystic "ship of life," sometimes a whale, sometimes a bird, and at other times simply a fish or a flying fish, "but at all times it is a spindle spinning out the cycle of life."[29] Over time "it came to be taken as a symbol of profound life, of the spiritual world that lies under the world of appearances, the fish representing the life force surging up."[30] In this design we see both a spinning-out and surging life force as an abundance of *Fish* leap forth from the water toward and almost into the hands of *Christ*. It is a striking illustration of exuberance and abundance. It demonstrates the authority of *Christ* over the natural elements and implies a desire on the part of the *Fish* to respond to his command. There is also an abundant catch of fish found in Luke 5:6–9.[31]

---

26. The initial letters of five Greek words: Iesous Christos Theou Uios Soter, form the word for fish: *ichthys*. This forms an acrostic title of Christ: Jesus Christ, Son of God, Savior.

27. Tertullian, *Bapt.* 1 (*ANF* 3:669).

28. Boris Matthews, *The Herder Symbol Dictionary: Symbols from Art, Archaeology, Mythology, Literature and Religion*, trans. Boris Matthews (Wilmette, IL: Chiron, 1986), 77.

29. Cirlot, *Dictionary of Symbols*, 106. The whale in which Jonah sailed might be thought of as a mystical ship of life: "But the Lord provided a large fish to swallow up Jonah; and Jonah was in the belly of the fish three days and three nights" (Jonah 1:17).

30. Cirlot, *Dictionary of Symbols*, 107.

31. In the Lukan account, the miraculous catch takes place during Jesus's earthly ministry, and there is a suggestion that they caught so many fish that "their nets

Fish appear frequently throughout the gospels and are often vital elements of miraculous events brought about by Jesus. There is the occasion of the discussion of the payment of taxes to Caesar in which Jesus instructs Peter to "go to the sea and cast a hook; take the first fish that comes up; and when you open its mouth, you will find a coin; take that and give it to them for you and me" (Matt 17:27). There are other accounts of the multiplication of fishes and loaves recounted with some varying details in the gospels (Matt 14:17–19; 15:34–36; Mark 6:38–43; 8:7; Luke 9:13–16; John 6:9–11). In Jesus's resurrection appearance to the disciples in Jerusalem, a direct link is made with the physical bodily presence of the risen Christ and the material form and food of fish: "They gave him a piece of broiled fish, and he took it and ate in their presence" (Luke 24:42–43).

The visual echo between the shapes of the *Fish* and leaves of the *Vine* profoundly connects the symbolic value of the *Fish* and the *Vine* in significant ways. Both are elements of the natural world that feature in Jesus's ministry. Both are divine food, food that has been the product of transformative miracles of Jesus: the wine of Cana (John 2:1–11) and the multiplications of the fishes and loaves. Both represent the material sustenance of the body found in Jesus's table fellowship. Both represent providence and abundance as signs of Jesus's care for his followers and friends. However, whereas the vine is a symbol that Jesus embraces and uses of himself in his reported speech ("I am the true vine," John 15:1), he never uses fish metaphorically to identify himself, but rather as a symbol of believers when he calls Simon and Andrew to become "fishers of men" (Matt 4:19; Mark 1:17; Luke 5:10). The *Vine* pattern is layered within the silhouette of *Christ*; an internal, self-identifying, and unifying metaphor. The *Fish*, the believers, called to "abide"—to become branches of "the true vine"—leap toward him in obedience and desire for transformation through the waters of baptism. This transformation is suggested in the almost identical shapes of the *Fish* and the leaves of the *Vine*, and emphasized in the change of color in the continuous line (vector moving toward *Christ*) from black to white at the edge of the silhouette.

There are two models of interpretation, elaborated at further length in Kress and van Leeuwen, about the function of a vector: those of trans-

---

were beginning to break" (Luke 5:6). By contrast, in the Johannine postresurrection account, "and though there were so many, the net was not torn" (John 21:11).

port (from one place to another) and those of transformation (from one thing into another). "And because one sign, the arrow, can represent both, the two meanings often become conflated: movement, transport *is* transformation; mobility *is* the cause of, and condition for, change, growth, evolution, progress."[32] Interestingly, in the case of the *Fish* and the *Vine*, these vectors are of both transport (the *Fish* are moving, leaping through the air, and the *Vine* is growing) *and* transformation. At the point where the *Fish* (Christians) cross over the boundary frame of the silhouette into *Christ*, they are transformed into flourishing branches (budding leaves) of the *Vine*. Spiritual transformation is the ultimate end of moving toward, abiding in *Christ*.

7.1.1.2. Waves, Water, and Net

Closely connected with the *Fish* is the *Net* in which they are caught (fig. 7.6). The net itself is a polyvalent symbol "of extensive interconnectedness, but especially of catching and gathering."[33] Jesus uses the metaphor of fishing to describe the evangelical task of his disciples: "And he said to them, 'Follow me, and I will make you fish for people'" (Matt 4:19; Mark 1:17). In the New Testament the net appears as a symbol of God's effects. In this

Fig. 7.6. Detail showing the *Waves/Net* episode.

sense a net with many fish represents the church. "Again, the kingdom of heaven is like a net that was thrown into the sea and caught fish of every kind" (Matt 13:47). The other possibility is to see the pattern as waves of water, water being another potent biblical symbol.

---

32. Kress and van Leeuwen, *Reading Images*, 62.
33. Matthews, *Herder Symbol Dictionary*, 138.

In Egyptian hieroglyphics, the symbol of water is a wavy line with small sharp crests, representing the water's surface. The same sign tripled represents a volume of water, that is, primeval ocean and prime matter.[34] A similar graphic pattern is replicated here to represent the Sea of *Tiberias* mentioned in the narrative of John 21.

> Water is the essential preserver of life. Limitless and immortal, the waters are the beginning and ending of all things on earth. The primeval waters, the image of prime matter, also contained all solid bodies before they acquired form and rigidity. The waters, in short, symbolize the universal congress of potentialities, the *fons et origo*, which precedes all forms and all creation. Immersion in water signifies a return to the pre-formal state, with a sense of death and annihilation on the one hand, but birth and regeneration on the other, since immersion intensifies the life-force.[35]

The simultaneous qualities of transparency and depth associated with water go far toward explaining the veneration of the ancients for this element, which, like earth, was a female principle. Water is, of all elements, the most clearly transitional between fire and air (the ethereal elements) and earth (the solid element). By analogy, water stands as a mediator between life and death, with a two-way positive and negative flow of creation and potential destruction. This apparent (and almost oxymoronic) dichotomy of "transparent depth," apart from other meanings, stands in particular for the communicating link between surface and abyss.[36]

In the gospels, water is richly symbolic of transformation and new life. Jesus himself is described as "coming up out of the water" during his baptism by John (Mark 1:10). Jesus presents himself to the woman at the well as "living water" that animates within believers "a spring of water gushing up to eternal life" (John 4:14). His promise is that "out of the believer's heart shall flow rivers of living water" (7:38). The wedding at Cana recounts the first transformative miracle of Jesus, whereby water is changed to wine (2:6–9). Jesus is presented as having authority over this primal element of water, be it in stone jars or the waters of the Sea of Galilee on which he walks and onto which he invites Peter (Matt 14:28), or the raging waters of the storm that threaten to sink the boat, which he brings

---

34. Cirlot, *Dictionary of Symbols*, 364.
35. Cirlot, *Dictionary of Symbols*, 365.
36. Cirlot, *Dictionary of Symbols*, 365.

under control (Luke 8:23–25). The cleansing quality of water comes into use as Jesus pours water into a basin and washes the disciples' feet (John 13:5). Finally, at the crucifixion "one of the soldiers pierced his side with a spear, and at once blood and water came out" (19:34).

7.1.2. Reactional Processes and the Disciples

Kress and van Leeuwen maintain, "When the vector is formed by an eyeline, by the direction of the glance of one or more of the represented participants, the process is reactional." In this instance, we no longer refer to actors but *reactors*, and not of goals but *phenomena*. "The *Phenomenon* may be formed either by another participant, the participant at whom or which the *Reactor* is looking, or by a whole visual proposition, for example, a transactional structure."[37] In *Easter*, a reactional process is evident in the group of *Tiberias* disciples. While this departs slightly from Kress and van Leeuwen's insistence on "visible eyes that have distinct pupils and are capable of facial expression,"[38] the gestures performed by the angles of the heads of the disciples strongly imply eyelines directed at the phenomenon of *Christ*. Were imaginary eyelines to be drawn from the invisible but implied eyes of the opaque, silhouetted disciples, they would land on the face or hands of *Christ*, most plausibly the hands, featuring the wounds of crucifixion, the gesture of *Christ*. The arms of some of the disciples perform a mimetic function, imitating the outstretched arms of *Christ* in

Fig. 7.7. Detail showing the *Emmaus* episode.

---

37. Kress and van Leeuwen, *Reading Images*, 67.
38. Kress and van Leeuwen, *Reading Images*, 67.

crucifixion. The other gestures, some perhaps with raised shoulders, suggest confusion and questioning; others might be read as submission or praise, as pointing to *Christ* as the answer to another's question. It is possible to imagine a conversation in the boat. This is a transactional reaction process, as the phenomenon is present and visible.

By contrast, the *Emmaus* disciples are not involved in a reactional process with *Christ*, as there is no direct eye contact between these disciples and *Christ*. They are engaged in two bidirectional transactional actions, the first with each other, a communication between the two of them, created by the diagonal vectors of their arm gestures and the strongly implied direct eyeline vector that connects them, a mutually reciprocated gaze (fig. 7.7). The second bidirectional transactional action is created by the doubled-headed vector that is formed by the road from Jerusalem. This may be perceived as emanating from the center of *Christ*. The road zigzags diagonally, first toward the disciple on the right, then the disciple on the left, then back toward the disciple on the right, before curving through and under that disciple to join up with the disciple on the left. The road also forms a vector pointing back to *Christ*. That movement toward *Christ* is reinforced in the diagonal vectors set up in the arm gestures of the disciples pointing in the direction of the road—toward *Christ*.[39] The end or vanishing point of the road almost connects with the long vertical ray of the *Light*, an emphatic symbol of Christ's presence.

---

39. In conversations with a few people to whom I showed this image, some felt this episode could just as easily be the appearance of Christ to Mary Magdalene in the garden (John 20:11–17), as it looks like a man and a woman; Christ could be telling Mary to go and tell the disciples that he is risen. I resist this interpretation, as that would fundamentally undermine the coherence of the design, the singularity of the large silhouette as the image and presence of the risen Christ in this design. There are also other biblical reception reasons to resist it too: the "tongues of fire" Pentecost symbol that appears in the middle of each disciple—a direct allusion to "did our hearts not burn within us?" (Luke 24:32). Some scholars propose that the unnamed person accompanying Cleopas (Luke 24:18) may be "Mary the wife of Clopas" named as present at the crucifixion in John 19:25 (allowing for such cross-referencing and difference in spellings). The absence of a second name has fueled speculation; see Joseph A. Fitzmyer, *The Gospel according to Luke*, AB (New York: Doubleday, 1970), 2:1563.

"The importance of the journey motif to the Lukan enterprise" makes the road a significant element of this visual episode.[40] The "way" (ὁδός) is for Luke a special designation for Jesus's salvific mission.[41] Fitzmyer writes,

> Christ comes to "walk with them" (*syneporeueto autois*, v.15). Note the double use of *en tē hodō*, "on the road" (vv.32,35). It is precisely the geographical setting in which Christ instructs them about the sense of the Scriptures. Thus at the end of the Lucan Gospel the appearance-story *par excellence* takes place, not only in the vicinity of the city of destiny, toward which Jesus' entire movement in the Gospel has been directed, but his final and supreme instruction ... is given "on the road."[42]

The *bidirectional* vector that is the road cleverly illustrates the journey the disillusioned disciples have made away from Jerusalem, the scene of the tragic execution of Jesus, accompanied by the unrecognizable stranger (the silhouette), now exclaiming excitedly to one another as they turn back, along the road, to Jerusalem and into new life in *Christ*.

7.1.2.1. The Light

The sun appears in three different forms in this design: as the large *Halo* behind the head of *Christ*; the radiating sun disc, the *Light*; and the rising sun emblem above the *Tiberias* episode, *Sunrise*. The sun is experienced as the dominant celestial body and by many as a numinous force, on which life on earth is dependent and so has therefore always carried religious meaning. The sun, along with its partner in the sky, the moon, animates the primal dichotomy of light and dark. Daylight symbolizes renewed life, truth, and logic. "As an all-seeing eye who travels the world, the sun acquired the character of a spy for the gods and therefore the stern judge of mankind."[43] In the gospels, the sun is often associated with

---

40. Joel B. Green, *The Gospel of Luke* (Grand Rapids: Eerdmans, 1997), 843.
41. Fitzmyer, *Gospel according to Luke*, 1:169.
42. Fitzmyer, *Gospel according to Luke*, 2:1558.
43. Jean Rhys Bram, "Sun," *ER* 14:134. Cirlot also points out: "On occasion, the sun appears as the direct son and heir of the god of heaven, and ... inherits one of the most notable and moral of the attributes of this deity: he sees all, and in consequence, knows all. In India, as Surya, it is the eye of Varuna; in Persia, it is the eye of Anuramazda; in Greece, as Helios, the eye of Zeus (or of Uranus); in Egypt it is the eye of Ra, and in Islam, of Allah. With his youthful and filial characteristics, the sun is

the effects of God in the world, especially ominous foretelling of the end times, "the sun will be darkened" (Mark 13:24), and the darkening of the sun at the crucifixion (Luke 23:45). Jesus is likened to the sun, and this is an image of glorification and illumination that is described in the transfiguration: "And he was transfigured before them, and his face shone like the sun" (Matt 17:2). Light is another metaphor that Jesus uses to refer to himself. "Again Jesus spoke to them, saying, 'I am the light of the world. Whoever follows me will never walk in darkness but will have the light of life'" (John 8:12).

> Images of light and darkness pervade the fourth gospel, creating what is probably its most striking motif. The prologue depicts God's Word as a source of life and light shining in the darkness (1:5). Later Jesus concludes his nocturnal encounter with Nicodemus with unsettling remarks about those who love darkness rather than light (3:19-21). Then the motif fades away until Jesus suddenly declares that he is "the light of the world" (8:12) and demonstrates the truth of his claim by enlightening the eyes of the man born blind (9:4–7). The healing of the blind man and its aftermath intensify hostility towards Jesus by many in Jerusalem, and shadows begin to fall over the period of daylight allotted for his ministry (11:9–10). With a final plea to believe in the light, Jesus vanishes from public view before plunging into the dark night of death (12:25–36, 46; 13:30). Afterward the motif is reduced to a glimmer, with but passing references to the glow of lanterns, a charcoal fire, and the predawn darkness of Easter morning.[44]

The ideational metafunction is shown here functioning in the many vectors creating transitional relations between episodes and participants within the narrative being construed. Lukan motifs such as the road, and many Johannine metaphors and symbols, have been brought into new relationships in exciting ways. The *Fish* leap out of the water toward *Christ* in response to his call. They are transformed through abiding in him and in love into flourishing branches of the *Vine*. These two symbols are not brought together in this way in the biblical text, yet Markell has imaginatively reconfigured their relationship here.

---

associated with the hero, as opposed to the father, who connotes the heavens, although the two, sun and sky are sometimes equated" (*Dictionary of Symbols*, 317).

44. Craig R. Koester, *Symbolism in the Fourth Gospel: Meaning, Mystery, Community* (Minneapolis: Fortress, 1995), 123.

7.2. The Interpersonal Metafunction in *Easter*

The interpersonal metafunction concerns the various relational dynamics set up within and through an image. A social semiotics of the visual analysis recognizes three possible relational dynamics within images, as "images also play a key role in the process of making interpersonal meaning."[45] The first is the relationship, set up through the image, between the interactive participants, that is, the producer of the image and the viewer; this concerns the communication of meaning intended by the producer and how it is received by the viewer. Artists make use of the specific semiotic resources available in the visual mode to establish communication with their viewers. In this context, the immediate producer is Markell, but there are other, more distant producers, too—namely, the Evangelical Lutheran Church in America, which commissioned the artist and supplied the brief for the desired communication to the intended viewer, who in this instance is a member of that church. The second relationship involves the represented participants; these are the people, places, and things illustrated *in* the image. These represented participants may be interacting with one another—as indeed is the case here in *Easter*. The third possibility is the interaction between the represented participants and the interactive participants or viewers. Kress and van Leeuwen distinguish four types of systems associated with the interpersonal function; these are image act and gaze; social distance and intimacy; horizontal angle and involvement; and finally, vertical angle and power. The four systems work interpersonally, as they show the way in which what is represented in a visual composition interacts with the viewer. *Easter* is a particularly striking example in the originality, power, and vivacity of its interpersonal engagement with the viewer.

7.2.1. The Image Act and the Gaze

> Seeing is powerful among humans and many higher mammals in part because it is a primary medium of social life. Communal relations are established and sustained in different kinds of looks—shy glances, bold stares, rapt gazes, or averted eyes interpret an encounter, confirm a relationship, or signal an intention with visceral force. Vision reveals authority and weakness, charisma and stigma, compassion and aggres-

---

45. Arsenio Jesús Moya Guijarro, *A Multimodal Analysis of Picture Books for Children: A Systemic Functional Approach* (Sheffield: Equinox, 2014), 91.

sion, and a host of other dispositions. Seeing collaborates with gesture, movement, touch, sound, and facial expression to form the basis of human communication. Vision also helps maintain social relations by linking individuals to the groups or social bodies that comprise their society—class, kin, tribe, ethos, folk, nation, monastic order, elect, redeemed, and damned.[46]

The interpersonal function considers how these social relations are established in images by analyzing the positioning of the viewer, an interactive participant, in relation to the person or people, the represented participants, depicted in the image. An imaginary and symbolic connection or interaction can be established between those depicted and the viewer.

This is achieved through eye contact or gaze. Eye contact is a form of direct address, in images as in life.[47] Kress and van Leeuwen write,

> There is, [then], a fundamental difference between pictures from which represented participants look directly at the viewer's eyes, and pictures in which this is not the case. When represented participants look at the viewer, vectors, formed by participants' eyelines connect the participants with the viewer. Contact is established, even if it is only on an imaginary level. In addition there may be a further vector, formed by a gesture in the same direction.[48]

Eye contact is accompanied by facial expression, gesture, and body language, all of which help the viewer discern whether this constitutes an offer or a demand. Kress and van Leeuwen write,

> This visual configuration has two related functions. In the first place it creates a visual form of direct address. It acknowledges the viewers explicitly, addressing them with a visual "you." In the second place it

---

46. David Morgan, *The Embodied Eye: Religious Visual Culture and the Social Life of Feeling* (Berkeley: University of California Press, 2012), 3.

47. The famous British World War I recruitment poster, designed by Alfred Leete, featuring Lord Kitchner pointing and staring directly at the viewer whilst the typographic message proclaimed "Your country needs YOU!" is one of the most well-known and explicit examples of this establishment of eye contact and the visual performance of direct address of the viewer, to powerful and memorable effect. See "Kitchener: The Most Famous Pointing Finger," BBC, August 4, 2014, https://tinyurl.com/SBL6710s.

48. Kress and van Leeuwen, *Reading Images*, 117.

constitutes an image act. The producer uses the image to do something to the viewer. It is for this reason that we have called this type of image a "demand," following Halliday (1985): the participant's gaze (and the gesture, if present) demands something from the viewer, demands that the viewer enter into some kind of imaginary relation with him or her. Exactly what kind of relation is then signified by other means, for instance by the facial expression of the represented participants.... The image wants something from the viewers—wants them to do something ... or to form a pseudo-social bond with a particular kind of represented participant. And in doing this, images define to some extent who the viewer is (e.g. male, inferior to the represented participant, etc.), and in that way exclude other viewers.[49]

The silhouette of *Christ* makes this a particularly interesting example to consider. We, the viewers (interactive participants), cannot see the eyes of *Christ*, as they are hidden in the silhouette. However, his eyes and his gaze at the viewer are forcefully implied by this powerful, direct frontal pose. As viewers, we understand intuitively that we are being gazed on by this imposing figure, that we are being held in his implied line of vision, and that we are being addressed. A demand is being made of us, the viewers, by *Christ*, to engage with him, to consider the implications of his presence in this image. Here I diverge from Kress and van Leeuwen, who maintain that it is essential that actual pupils be visible in the rendering. In this image, there are other commanding vectors emanating from *Christ* to contend that a powerful direct address is being made to the viewer. The most powerful of these implied vectors, which may stand in for the eyeline vectors, is the *Light* that appears directly, centrally, in the upper chest area of *Christ* (see fig. 7.8). As I noted in exploring the ideational function of the *Light* episode, this is a polyvalent symbol; the sun is the divine eye, and here it stands in for the actual eyes of *Christ* in a profoundly symbolic way and functioning *interpersonally* as such. This heightens the quality and impression of being addressed by *Christ* as a transformed, transcendent being, the resurrected Lord, a divine being, God.

This *Light* has many vectors, white rays, emanating from it in all directions and, it is implied, in a three-dimensional direction out toward the viewer too. Josef Albers in his extensive studies of the interactions of colors, one with another, shows that red and white (and other contrast-

---

49. Kress and van Leeuwen, *Reading Images*, 118.

Fig. 7.8. Detail showing the *Light* episode and the optical illusion of vibration set up by the high contrast between red and white.

ing pairings of colors), when they are brought into very close proximity with each other, create a visual vibration.[50] Immediately around the central disc of this sunburst, the wedges of the white rays are extremely thin, and the inverse red wedges between them likewise so thin, due to the density of the rays radiating from the disc, that this visual effect is created. The *Light* shimmers ever so slightly and yet perceptibly. This profoundly enhances its semiotic effect as a vector and, hence, the demand made of the viewer by *Christ*. The light of Christ is shining at or on the viewer, and this markedly intensifies the direct address, its impact, attraction, and meaning.

This relational interaction between depicted holy figures and viewers is not new—it has been practiced for centuries. According to art historian Hans Belting, "The suggestion of reciprocity between the viewer and the person depicted in the image" had an explicitly devotional purpose in

---

50. Albers, *Color*, 61. "The conditions for these varying effects occur between colors which are contrasting in their hues but also close or similar in light intensity.... Often under the same conditions it is perceived by some people and not by others."

Christian art of the Middle Ages.[51] Turning to the gesture of *Christ*, his outstretched arms and out-turned palms are also a demand made of the viewer to engage with him directly. This gesture is an invitation to belief —it says something like, "See, I am risen." Consistent with the gospel narratives this image references, *Christ* offers his wounded hands for inspection. In this image *Christ* makes a resurrection appearance to the viewer.

7.2.2. Social Distance and Intimacy

"What kinds of people are allowed to look out of the frame and engage with us and what kinds are not?" asks David Machin.[52] This brings us to the other type of image, where the represented participants do not attempt to make contact with the viewer and are the objects of the viewer's "dispassionate scrutiny." In this instance, Kress and van Leeuwen write,

> The viewer's role is that of an invisible onlooker. All images which do not contain human or quasi-human participants looking directly at the viewer are of this kind. For this reason we have, again following Halliday (1985), called this kind of image an "offer." It "offers" the represented participants to the viewer as items of information, objects of contemplation, impersonally, as though they were specimens in a display case.[53]

I have explored above the various ways in which *Christ* makes a demand of the viewer, makes contact with the viewer of this image. Interestingly, by contrast, the two episodes featuring the other human represented participants, the disciples, do not function as demand images but as offer elements within this system. In the *Emmaus* episode, the two disciples are directly facing each other and gesturing toward each other in their body language. This is a bidirectional transaction between these two disciples. The *Tiberias* fishermen likewise do not engage the viewer and are in a transactional system with the silhouetted *Christ* themselves as a collective group. Both of these episodes feature human characters available

---

51. Hans Belting, *The Image and Its Public in the Middle Ages* (New York: Caratzas, 1990), 57. The incredibly lifelike wooden statues of thirteenth- and fourteenth-century Italy are a case in point.
52. David Machin, *Introduction to Multimodal Analysis* (London: Bloomsbury, 2007), 111.
53. Kress and van Leeuwen, *Reading Images*, 119.

to the viewer for scrutiny and consideration. By way of contrast with the *Easter* artwork, Markell's signature design of this series "Christ" (fig. 1.8), discussed in chapter 1, shows the majesty of the glorified Christ offered for the viewer's contemplation, but no demand is made in terms of an emotional response.

Returning to *Easter*, I suggest that there are two similar yet distinct points of view set up for the viewer in relation to the disciple episodes: *Emmaus* and *Tiberias*. The stronger of the two is the lower angle, where the eyeline of the viewer is approximately on a level with the disciples in the boat of the *Tiberias* episode (fig. 7.9). The viewer is placed at some distance from the scene, on the other side of the water that extends in front of the boat. The only two hints at perspective in this very flat, two-dimensional work are created by the *Waves* and the road in the *Emmaus* episode. The depth of the wave curves decreases as they move out away from the boat. The curves also lengthen horizontally, becoming shallower, as it were, and this creates perspective. If one were to draw straight lines connecting the outermost and uppermost peaks of the waves, they would converge in a vanishing point in the center of the lower-middle disciple silhouetted in white. This informs us approximately as to our point of view as the interactive participant. We are placed on a level with the disciples in the boat.

This is significant in terms of the interpersonal address being made to us through the image by the producers of the image. The viewer is addressed as one on a par with the disciples. There is a spatial distance between ourselves and the disciples, but we are configured, through this point of view, to be equal to them, on the same level, in terms of being addressed by the *Christ* figure. In the *Emmaus* episode with the disciples on the road, another vanishing point is created by the road, at waist level, in the middle between the two conversing disciples. This vanishing point elevates our point of view to that vanishing point, but that is as high as we can go, in this image. The first vanishing point brings us up to the boat, in front of the unseen feet of *Christ*, and the second brings us right into the *Christ* figure, to a point on a road that disappears into the infinite opaque depth of the silhouette of *Christ* (fig. 7.10). The disciples are the same size in both episodes.

> There are, then, since the Renaissance two kinds of images in Western cultures: subjective and objective images, images *with* (central) perspective (and hence with a "built in" point of view) and images *without* (central) perspective (and hence without a "built in" point of view). In

Fig. 7.9. Diagram showing perspective lines created by the *Wave* pattern that create a vanishing point in the lower central disciple of the *Tiberias* episode.

Fig. 7.10. Diagram showing the second vanishing point created by the *Emmaus* road.

subjective images the viewer can see what there is to see only from a particular point of view. In objective images, the image reveals everything there is to know (or that the image produced has judged to be so) about the represented participants, even if, to do so, it is necessary to violate the laws of naturalistic depiction or, indeed, the laws of nature.[54]

The genius of this design is the positioning of the viewer. We are placed on a par, as it were, with both groups of disciples. The laws of naturalistic depiction have been subverted here most obviously in the scale of *Christ*, in the first instance, and then in the setting up of two independent narrative episodes with slightly different, yet central viewer perspectives. We are addressed, in this image, by the same *Christ* who appeared before the disciples on the road to *Emmaus* and those out fishing on the sea of *Tiberias* at dawn. So, while we are at a remove, separated from these first-century disciples in space and time, we are all now addressed in our common humanity (and baptism, possibly, or membership of the Christian community) by the same risen *Christ* in the interpersonal relations set up in this design. The viewer's primary engagement is with *Christ*, not with the disciples; we remain somewhat detached from the disciples, who are presented to us in the offer relation for consideration. There is no invitation to engage emotionally with the disciples in a direct way.

In terms of distance, a medium-range position shows the full figure. In the long-range position, the human figure occupies about half the height of the frame, and the very long range is anything wider than that.[55] In the *Easter* image, the designer has cleverly mixed up the ranges and perspectives, and they are significant in bearing out further the interpersonal engagements set up in the demand/offer system. The disciples are in the very long range. Even within the frame of the silhouette, they are less than a third of the height of the frame. *Christ* is in the long range, his full figure is visible, and his figure constitutes about half the height of the frame in the sense of the extent of the page. Neither *Christ* nor the disciples are available to the viewer at intimate or close personal distance. The extended arm gestures of the *Emmaus* disciples suggest dialogue: questioning and explanation in the implied conversation taking place between them. The *Tiberias* disciples in the boat make expansive body gestures, their arms and hands extended (fig. 7.11). These gestures may be read as either praise

---

54. Kress and van Leeuwen, *Reading Images*, 130.
55. Kress and van Leeuwen, *Reading Images*, 124.

Fig. 7.11. Detail showing the *Tiberias* episode (with Peter as the upper-central figure in the back row, with arms widely outstretched). I suggest the Beloved Disciple is featured as the lower-central figure with his arms crossed over his body.

for *Christ* or astonishment and surprise. The lower white figure in the center is the exception; his arms cross over his body in an intriguing gesture of gathering in, of awe and wonder, as he looks up at *Christ*. It may seem implausible to assign identities to the disciples in the boat; however, I venture to suggest that the uppermost central figure in white represents Peter, characterized in the gospels as given to impetuous and spontaneous actions and proclamations, whose mandate as leader or shepherd of this fledgling community of faith is reasserted by Christ (John 21:15–17). The manner of his own death (by crucifixion in Christian tradition) is perhaps alluded to in verse 18 and illustrated in his expansive gesture here. The lower disciple, also in white and in the center, has completely contrasting gestures: his arms are both contained within his silhouette, and his hand on his heart is indicative of a contemplative disposition.

Sandra Schneiders, discussing John 21, draws out marked differences in personality between the Beloved Disciple and Peter and interprets these as "the two constitutive activities of the church: contemplation and ministry."[56] She presents the Beloved Disciple as "the paradigmatic embodiment of contemplative openness to the revelation of Jesus."[57]

---

56. Sandra M. Schneiders, *Written That You May Believe: Encountering Jesus in the Fourth Gospel* (New York: Crossroad, 1999), 204.

57. Sandra M. Schneiders, "John 21:1-14," *Int* 43 (1989): 70–75.

In this pericope we are told specifically that Jesus manifested or revealed himself to the disciples, just as he had promised before his death that he would manifest himself to those who loved him and kept his word (see 14:18–23). It is the Beloved Disciple who recognizes him with perfect clarity and proclaims him authoritatively. Simon Peter's recognition of and coming to Jesus is a response to that proclamation which, in this sense, grounds his pastoral leadership. This same proclamation also illumines the ignorance of the other disciples (see v.4), who never seem to have the same clarity or certitude that the Beloved Disciple does (see v.12). Contemplative receptivity to the life-giving revelation of Jesus is the source of the church's proclamation, which grounds both the faith of the disciples and the church's mission to the world. In this final chapter the evangelist reaffirms the priority of love as the basis of spiritual insight that has been assigned to the Beloved Disciple throughout the gospel but now clarifies the relationship of church leadership, recognized in Peter, to this primacy of revelatory contemplation.[58]

This "primacy of revelatory contemplation" in the Beloved Disciple is the vanishing point for the viewer in this offer relation. Of the many responses possible to the revelation of *Christ*, this is modeled for the viewer as the first and most desirous.

7.2.3. Horizontal Angle and Involvement

The difference between the oblique and the frontal angle is about encoding involvement or detachment into the viewer's implied response to the image. The horizontal angle encodes whether the viewer is involved with the represented participants or not. The frontal angle says, as it were, "What you see here is part of our world, something we are involved with." The oblique angle says, "What you see here is *not* part of our world, it is their world, something we are not involved with."[59] In *Easter*, the relation of the frontal plane of represented participants is aligned with the frontal plane of the viewer, and so it has a frontal, as distinct from an oblique, point of view.[60] This is most forcefully felt in the imposing sil-

---

58. Schneiders, *Written That You May Believe*, 204.
59. Kress and van Leeuwen, *Reading Images*, 136.
60. Kress and van Leeuwen, *Reading Images*, 134–35. The criterion for defining a frontal angle is that the vanishing point(s) still fall(s) within the vertical boundaries of the image (they may fall outside the horizontal boundaries).

houette of *Christ*. The disciples in the *Emmaus* episode are very slightly oblique, engaged as they are in conversation but essentially oriented outward, turned toward the viewer and opening up in their body language with broad gestures into the space around them and between them. The disciples below are depicted frontally. The disciples echo then the frontal engagement of *Christ*. As viewers, we are again drawn into this compelling image through this frontal engagement, which suggests this is a narrative in which we are involved.

Those aspects of the interpersonal function that are at work in this design include demand and offer, middle and long shots, frontal angle and lowered eye-level angles. The **invitation** made directly through dynamic *Light* to the viewer is to become a disciple, in imitation of those depicted: to respond to the gesture of revelation and appearance of the risen *Christ*, to make one's way into and through the waters of baptism, to join the *Fish* transformed in the *Vine*, a believer who has chosen the way and abides in *Christ's* love.

7.3. The Textual Metafunction in Easter

The third metafunction is known as the textual metafunction and deals with composition and the integration of the elements into a coherent whole. Composition brings the ideational or representational meanings of the image into relationship with the interactive or interpersonal meanings through three interrelated systems:

1. Information value. The placement of elements (participants and syntagms that relate them to each other and to the viewer) endows them with the specific informational values attached to the various zones of the image: left and right, top and bottom, center and margin.
2. Salience. The elements (participants as well as representational and interactive syntagms) are made to attract the viewer's attention to different degrees, as realized by such factors as placement in the foreground or background, relative size, contrasts in tonal value (or color), differences in sharpness, and so on.
3. Framing. The presence or absence of framing devices (realized by elements that create dividing lines, or by actual frame lines) dis-

connects or connects elements of the image, signifying that they belong or do not belong together in some sense.[61]

7.3.1. Information Values: Given/New, Ideal/Real, Center/Margin

Easter is a composition that has a dominant central focus. It may be described as having a triptych formation. Most of the narrative visual episodes are located in the center, with two almost identical and mirroring side panels. This triptychal composition is symmetrical and therefore not polarized in the marginal side panels. There is one small but significant and noticeable difference in the design between the left and right panels: on the left, over the arm of *Christ*, is the resurrection cross: a thin cross bearing a red flag or pennant featuring a cross pattern in white.[62] This banner is a symbol of the resurrection that emerged in medieval art and was popularized during the Renaissance.[63] A quotation or an echo of the composition of many well-known Renaissance paintings, such as Piero della Francesca's *The Resurrection*, is at work here. In these paintings Christ triumphantly steps forth from a sarcophagus holding a cross with a flying pennant. In the left position of this composition, which makes use of the horizontal axis, the resurrection cross occupies the *given* position. In other words, "it is presented as something the viewer already knows, as a familiar and agreed-upon point of departure."[64]

Correspondingly, in the *new* position, in the same place on the right side, is a flowering and fruit-bearing shoot of the *Vine*, the *Sprouting Vine Shoot*. Two of the three leaves of this shoot point to the right, the future, further enhancing the effect of illustrating the new reality, the outcome of the resurrection. The emergence of this organic *Vine* sprouting into this

---

61. Kress and van Leeuwen, *Reading Images*, 177.

62. Most conventionally, this is a white flag with a red cross, but in this design, given the white background, this has been reversed for better effect (a red flag certainly has a precedent in art history).

63. Examples of the resurrection cross in art may be seen in Giotto, *Resurrection (Noli Me Tangere)*, ca. 1300–1305; Piero della Francesca, *The Resurrection*, ca. 1463–1465; Sandro Botticelli, *Resurrection of Christ*, 1490; Pietro Perugino, *Resurrection of Christ*, 1502–1506. A completely white flag may be seen in El Greco, *Resurrection of Christ*, 1597–1600. A completely red flag may be seen in Deiric Bouts, *Resurrection*, 1455, and Peter Paul Rubens, *The Resurrection of Christ*, ca. 1611/1612.

64. Kress and van Leeuwen, *Reading Images*, 181.

white space outside the silhouette symbolically reflects the wood of the cross on the other side with a powerful message about the new life generated through Jesus's death on the cross. This symbolic mirroring of the *Cross* and the *Vine* is accentuated by the continuation of the vertical black line of the *Cross* into a white branch of the *Vine* in the silhouette. The organic, curving, tendril-like *Vine* may also be seen as a root system in the fertile ground of the mediating silhouette of *Christ*. In this sense, the white *Vine* functions visually like a narrative arc linking the *Cross* and the *Sprouting Vine Shoot*.

This design is a modern iteration of a classic composition in Western Christian art going back to the medieval period. *Christ* is presented in the center as the Mediator and Savior, with the crucifixion symbolized on the left, also sometimes understood in medieval art to portray the "bad side" and resurrection on the right, the "good side."[65] In the same way as left and right operate compositionally to express different values, so do the upper and lower realm of the image. The informational values assigned to the upper and lower regions are summarized by Kress and van Leeuwen as follows:

> If, in a visual composition, some of the constituent elements are placed in the upper part, and other different elements in the lower part of the picture space or the page, then what has been placed on the top is presented as the Ideal, and what has been placed at the bottom is put forward as the Real. For something to be Ideal means that it is presented as the idealized or generalized essence of the information, hence also as its ostensibly, most salient part. The Real is then opposed to this in that it presents more specific information (e.g. details), more "down-to-earth" information (e.g. photographs as documentary evidence, or maps or charts), or more practical information (e.g. practical consequences, directions for action).[66]

This dynamic is evidently at work in this design as the upper third deals with the ideal: the divine, the illuminated head of the risen *Christ*, and the various symbolic elements that signify resurrection. The lower two-thirds feature the real, the world of humans. The *Emmaus* episode documents a mystical encounter with the risen *Christ*, and the bottom third, the *Tibe-*

---

65. Kress and van Leeuwen, *Reading Images*, 198.
66. Kress and van Leeuwen, *Reading Images*, 186–87.

rias episode—with the most humans—in their boat at sea level is the realm most grounded in the real, as we know it.

Christ is anchored on the page by the black horizontal bar of the boat. He is visually top-heavy (the spread of his arms and tunic creating a larger space), and this is significant in the top-bottom relationship. Vertical elongation creates a more pronounced distinction between top and bottom and hence a bias toward hierarchy, and toward opposition generally (what is most important or otherwise dominant goes on top; what is less important or dominant is relegated to the bottom). In this composition, the ideal-real opposition works to further emphasize the distinction between the transcendent: the transformed and risen *Christ*, and the disciples, located in the real world, grappling to come terms with the enormity of this event.

The other episode that features in the lower half of the design and in the outer thirds of the triptych are the leaping fish episodes. The movement of the *Fish*, signaled by their majority direction, is upward, out of the water toward *Christ*. There are minor chiastic structures in the coloring of the *Fish*: (vertically) black-black-red down the left, and red-black-black down the right, or, alternatively (horizontally) black-red-black-black-red-black, back and forth, across the image, visible in the three inner groupings of *Fish*. The change in color pattern does not add to the meaning of the *Fish* but breaks the absolute symmetry of the pattern on either side of *Christ*, thereby lending a greater dynamism to their movement.

> Rhythm and balance also form the most bodily aspects of texts, the interface between our physical and semiotic selves. Without rhythm and balance, physical coordination in time and space is impossible. They form an indispensable matrix for the production and reception of messages and are vital in human interaction. Moreover, it is to quite some degree from the sense of rhythm and the sense of compositional balance that our aesthetic pleasure in texts and our affective relations to texts are derived.[67]

In terms of center and margin, the center is the primary position of dominance, power, and authority, but it has a temporal dimension too: "a sense of permanence goes with the central position."[68]

---

67. Kress and van Leeuwen, *Reading Images*, 203.
68. Arnheim, *Power of the Center*, 73.

7.3.2. Salience

Composition is not just a matter of formal aesthetics and of feeling, or of pulling readers' attention (although it is that as well); it also marshals meaningful elements into coherent texts, and it does this in ways which themselves follow the requirements of mode-specific structures and themselves produce meaning.[69] Much has been written already about the salience given to *Christ* through the use of the mode of silhouette in the previous chapter. The salience of *Christ*, his visual dominance and weight in the composition, is established through many means: the central position; the bold, dynamic red color; the amount of space this form occupies in the composition; and, primarily, the use of silhouette creating a solid, weighty form. It is further elaborated through the perspective set up in the waves, with a vanishing point behind the *Tiberias* disciples at the feet of *Christ* and the leaping fish that point toward *Christ*. Finally, there is the second most salient episode, the radiating sunburst that emanates from the center of *Christ* and operates as a striking focal point for the entire composition.

7.3.3. Framing

The previous chapter, on silhouette, has dealt with the framing qualities of silhouette and its use to effect in this work. The silhouetted *Christ* serves as a frame in many ways. It provides the frame for the two episodes of the *Emmaus* and *Tiberias* events. The *Vine* and *Fish* episodes also serve as frames for these events. Cleverly, the curves of the *Fish* expand the space around the *Tiberias* disciples and connect them with the water and with the *Christ* silhouette. The *Sunrise* above the *Tiberias* episode also functions to frame the *Tiberias* episode. The vine pattern almost meets in the middle of the silhouette, in the middle of the vertical space between the *Emmaus* and *Tiberias* episodes; it separates the two scriptural passages, the two different narratives of encounters with the risen *Christ*, a Lukan one and a Johannine one.

If we are to read the *Light* as a graphic partner in a pairing with the *Sunrise* over the *Tiberias* episode, they may be indicating times of day, noon and morning, respectively. There is an upward vertical reading made possible through the three symbols of light. It begins with the *Sunrise* over the

---

69. Kress and van Leeuwen, *Reading Images*, 203.

Tiberias episode, moves up into the fully radiating midday *Light* over the *Emmaus* episode, and then goes into the fullness of light that illuminates *Christ* and is symbolized by the *Halo* around his head, which expands into the glory of the divine light of white ground all around him. It is a vertical, upward movement from the confusion of the *Tiberias* disciples to illuminated truth and realized transcendence in the glorified *Christ*.

7.4. Conclusion

Of course, not every viewer will see all of these allusions to the scriptural texts. It is also possible that the artist too may not have intentionally designed in all of the semiotic functions, compositional dynamics, symbolic aspects, and affordances of meaning with such precise and conscious deliberation as has been drawn to the surface through this semiotic analysis. An artwork itself can evolve in certain directions once certain elements appear, and, no doubt the dominant silhouette played a role in determining the compositional dynamics to some extent. Making use of the visual modes of color, silhouette, and image, the artist has wrought together many metaphors, metonyms, and symbols from the Easter gospel accounts, through the use of visual narrative structures, interpersonal relations, and composition to create a thoroughly engaging design. Significantly, this design functions semiotically as a profoundly sophisticated and moving invitation, extended to the attentive viewer, to become a contemporary disciple, a member of the church, to enter the communal life of the body of *Christ* through the waters of baptism. The risen and ascendant *Christ* of the Easter narratives of the Christian Scriptures opens his arms and invites the viewer to come and abide in him, the true *Vine* and *Light* of the world. I conclude with a final word from Markell: "Images of mystery build a bridge between what we see and what we believe. Through images of mystery we enter into the Divine, God's personal life where time and space are changed. Here the poetry of the eternal and the ritual of heaven transfigure our imagination."[70]

---

70. "Images," Markell Studios, https://tinyurl.com/SBL6710t.

8
A Semiotic Analysis of the Graphic Design
Christ Yesterday and Today by Meinrad Craighead

> Liminality may perhaps be ... a realm of pure possibility whence novel configurations of ideas and relations may arise.
> —Victor W. Turner, *The Forest of Symbols*

Christ Yesterday and Today is a graphic illustration designed by contemporary American artist Meinrad Craighead for *The Sunday Missal* of the Roman Catholic Church, printed by Collins in 1975 (fig. 8.1).[1] Meinrad Craighead was commissioned to produce a series of graphic designs for inclusion in both the Sunday and weekday missals. The design titled *Christ Yesterday and Today* appears on the left-hand (verso) page of a double-page spread in *The Sunday Missal*, facing the Easter season section. It comes after the end of the Good Friday service and before the solemn Easter Vigil (figs. 5.1–2). It may be understood as functioning semiotically to hold the space of Holy Saturday in the missal. There is no liturgy on Holy Saturday in the Roman Catholic Church.

> On Holy Saturday the Church waits at the Lord's tomb, meditating on his suffering and death. The altar is left bare, and the sacrifice of the mass is not celebrated. Only after the solemn Vigil during the night, held in

---

1. *Christ Yesterday and Today* appears on page 206 of *The Sunday Missal*. The missal text was approved for use in England and Wales, Scotland, Ireland, and Africa in 1974. It was first published in 1975. New impressions were published every year up to a sixth impression in 1977. Thereafter the missal was reprinted almost every year, featuring Meinrad's illustrations, until the issue of the new Missal in 2011. See *Sunday Missal*, 206. Turn to ch. 5 to see photographs illustrating the relationship between the illustration sited as it is between the liturgical texts of Good Friday and the Easter Vigil.

Fig. 8.1. Meinrad Craighead, *Christ Yesterday and Today*. © Meinrad Craighead. All Rights Reserved.

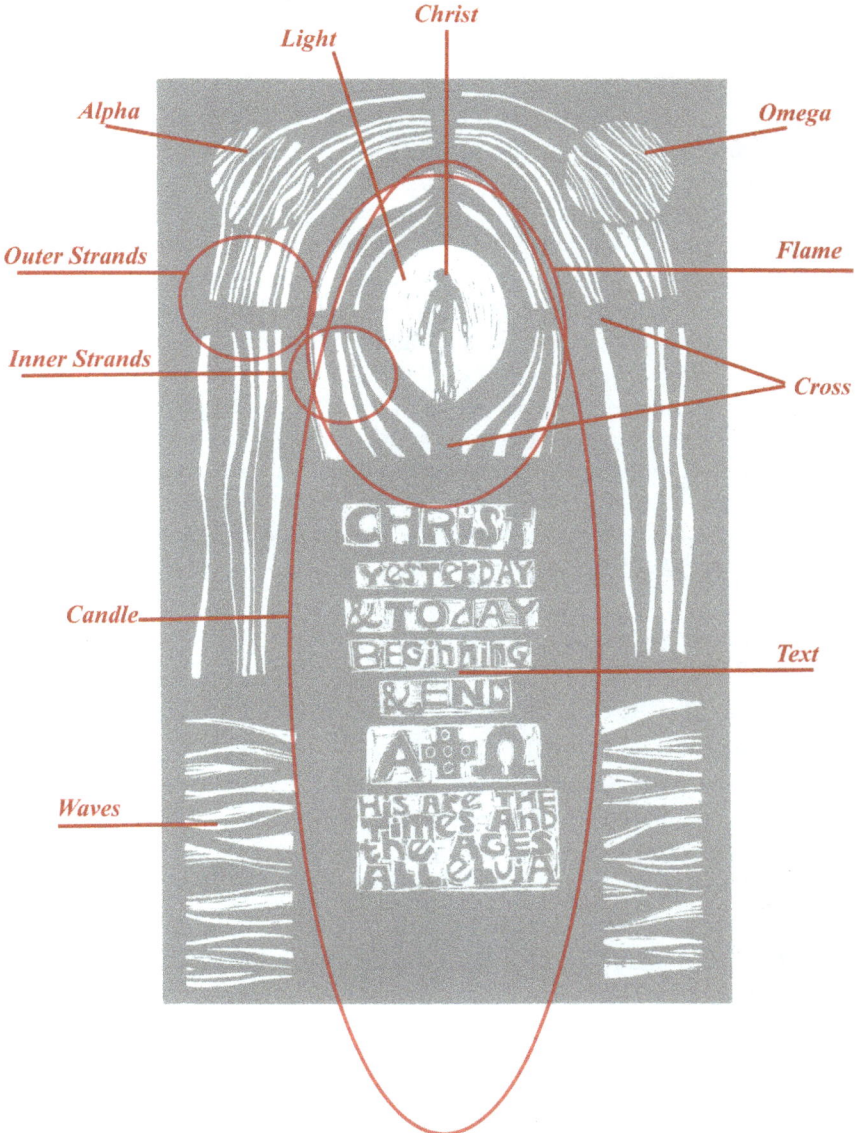

Fig. 8.2. *Christ Yesterday and Today* with labels as detailed sections are referred to throughout the chapter. © Meinrad Craighead. All Rights Reserved.

anticipation of the resurrection, does the Easter celebration begin, with a spirit of joy that overflows into the following period of fifty days.[2]

In his seminal work on Holy Saturday, theologian Alan Lewis writes,

> The second day appears to be a no-man's-land, an anonymous, counterfeit moment in the gospel story, which can boast no identity for itself, claim no meaning, and reflect only what light it can borrow from its predecessor and its sequel. Or, alternatively, does the precise locus of this Saturday, at the interface between cross and resurrection, its very uniqueness as the one moment in history which is both after Good Friday and before Easter, invest it with special meaning, a distinct identity, and the most revealing light? Might not the place dividing Calvary and the Garden be the best of all starting places from which to reflect upon what happened on the cross, in the tomb, and in between? The midway interval, at the heart of the unfolding story, might itself provide an excellent vantage point from which to observe the drama, understand its actors, and interpret its import. The nonevent of the second day could after all be a *significant* zero, a *pregnant* emptiness, a silent nothing which says *everything*.[3]

This design serves as a contemplative, visual marker of the liturgical, verbal silence of Holy Saturday, appearing as it does between Good Friday and the Easter Vigil: the start of Eastertide in the church's liturgical calendar. While I will focus on this full-page illustration, I wish also to reference a smaller design: *Christ, Image of God* (fig. 8.3). This design appears as a quarter-page banner at the beginning of the Christmas season.[4] This smaller artwork introduces or headlines the other major liturgical season in the Christian calendar. *The Sunday Missal* is a small, light volume weighing around three hundred grams, slightly smaller than an average paperback and produced to a high-quality finish, including a leatherette cover with gold-foil lettering and gilded edges.

---

2. *Sunday Missal*, 205.

3. Alan E. Lewis, *Between Cross and Resurrection: A Theology of Holy Saturday* (Grand Rapids: Eerdmans, 2001), 3.

4. *Christ, Image of God* appears on (recto) pages 93, 402, and 568 of *The Sunday Missal*. This design appears in the missal three times, once in each liturgical calendar year (A, B, and C), whereas the full-page *Christ Yesterday and Today* appears only once. The Scripture lections for the Easter Vigil liturgy do not change; it features the same readings every year regardless of the cycle.

Fig. 8.3. *Christ, Image of God*, by Meinrad Craighead. © Meinrad Craighead. All Rights Reserved.

Craighead, the artist, was presented in the introduction along with her full-page design *Christ Yesterday and Today*—the focus of this chapter's in-depth analysis using the social semiotics of the visual methodology developed by Kress and van Leeuwen. This is a multimodal text; the modes in use are image, color, and text.[5] Using the three metafunctional categories outlined in previous chapters, I will analyze the semiotic functioning of this design, with occasional reference to the smaller design *Christ, Image of God*. A small number of biblical texts are given prominence in these artworks and will be considered in relation to the images.

8.1. The Ideational Metafunction in *Christ Yesterday and Today*

The ideational metafunction "embodies experiential (participants, processes and circumstances) and logical (connections between different structures) meanings."[6] Understood within the ideational function, this design is characteristically *conceptual*, a different category and set of processes to narrative. Conceptual images represent "participants in terms of their more generalized and more or less stable and timeless essence, in terms of class, or structure or meaning."[7] Within conceptual images are classifying and identifying processes known as *relational*. These are

---

5. Chapters 5 and 6 demonstrate how color and silhouette are visual semiotic modes in their own right.
6. Moya Guijarro, *Multimodal Analysis*, 62.
7. Kress and van Leeuwen, *Reading Images*, 79.

processes of having, being, or becoming in which the participant is identified or situated circumstantially.[8] Some relational processes are described as *attributive*. The participant is referred to as a *carrier* to which these symbolic attributes are attributed. In this design, *Christ* is a carrier in a relational process, identified explicitly in the central *text* as possessing symbolic attributes such as "Alpha and Omega" and "(his are) the times and the ages."[9] These symbolic attributes are represented visually around *Christ* in shapes and patterns and through the contrasting use of black and white. The wavy lines, discs, cross shape, and circle of light are abstract, but they are not simply decorative. They mean something in relation to *Christ*. These participants, in the design, are the symbolic attributes of this central *Christ* figure.

> Human participants in Symbolic Attributive processes usually pose for the viewer, rather than being shown as involved in some action. This does not mean that they are necessarily portrayed front on and at eye level, or that they necessarily look at the viewer, even though all of these may be the case. It means that they take up a posture which cannot be interpreted as narrative: they just sit or stand there, for no reason other than to display themselves to the viewer.[10]

This ambiguous *Christ* figure is on display available for our contemplation but not demanding an emotional response in the way that a direct gaze or gesture might in the narrative process—as observed in the Markell piece.

8.1.1. Symbolic Attributes

This design is a symbolic process—meaning it is about what a participant means or is.[11] In this image *Christ* is a carrier, a participant whose meaning or identity is established in relation to other participants, here the graphic elements of alternating bands or strands that curve around a central cross framing a disc of *Light*. These other participants "represent the meaning

---

8. Halliday, *Functional Grammar*, 259.
9. I will elaborate in greater depth on the *intersemiosis* between image and word later in this chapter.
10. Kress and van Leeuwen, *Reading Images*, 105–6.
11. Kress and van Leeuwen, *Reading Images*, 105.

or identity itself, the *symbolic attribute*." Kress and van Leeuwen describe *symbolic attributes* thus:

> (1) They are made salient in the representation in one way or another; for instance ... through their conspicuous color or tone.
> (2) They are pointed at by means of a gesture which cannot be interpreted as an action other than the action of "pointing out the symbolic attribute to the viewer"—here we can include also the arrows which can connect visual realizations of participants with verbal realizations of the same participant, or vice versa, [...] for these also establish a relation of identity through "pointing."
> (3) They look out of place in the whole, in some way.
> (4) They are conventionally associated with symbolic values.[12]

Both the *Inner* and *Outer Strands* (fig. 8.4) are visual representations of the symbolic attributes of the carrier: *Christ*. Both sets of *Strands* are strikingly salient, white on black, as they frame the central *Light*. As time is a symbolic attribute appointed to Christ repeatedly in the central text, the wavy, ribbon-like *Strands* represent the concept of time. The *Strands* radiating around the central *Christ* symbolize divine, cosmic time. "Yesterday and Today, Beginning and End, Alpha and Omega" are *symbolic attributes* of Christ in the text. The *Outer Strands*, which flatten out into vertical stripes, symmetrically balanced down either side of the design, represent past and future time, stretching to eternity in both directions. These are the "times and the ages," the eras and epochs, the symbolic attributes of time represented here metaphorically like the growth rings found on a tree. Time is at the crux of the Christ event, the manifestation of the eternal in the temporal.

Fig. 8.4. Detail from *Christ Yesterday and Today* showing a section of the *Outer* and *Inner Strands*. The *Outer Strands* are those thinner strands around the edges within which the circular discs are found. The *Inner Strands* are those in the lower center here (closest to the *Christ* figure). © Meinrad Craighead. All Rights Reserved.

---

12. Kress and van Leeuwen, *Reading Images*, 105.

> Time is the context and content of reality, at once the eternal, unchanging environment of our being and its momentary, ever changing mode of expression. Conceived absolutely, it is timeless; perceived relatively, it is timely. And it is the paradoxical relation of these two that is the significant focus of much of the world's religions. Not only, along with science, does religion seek to mark such stages of relative time as it can denote, but religion goes beyond science in attempting to understand the translogical connection of relative temporal stages to timeless eternity itself. Beginning and ending with the absolute (the eternal), religion tries to perceive the particular and relative (the moment and history) in its light.[13]

Like Jews, Christians find eternity not only manifest in history but also "evinced in the moment."[14] John's Gospel records the paradoxical message that eternal, absolute reality is always present, here and now, in the timely. Portrayed in that gospel as the beginning, end, and center point of time, Christ announces himself as the eternal "I am" (John 8:58).

In Craighead's design, these *Strands* look out of place in the whole in some way, awkward and aesthetically slightly jarring. At a literal level they make no sense. They are abstract and symbolic. The temporal dynamic "Yesterday and Today"—a more immediate or short-term time period—plays out radially in the *Inner Strands* intensified around *Christ*.[15] By contrast, the beginning may be represented emerging far away, down on the left, and the end is represented far away, down on the right. Time curves around *Christ*.[16] The *Light* is (the unseen) God. The two further discs in the upper two quadrants are the symbolic attributes: "Alpha and Omega," left and right, respectively. *Christ* is suspended in this central position in time, the present moment, the already-but-not-yet manifestation of the reign of God. Symbolically, the center of the *Cross* marks the perfect meeting point of these two axes: the vertical (the divine) and the horizontal (the human). Here, these directions are symbolic attributes of *Christ* as time, divine, cosmic time, the "Beginning and End," and immediate, earthly, human time: "Yesterday and Today." The central circle of the *Cross* acts as a keyhole or portal through which we see *Christ* as this focal

---

13. Barbara C. Sproul, "Sacred Time," *ER* 12:535.
14. Sproul, "Sacred Time," 539.
15. I will elaborate on this in the section on the textual function.
16. In 1915 Einstein put forward his general theory of relativity, in which he maintained that time and space are curved.

point in which both the vertical/heavenly and horizontal/earthly axes of time meet and are found.

Christ, Image of God (fig. 8.3), the Christmas banner, may be described as divided horizontally (two-fifths over three-fifths), with the image in the upper section and typography in the lower section. The illustrative strip across the top of this design features undulating wavy lines running behind three equidistant circles with thick black outlines. The outer circles consist of wavy lines running vertically/diagonally counter to the prevailing pattern but identical to it. The diagonal lines lean inward (toward the center). The two discs—one left, one right—suspended in wavy lines are symbolic attributes for the Alpha and Omega points in time. In the center, the third circle contains the silhouette of a human figure. As the banner headlining the Christmas season, this design clearly illustrates the incarnation, the central figure signifying *Christ* as an infant or child and yet also hinting at the crucifixion through his outstretched arms. The use of this graphic device—a silhouette of a human form suspended in a white circle with a strong black outline—alerts viewers that a symbolic identification and resonance is clearly intended by the artist between this design and *Christ Yesterday and Today* (fig. 8.1). This symbol, a silhouette of *Christ* in a framed white circle, at these two most significant feasts in the church's calendar, the incarnation (*Christ, Image of God*) and death/resurrection (*Christ Yesterday and Today*) of Christ, is striking in its transformation and visual power.

8.1.2. The Biblical Text and the Text

"The Alpha and the Omega" is a phrase that appears three times in Revelation, twice as a self-designation of God (1:8; 21:6) and once as a self-designation of Christ (22:13). In Rev 1:8 this description of God is expanded with "who is and who was and who is to come, the Almighty." Christ identifies himself as "the Alpha and the Omega, the first and the last, the beginning and the end" (22:13). The juxtaposition of the terms *alpha* and *omega* unites creation and eschatology. The same God who brought the world into existence will bring it to completion. Everything has its origin in God, as Alpha (4:11). As Omega, God is acknowledged as the sustaining power in which all things find meaning and purpose until brought to their final consummation at the end of time. That which was brought in to being "in the beginning" (Gen 1:1) will be resolved in God at the end. The designation "the Alpha and the Omega" does not restrict God to beginning and end but is a declaration of the totality of God's power and control over all time: past, present, and future.

> The author of Revelation, because of his exalted Christology, can apply the same phrases to Christ that he used for God. He too is the first and the last, the beginning and the end, the Alpha and Omega. Elsewhere in the NT, Christ's role in creation is explicitly stated (John 1:3; Col 1:16). The idea of Christ as Omega or the end is particularly appropriate in Revelation which depicts Christ as the means through which God's purposes are accomplished.[17]

The designation "yesterday and today" as symbolic attributes of Christ has been drawn from the letter to the Hebrews: "Jesus Christ is the same yesterday and today and forever" (Heb 13:8).[18] It echoes the affirmation of Christ's eternal sameness found in Rev 1:8; 10–12. This sameness does not refer to "metaphysical immutability but to constancy of purpose, reliability, faithfulness to promises."[19] The phrase may be influenced by other liturgical expressions found in Rev 1:4, 8; 4:8. Phrases such as "to the ages" and "forever" are common in early Christian praise, for example, Luke 1:33; Rom 1:25; 9:5; 11:36; Phil 4:20; Heb 13:21. Richard Bauckham writes,

> We should notice how closely it corresponds to the citation from Ps. 102, understood as addressed to Christ, in the first chapter of Hebrews. That quotation affirms the full eternity past and eternity future of the divine Christ, and very strikingly, it uses the same phrase as Heb 13:8 to affirm

---

17. Mitchell G. Reddish, "Alpha and Omega," *ABD* 1:162.

18. The distinctiveness of Heb 13 has raised questions about the relationship of this chapter to chs. 1–12. Some scholars, such as Wedderburn, argue that all of ch. 13 was added by a later redactor. See Alexander J. M. Wedderburn, "The 'Letter' to the Hebrews and Its Thirteenth Chapter," *NTS* 50 (2004): 390–405. Others, such as Thompson, suggest the two segments, 13:1–6 and 13:18–25, have "the common characteristics of a Pauline letter," while 13:7–17 is distinct and "maintains the style of the first twelve chapters and recapitulates the argument of its central section (7:1–10:18)." See James W. Thompson, *Hebrews*, PCNT (Grand Rapids: Baker, 2008), 273.

19. Richard Bauckham, "The Divinity of Jesus Christ in the Epistle to the Hebrews," in *The Epistle to the Hebrews and Christian Theology*, ed. Richard Bauckham et al. (Grand Rapids: Eerdmans, 2009), 36.

that he is "the same," that is, he retains his own integrity throughout eternity.[20]

Moreover, Sean McDonough maintains that a threefold formula referring to divine identity as past, present, and future is widely found in ancient Hellenistic, Jewish, and Christian literature.[21] He suggests that it is part of the definition of a true deity and consistent with Jewish appreciations of the name of God as seen in the Targums (e.g., Tg. Ps.-J.; Deut 32:39).[22] It is pertinent that the Easter Vigil blessing of the candle, a prominent part of the Service of Light, contains a threefold formula of naming Christ: "Christ, yesterday and today, the beginning and the end, Alpha and Omega."[23] Here the third temporal aspect, "forever," has been dropped, as has "the same" from Heb 13:8. This allows for three neatly matching pairs—"yesterday and today, the beginning and the end, Alpha and Omega"—that in turn create a new threefold formula that reiterates and implies all that is contained in the Hebrews verse.

The vigil blessing continues, "All time belongs to him, and all the ages; to him be glory and power, through every age and for ever. Amen."[24] This has been paraphrased in the lowest section of Craighead's woodcut text as "His Are The Times And the Ages Alleluia" (fig. 8.5). This is not a direct quotation of any one particular Scripture passage but rather a synthesis of the temporal dimension of Rev 22:13 and many other texts that place Christ as sovereign over

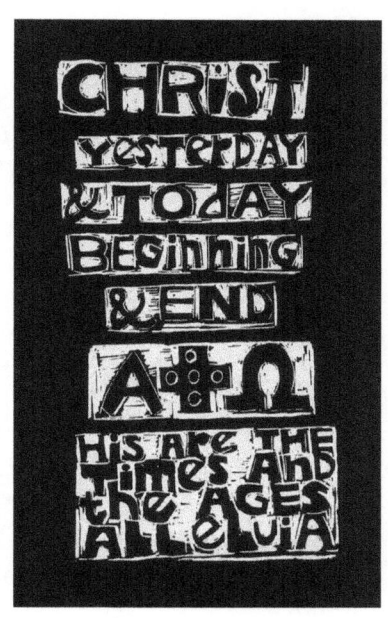

Fig. 8.5. Detail of text from *Christ Yesterday and Today*. © Meinrad Craighead. All Rights Reserved.

---

20. Bauckham, "Divinity of Jesus Christ," 34.
21. Sean M. McDonough, *YHWH at Patmos: Rev. 1:4 in Its Hellenistic and Early Jewish Setting*, WUNT 2/107 (Tübingen: Mohr Siebeck, 1999), 41–57, 187–92.
22. McDonough, *YHWH at Patmos*, 183–85.
23. *Sunday Missal*, 209.
24. *Sunday Missal*, 209.

time (Matt 28:20; Eph 1:21; 1 Tim 1:17; 2 Tim 1:9) and reigning in glory forever (Luke 1:33; Rom 1:25; 9:5; 11:36; Phil 4:20; Heb 13:21).

In the Christmas design *Christ, Image of God* (fig. 8.3) the text contains a slight adaptation of Col 1:15 ("He is the image of the invisible God, the firstborn of all creation") and a paraphrasing of the second part of the statement laid out in Col 1:16 ("for in him all things in heaven and on earth were created, things visible and invisible, whether thrones or dominions or rulers or powers—all things have been created through him and for him"). This is a cosmic vision of Christ as the "one who supremely makes the invisible God visible," who is the manifestation of the divine in human reality.[25] This assertion about Christ dynamically draws the spheres of creation and redemption together. Andrew Lincoln writes:

> Although the first part of the hymn speaks of Christ's agency in creation, it is what was first believed about his role in redemption that enabled early believers to make claims about his role in creation. In 1 Cor 15:49 and 2 Cor 4:4 Paul had used the term "image" (eikon, *eikon*) for the resurrected and exalted Christ, who as the last Adam now represented humanity as God has always intended it to be. This notion was then pushed back as far as it could go. If the resurrected Christ was the supreme expression of the image of God, then he must always have been so.... The sort of language that had been employed of Wisdom in Wis 7:26 ("she is a reflection of eternal light, a spotless mirror of the working of God, and an image of his goodness," NSRV) becomes a resource for expressing this belief about the status of Christ in God's purposes.[26]

Eduard Schweizer notes, "In Wisdom of Solomon 7:25, it is the full presence of God in his wisdom that is described: For she is a breath of the power of God, and a pure emanation of the glory of the Almighty."[27] Personified Wisdom is also related to the primordial act of creation: "The Lord by wisdom founded the earth" (Prov 3:19). Elizabeth Johnson expands,

> The great poem of Proverbs 8:22–31 unfolds this association in detail. Sophia existed before the beginning of the world as the first of God's works. Then she is beside God at the vital moments of creation as either a master craftsperson or God's darling child (the text is disputed). In

---

25. Andrew T. Lincoln, "Colossians," *NIB* 11:597.
26. Lincoln, "Colossians," 597.
27. Schweizer, *Colossians*, 64.

either case, God takes delight in her. Conversely she always rejoices in God's presence, plays everywhere in the new world, and takes delight in human beings.[28]

Here in the great hymn of Colossians, in 1:15b, Christ is placed in this role as the firstborn of all creation. Christ is recognized as the (feminine) Jewish symbol of personified Wisdom made manifest in his earthly incarnation.[29] Breath, a pure emanation of glory, reflection of eternal light, a spotless mirror—these are extraordinary symbols to bring to life in an image. It is precisely this Wisdom imagery that Craighead has put to work in her design *Christ, Image of God*. The circular *Light* in which *Christ* is placed is this spotless mirror reflecting the eternal light, a pure emanation of the glory of God. This circular *Light* is repeated in the design *Christ Yesterday and Today*.

8.1.3. The *Candle*

There is no perspective in this design; it is a flat, abstract, and symbolic work. However, there is a sense in which the *Inner Strands* create an idea of distance in an abstract and symbolic way, construed through these rings or strands. *Christ* in the *Light* is far away. He is located in another realm of time and space beyond human reach and reckoning. Spatially, this place has no real equivalent and cannot be depicted in conventional spatial relations or perspective; it can only be implied visually in an abstract and symbolic way, as done here. Color works powerfully here to symbolize sacred space and time. The deep, expansive black is the originary dark and formless void from which the unseen God brings into being the universe, in and through *Christ* (Gen 1:2; John 1:1–5; Col 1:16). White in its many dimensions functions to symbolize time. Black may be seen as representing the spatial dimension and white the temporal dimension.

Within the design there is another symbol, composed of many participants, that is almost imperceptible: a candle (fig. 8.6). If one focuses on the vertical center, it is possible to discern a *Candle*, the body of which is a black rectangle that contains the text and the *Flame*, as previously outlined, at the

---

28. Johnson, *She Who Is*, 88.
29. Elisabeth Schüssler Fiorenza, *Jesus, Miriam's Child, Sophia's Prophet: Critical Issues in Feminist Christology* (New York: Continuum, 2004), 152; Johnson, *She Who Is*, 150.

Fig. 8.6. Detail from *Christ Yesterday and Today*. It is possible to see a candle in the design, complete with body, wick, and radiating *Flame*. © Meinrad Craighead. All Rights Reserved.

top, with the *Inner Strands* perceived as rays of light emanating from the central illumination.[30] The text in this case is the words of both Scripture and the ritual Service of Light that marks the blessing of the paschal candle at the Easter Vigil.

8.1.4. Liminality

Liminality is a concept that finds its origin in the social science of anthropology, most particularly the work of Victor Turner, building on the earlier work of Arnold van Gennep.[31] The Latin root, *limen*, of the term *liminality*, means "threshold" and refers, in the first instance, to a middle stage in the process of ritual.[32] When an individual or a group is in this process of transition from one status to another, there is a threefold structure to the entire process or ritual, including a preliminal rite, in which the old status is acknowledged and symbolically discarded; a metaphorical death may occur. The liminal stage is a period of disorientation and ambiguity that must be gone through in order to successfully transition into the new status and identity. Finally, there is a postliminal stage, in which the initiate is conferred with their new status and reincorporated into the group, tribe, community.

The liminal threshold is about the space between the old and the new status or reality. Liminality is characterized by loss of status, a fundamental equality between initiates regardless of their age, wealth, education, gender, or any other markers of hierarchy conventionally held in the society.

---

30. Standing alone, this *Candle* looks decidedly phallic. Yet, I suggest that a yonic symbol may be read in the *Flame*. In this sense, the complete symbol may be seen as containing both male and female energies.

31. Victor W. Turner, *The Ritual Process* (New York: de Gruyter, 1969).

32. Early anthropological work done by van Gennep and Turner focused on coming-of-age or leadership rituals in traditional societies. More recently, usage of the term has broadened to describe political and cultural change as well as rituals.

Absence of rank and property, homogeneity and anonymity, minimization of gender difference, humility, simplicity, unselfishness: these are all qualities of liminality.[33] Every society and religious grouping has liminal people, groups, and individuals, whether by accident or design, who live outside the conventions of their society. Homeless people, street children, hermits, monks, and gurus are all characteristically liminal in their lifestyles, as indeed are Jesus and his cousin John the Baptist. "Liminal people occupy ambiguous social positions. They exist apart from ordinary distinctions and expectations, living in a time out of time," writes Conrad Kottak.[34]

Liminality is also very much about space and place. Rituals involving experiences of liminality invariably happen beyond the village or city, in other places, often in natural and designated sacred spaces, such as forests or wilderness areas. Liminal time also happens outside the conventional social structures of time. That period of three days between the death and resurrection of Christ is understood as a profoundly liminal time, an inexplicable time of transition from Jesus being tortured to death by crucifixion and his resurrection on the third day. *Christ Yesterday and Today* is undoubtedly a striking depiction of the liminality of the tomb. The inner circle contained within the eye of the *Cross* conceptually represents that liminal moment after "he bowed his head and gave up his spirit" (John 19:30). It is simultaneously the descent to the dead (Acts 3:15; Rom 8:11; 1 Cor 15:20; cf. Heb 2:14; 13:20) and the ascent to new life (Acts 13:32–33). The thick black circle of the *Cross* marks the threshold. The *Light* signifies the liminal space of the tomb and the liminal time out of time that is the three days spent there. It is sacred space-time. *Christ* can be read as both descending and ascending. The thick black bars of the *Cross*, that cross over time, mark this out as a place that is held between the vertical and horizontal, heaven and earth. Semiotically, this is a place of mediation, and *Christ* is the Mediator.

8.2. The Interpersonal Metafunction in *Christ Yesterday and Today*

The interpersonal metafunction concerns the various relational dynamics set up within and through an image. It places the implied viewer in a

---

33. Conrad Phillip Kottak, *Cultural Anthropology*, 9th ed. (New York: McGraw-Hill, 2002), 308.
34. Kottak, *Cultural Anthropology*, 309.

certain relationship with the represented participants of the image. Unlike in the demand made of us in Markell's design, this *Christ* figure is quite different, with head bowed, dead, limp, and passive, portrayed as suspended in a liminal time and space, between death on the cross, descent and entombment, and the resurrection of Easter. This *Christ* is an offer image, available for our contemplation but not demanding an emotional connection with us.

The figure of *Christ* is small on the page, almost a seventh of the height of the design. The viewer is held a long way back from Christ, as the only human represented participant in the design. The social distance construed here is impersonal. It also implies cognitive distance in the sense of something not easily understood, a mystery. The distance is not simply social and impersonal—it is also temporal and spatial. *Christ* is out of the viewer's reach both physically and emotionally, but also in a spatial and temporal sense. He is in an alternative spatial and temporal zone, implied by the portal of the circular eye of the *Cross* and the tunnel-like (albeit flat) perspective rendered by the *Inner Strands* around it. The attitude taken is one of subjective involvement. Despite there being no direct gaze, there remains some direct engagement with the viewer through the frontal positioning of his body. As Kress and van Leeuwen write,

> In the depiction of humans (and animals), "involvement" and "detachment" can interact with "demand" and "offer" in complex ways. The body of the represented participant may be angled away from the plane of the viewer, while his or her head and/or gaze may be turned towards it—or vice versa. The result is a double message: "although I am not part of your world, I nevertheless make contact with you, from my own, different world"; or "although this person is part of our world, someone like you and me, we nevertheless offer his or her image to you as an object for dispassionate reflection."[35]

The body of *Christ* is angled toward the plane of the viewer in a frontal way, but the tilt of the head is turned down and thus disengaged from the viewer. The double message here then is something like, "Although I am/was part of your world, I cannot make contact with you as I am presently in my own, different world." There is a withdrawal from direct emotional engagement with the viewer, but some involvement is maintained through

---

35. Kress and van Leeuwen, *Reading Images*, 138.

the frontal offer of the body of Christ to the viewer. In *Christ, Image of God*, the figure of the infant or child *Christ* faces toward the viewer. Interestingly, in both of these designs, the viewer position is one of equality with the figure of *Christ*; we neither look up nor down at the figure, but rather it is placed squarely in front of the viewer—at the mid-eye level. This enhances the viewer's involvement and may compensate in some way for the impersonal social distance created.

8.3. The Textual Metafunction in *Christ Yesterday and Today*

The third metafunction, the textual, deals with composition and the integration of the elements into a coherent whole. Composition brings the ideational or representational processes of the image into relationship with the interpersonal or interactive processes through three interrelated systems: (1) information value, (2) salience, and (3) framing, and I will consider Craighead's design through all three.

8.3.1. Information Values: Given/New, Ideal/Real, Center/Margin

Christ Yesterday and Today is a composition that has a dominant central focus. However, I resist the possibility of seeing this as a triptych with three clearly demarcated (and symmetrical, outer) vertical panels. Rather, there is a strong mediator to polarized process evident here in the central eye of the *Cross, Light*, and *Christ* participants. In the top half of the composition two dynamics are at work simultaneously. First, there is the dominant *Flame*. Second, though a much weaker visual dynamic, the upper half is divided by the vertical of the *Cross*. The *Flame* dominates both the center and upper half of the design. *Christ* in the center of the *Light* mediates to link the polarized participants of the *Alpha* and *Omega* in the upper left and right corners with the text and the horizontal *Waves* in the bottom left and right corners into a coherent, meaningful whole.

The horizontal *Waves* are interrupted by the vertical black rectangle of the *Candle* in which the text sits. Nonetheless, despite this vertical interruption, horizontal continuity is strongly implied visually in the *Waves*. Viewers intuitively understand the *Waves* as a continuous flow (through or) behind the *Candle*. The *Waves* are in the lower third of the composition. This is the realm of the real or the earthly. If one accepts the *Waves* as similar to the *Strands*, and symbolically and abstractly representing the concept of time, then their being both horizontal and situated at the base of the composition visually implies that the *Waves* represent time in the earthly or human realm. By contrast, the *Outer Strands* on the vertical divine axis symbolize cosmic time. Time curves around *Christ* as the pivot—the center point of time.

8.3.2. Salience

Salience creates a hierarchy of importance among the elements, selecting some as more important than others, more worthy of attention than others, regardless of their placement in the composition.[36] *Christ* in the *Light* is the most salient point of the composition. The white *Inner* and *Outer Strands* are also visually striking and compelling in their vibrancy against the black background but secondary to the *Light* and *Christ* in their salience. The text for all its complexity and central position is the least salient element in the design, with the various weights of the *Inner* and *Outer Strands* and the *Waves* carrying greater visual potency.

8.3.3. Framing

That most salient point, *Christ* in the *Light*, is framed by a thick black circle that forms the center of the *Cross*. This framing device serves to enhance the salience of the *Christ* in the *Light* in the upper center of the composition. The *Outer Strands* and the *Waves* together frame the *Candle*. The symbols of time frame the liturgical symbol of the resurrection: the paschal candle lit in the Service of Light at the opening of the Easter Vigil.

A subtle but interesting semiosis is detectable in the framing of the two symbolic discs of *Alpha* (left) and *Omega* (right). The *Alpha* disc does not have a continuous black border; it is porous. Two of the white *Outer Strands* move seamlessly and uninterrupted in a continuous line through the disc, parallel to those lines contained within the disc. However, on the other side, the *Omega* disc is fully contained within a black border, signifying completion. It is a visual full stop, the end of time.

---

36. Kress and van Leeuwen, *Reading Images*, 200.

8.4. Materiality

An aspect of graphic design that has received less attention from semioticians is that of materiality and its semiotic relation to or function in meaning making. The two major designs considered in this study are materially quite different. Markell's illustration is clearly generated through a digital illustration program that enables perfectly crisp edges, lines, and curves. Technologically, it belongs to the means of production of the twenty-first century. Yet, while it would be entirely possible to manually recreate that design with the aid of technical drawing equipment, it is an aesthetic that would be foreign to a person living a few centuries ago. Meinrad's woodcut, however, sits in a tradition that points back to the beginning of printing, whatever the surface and substrate, almost two thousand years ago.[37] The visual results of these different technologies, digital and hand-carved woodcut, do different work semiotically. As Kress and van Leeuwen write,

> Materiality matters: oil- and water-based paints offer different affordances, and hence different potentials for making meaning. The manner of production also matters. If we ask the seemingly simple question "What is a text?" or "Is a written text the same object or a different one when it is written with a pencil or with a pen and ink or is word-processed?," the answer of most *linguists* would be "No question. It is the same text." The material, graphic expression of the text would not be seen as a relevant issue. If we asked a non-linguist the same question, the answer might be different.... Like us, they would see "presentation" as a significant part of the making of the text, increasingly often equal to, or even more important than, other aspects. For them, as for the painter or the viewer of a painting, the medium of inscription changes the text.[38]

The woodcut letters of the biblical text appear decidedly different in this form than they do in the mechanically typeset pages of a Bible or missal.

---

37. The ancient civilizations of Mesopotamia and China both produced examples of rudimentary forms of relief printing from carved stone and other materials. The real development of woodblock printing on paper is attributed to the Chinese in the second and third centuries. Ts'ai Lun, a second-century Chinese government official, is credited with the invention of paper in 105 CE, and this marked a turning point in the advance of woodcut printing. In Western Europe, this technique became popular around the beginning of the fifteenth century (Meggs, *History*, 23–35).

38. Kress and van Leeuwen, *Reading Images*, 216.

In the first instance, reading it requires a different degree of attentiveness, almost like working out a puzzle. The typography is unorthodox; it breaks the rules of conventional lettering, mixing upper- and lowercase letters within words. Lowercase letters may be smaller than capitals and may begin words that contain capitals. The uneven boldness and varied juxtaposition of letters lend accent and emphasis in new ways. In the ideational function a woodcut speaks to an age-old tradition of human image-making. In the social-semiotic context of religious books, the viewer is reminded of the earliest illustrations to appear in print, black-and-white woodcuts. Woodcuts are old, organic, Germanic, and expressive. They work in reverse, meaning it is the negative space that is being cut away, rather than the positive line that is being carved. This adds to their guttural and expressive quality. Meinrad's woodcuts are fluid and raw. In this instance, there is something symbolically profound about a design that illustrates the concept of cosmic time through a pattern something like tree rings, being carved out of wood.

In the interpersonal function it is about the intimacy and immediacy of an image carved by the artist's hand. The viewer is in close proximity to the original mark making of the artist. Chiseling the organic substrate of wood by hand with an awl or other simple carving implements is a process that requires little mechanical intervention. The artist's imagination, gift for drawing, and translating it into carving, with the unique softness, hardness, and grain of the wood block, collude to bring forth an image. The production of a woodcut is a very physical process, each groove a deliberate, conscious, and active gesture. The second part—the printing of the image—requires strength and effort in the handling of a press: repeatedly shifting block and paper back and forth into position and pulling a weighty press. It involves physicality at every stage. With a woodcut the viewer is close to that process.

In the textual or compositional metafunction, social-semiotic analysis suggests that the organic nature of the process speaks its own language. The wood block itself plays a part in the creation, its quality, density, and grain guiding or resisting certain marks. It is not a wholly pliant or manipulable material. It lends its unique character to the process and to the finished product, where its grain is visible in the prints. Leaving visible strains of wood grain around objects and letters—in the carved-out (negative) areas—is fundamental to the technique, a respect for the wood and the quality it brings to the physical act of mark making in wood. Some of the woodgrain quality is sadly lost in the large-scale mechanical printing such as for *The Sunday Missal*. In the original prints that would have been pulled of this design it would have no doubt been apparent that this was created from elemental matter, with the grain of the wood visible, like a watermark in the glossy black ink. As it displays in the missal, the contrast in quality of line—expressive, fluid and organic, and striking dense black with the printed pages—adds to the salience and power of the designs.

8.5. Intersemiosis

More recent scholarship using this visual grammar set out by Kress and van Leeuwen has raised the issue of the relationship between the visual text and the verbal text: bimodal texts, as Clare Painter labels them.[39] Both of the designs by Craighead featured here qualify as bimodal texts, having text as a contributory element and represented participant in the design. These two semiotic systems are different in the way that they afford meaning. Painter elaborates:

> A verbal text unfolds over time in a dynamic, sequential way and language has a rich potential for the control of temporal deixis, sequencing, location, phasing and aspect. This is in contrast with the "instantaneous" holistic apprehension of an individual image and the corresponding potential of the visual semiotic for non-sequential spatial and comparative relationships. Recognition of such differences suggests some of the more obvious ways meanings might be expected to be "shared out" in a bimodal text. But complementarities in affordances are also to be found in areas where language and image are equally well-suited, as for example in the construal of human emotion. Here each semiotic can create a similar kind of meaning while drawing on its own distinct range or configuration of options. In such areas, a bimodal text may make use of either or both semiotics depending on whether sharing the semantic load, amplifying a common meaning or some more complex kind of counterpointing is being managed.[40]

Lee Unsworth points out, "Current research indicates that articulating discrete visual and verbal grammars is not sufficient to account for meanings made at the intersection of language and image."[41] That potential

---

39. Painter, Martin, and Unsworth, *Reading Visual Narratives*, 133.
40. Painter, Martin, and Unsworth, *Reading Visual Narratives*, 133.
41. Lee Unsworth, "Towards a Metalanguage for Multiliteracies Education:

affordance of meaning at the point of synergy between visual and verbal text has not yet been fully developed into a specific functional metalanguage.[42] Arsenio Jesús Moya Guijarro has made a start at laying out some early theoretical proposals building on Unsworth and within the familiar visual semiotic structure of Kress and van Leeuwen (fig. 8.7).[43] Within the ideational metafunction, they suggest three types of visual/verbal or bimodal interplay: concurrence, complementarity, and connection. Moya Guijarro states: "*Ideational Concurrence* takes place when the verbal and the visual modalities are equivalent in ideational meaning and, thus, the inference required from the viewer to understand the coherence established between words and images is minimal."[44] This category is then broken down into two further stages: equivalence and instantiation.

The second type of interplay is ideational complementarity.[45] "In this verbal and visual intersection, either words or images provide information that is missing in the other semiotic component."[46] Unsworth differentiates between two subtypes of ideational complementarity: augmentation and divergence.[47] A third type of intersemiotic coherence is drawn from the work

---

Describing the Meaning-Making Resources of Language-Image Interaction," *ETPC* 5.1 (2006): 56.

42. Roland Barthes distinguished two image-text relations, elaboration and relay, to define the inter animation between verbal and visual codes. See Barthes, *Introduction to the Structural Analysis of Narratives: Image—Music—Text* (London: Fontana, 1977). In elaboration the textual component restates the meanings of the image or vice versa in such a way that both the verbal and the visual codes express the same meaning; in relay, the verbal component expands the meanings transmitted by the images or vice versa. In relay each code adds new meanings to complete the message going beyond the information transmitted in one of the two components.

43. Moya Guijarro adapts specifically from Lee Unsworth, "Towards a Metalanguage"; Unsworth, "Explicating Inter-modal Meaning-Making in Media and Literary Texts: Towards a Metalanguage of Image/Text Relations," in *Media Teaching: Language, Audience, Production*, ed. Andrew Burn and Cal Durrant (London: AATE-NATE and Wakefield Press, 2008), 48–80; and Unsworth, "Multiliteracies and Metalanguage: Describing Image/Text Relations as a Resource for Negotiating Multimodal Texts," in *Handbook of Research on New Literacies*, ed. Donald J. Leu, Julie Corio, Michele Knobel, and Colin Lankshear (Mahwah, NJ: Erlbaum, 2008), 377–405.

44. Moya Guijarro, *Multimodal Analysis*, 69.

45. Unsworth, "Towards a Metalanguage," 62.

46. Moya Guijarro, *Multimodal Analysis*, 71.

47. Unsworth, "Towards a Metalanguage," 63–64.

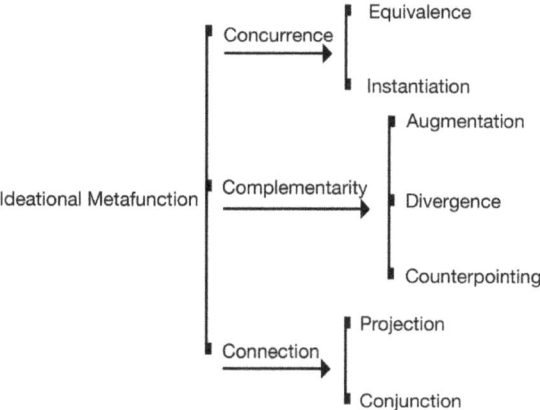

Fig. 8.7. Intersemiotic systems within the ideational metafunction. Source: Arsenio Jesús Moya Guijarro, *Multimodal Analysis*, 70. © Equinox Publishing Ltd 2014.

of Maria Nikolejeva and Carole Scott and is named counterpointing.[48] Finally, Unsworth also distinguishes another type of intersection between words and images: connection. This in turn is subdivided into two further categories: projection, which involves quoting speech and reporting thoughts, and conjunction, subdivided into causal, temporal, and spatial relations.[49]

With regard to Meinrad's graphic design *Christ Yesterday and Today* featuring text, a composite of short passages of Scripture texts within the woodcut image, the above analysis suggests that they all fall within the range of complementary augmentation. The synergy between visual and verbal goes beyond concurrence. The visual element is not simply illustrative, nor is the verbal element simply explanatory. As in all instances the visual is symbolic attributive, and this may itself imply augmentation. "In augmentation each modality provides additional information which is consistent with the other mode."[50] Each modality specializes in the transmission of specific meanings. As Jeff Bezemer and Kress point out, each has its own epistemological commitment or unavoidable affordances, which are inherently linked to it.[51]

---

48. Maria Nikolejeva and Carole Scott, "The Dynamics of Picture Books Communication," *CLE* 31.4 (2000): 232.
49. Unsworth, "Towards a Metalanguage," 66.
50. Moya Guijarro, *Multimodal Analysis*, 73.
51. Jeff Bezemer and Gunther Kress, "Writing in Multimodal Texts: A Social Semiotic Account of Designs for Learning," *WC* 25.2 (2008): 176.

8.6. Conclusion

Situated in *The Sunday Missal* between Good Friday and the Easter Vigil, this design semiotically marks the ritual silence of Holy Saturday. Against the black of primordial sacred space, white signifies the eternal presence of Christ, who was with the unseen God in the beginning.

> In the beginning was the Word, and the Word was with God, and the Word was God. He was in the beginning with God. All things came into being through him, and without him not one thing came into being. What has come into being in him was life, and the life was the light of all people. The light shines in the darkness, and the darkness did not overcome it. (John 1:1–5)

From this radiant center point of *Light*, Christ mediates the sacred convergence of time, eternal and temporal, in his passion, death, and resurrection. What may seem at a first glance as rough and awkward lines that are difficult to comprehend augment some of the richest lines of Scripture, in an intersemiotic dance of bimodal meaning between word and image. This is a conceptual image where *Christ* is a carrier of complex symbolic attributes, carved out of wood, in what is at once a striking and simple design of profound depth. Set against the formality of perfectly set Roman serifs in the accompanying printed texts—the rubrics of ritual—are expressive, unorthodox letters etched in organic matter. A design that, in its textual function, renders every modality (color modulation, variance, tonality, etc.) in its lowest possible register speaks to the essential truth held by Christians. As viewers contemplate, in this liminal design, a compelling convergence of many biblical texts, symbolic attributes, and liturgical rite, they might hear echoed in the dark the refrain "Lumen Christi."

9
Conclusion

Seeing comes before words.

—John Berger, *Ways of Seeing*

9.1. Graphic Design in the Lectionary

The Bible has always been "illustrated." It has always been both verbal and visual in its reception and its expression, even in its precanonical forms, be it the *ichthys* (ΙΧΘΥΣ) fish symbol, relief carvings on sarcophagi, mosaics in ancient house churches, or frescoes in the catacombs. This new orientation toward the visual history and reception of the Bible is emblematic of the visual turn in the humanities generally—reflecting the cultural proliferation of images and exponential increase in the importance of the visual in the newly globalized and multimodal realms of communication. O'Kane and Exum, among others, have observed this lacuna in the work of the academy and have pioneered a path of fruitful dialogue between biblical word and biblical image.

Meanwhile, semioticians Kress and van Leeuwen have expanded Halliday's foundational *Systemic Functional Grammar* and demonstrate how a social semiotics of the visual may provide a powerful method for exploring how images work to make meaning. Contra Saussure, they have developed a systemic functional semiotics away from the notion that the relationship between the signifier and the signified in the sign is *arbitrary*, preferring to recognize that relationship as always *motivated* and *conventional*. "We wish to assert the effects of the transformative role of individual agents, yet also the constant presence of the social: in the historical shaping of the resources, in the individual agent's social history, in the recognition of present conventions, in the effect of the environment in which representation and communication happen." In other words, they start from the premise that sign makers have agency and desire their messages be maximally understood in a particular context, and therefore choose forms of expression that they see as most apt and plausible, and "which they believe to be maximally transparent to other participants."[1] The social context of this semiotic activity is always vitally significant and contributes to the semiotic choices made by the sign maker. "The context may either have rules or best practices that regulate how specific semiotic resources can be used, or leave the users relatively free in their use of the resource."[2]

This valuing of the desire of the sign maker to choose the most criterial aspects of the object, event, or idea to be communicated—alongside the influences of social convention in shaping the semiotic resources, affordances, and potentials available to both producer and receiver—make this a particularly viable approach to artworks designed to illustrate biblical lections in books used in the liturgies of the church. The social context of Christian liturgy is highly orchestrated. It is one in which the semiotic modes of language, gesture, dress, and behavior are highly ritualized, conventional, well-defined, historical, traditional, and, most importantly, communal and community forming. This is the social context for this semiotic act of expression—graphically designed images illustrating the Scriptures held in esteem by those participating in the ritual.

Significantly, for this study, liturgy is also a major site for the reception of the Bible. In this social-semiotic context, that reception is multimodal; the Scriptures are a prominent component of the ritual and are repeated throughout in many ways, through many different modes (verbal, visual, audio, gesture). The semiotic resource, the material artifact that physically manifests the Scriptures in this context, is the lectionary (and its pew accompaniments in the ELW *Worship* book and Roman Catholic *Sunday Missal*). Redolent with the semiotic signifiers of the Bible—large, weighty, gilt-edged, embossed, and decorated with bright silk bookmarks—the lectionary ritually performs the semantic and iconic authority of the Bible in the communal arenas of Christian worship. As such, lectionaries themselves are iconic books in their own right as they are displayed, incensed, blessed, kissed, venerated, read aloud, and preached from.

The lectionary is at once an iconic book, a hermeneutical approach, and a liturgical structure. Many hermeneutical threads and motifs animate the

---

1. Kress and van Leeuwen, *Reading Images*, 12–13.
2. Van Leeuwen, *Social Semiotics*, 4.

lectionary through the curation and arrangement of biblical texts drawn from both Testaments. As the primary site of the church's *Wirkungsgeschichte* of the Bible, the lectionary projects an explicit Christocentric hermeneutic intended to be formative of Christian community. Somewhat ironically, while this complex reception of biblical texts is the focus of many Christians' attention every Sunday, the lectionary has not yet been fully acknowledged for the immense richness it holds out to biblical reception scholars.

> In social semiotics resources are signifiers, observable actions and objects that have been drawn into the domain of social communication and that have a *theoretical* semiotic potential constituted by all their past uses and all their potential uses and an *actual* semiotic potential constituted by those past uses that are known to and considered relevant by the users of the resource, and by such potential uses as may be uncovered by the users on the basis of their specific needs and interests. Such uses take place in a social context.[3]

From a social-semiotic perspective, everything about lectionaries—the materials used, the languages in which they are written, the typefaces chosen (majuscule, minuscule, or script, Roman or Gothic), the amount of white space on the page, the density of text, the number of columns, the use of particular colors (black, red, and white), the ratio of text to image, the placement and style of illuminations—relate to the most apt and plausible choices being made with the semiotic resources available at a particular time and place, in order to make meaning, in the social context of a particular community of people.

The color triad of red, black, and white presents itself as a semiotic resource, indeed a sociochrome, that has evolved out of a lengthy tradition and has functioned, in ways consistent with its present uses, for diverse groups of religious readers down through the ages. In a powerful way the colors collude, each strengthening the other to perform the semiotic functioning of the other. The triad forms a confluence of complementarity. In the graphic designs considered here, color contains and brings together metonym, metaphor, symbol, and text, creating interactions and depths of meaning beyond the purely verbal text. Applying Kress and van Leeuwen's metafunctional approach reveals how these designs employ color in

---

3. Van Leeuwen, *Social Semiotics*, 4.

profound ways, within the context of the Scriptures surrounding them in the books within which they appear, to dramatically enhance their communicative potential. The color triad black, red, and white is a constitutive element formative of meaning in the iconic liturgical book.

Silhouette has deep historical origins as a visual device for contouring bodily absence and illusive, mysterious presence. This makes it a particularly powerful visual metonym for the risen Christ. Beyond this, the imaging of Jesus is a politicized area in contemporary Christianity. Both Markell and Craighead have made use of silhouette in ways that creatively circumvent these contests while simultaneously expressing the gospel value of inclusivity, ideally at the heart of Christian community. Visually, silhouette is about simplicity, about reducing something to its most essential shape for an immediate apprehension of its significance. Yet, paradoxically, silhouettes are opaque, dense, and impenetrable. They are containers, receptive wells for the narratives, memories, and ideas projected into them. Silhouette is a vehicle for the visual representation of the biblical invocation of an inclusive model of community (Gal 3:28). Both Markell and Craighead have used silhouette as a semiotic resource to subvert contentious issues of embodied difference by refusing to delineate either race or gender. As such, christological and ecclesiological proposals about the universal salvific significance of Christ, as proclaimed in the biblical texts, are made through the use of silhouette in this context.

Markell's *Easter* is an extraordinary visual reception of selected resurrection pericopes. Centered on the powerful, vibrant, red silhouette of the risen *Christ*, this design creatively converges many biblical metaphors, metonyms, and symbols from the Easter gospel lections, through the use of visual narrative structures, interpersonal relations, and composition to create a thoroughly engaging design. Significantly, this design functions as a profoundly sophisticated and moving invitation, extended to the attentive viewer, to become a contemporary disciple, a member of the church, to enter the communal life of the body of *Christ* through the waters of baptism. The risen and ascendant *Christ* of the Easter narratives invites the viewer to abide in him, the true *Vine* and *Light* of the world.

Craighead's *Christ, Yesterday and Today* marks the silent liminality of Holy Saturday in the Triduum. *Christ*, suspended between his death on Good Friday and his resurrection on Easter Sunday, in a radiant nucleus of divine *Light*, mediates the sacred convergence of time: eternal and temporal. Offset against the formality of the red Roman rubrics of ritual are expressive, unorthodox letters, words of Scripture carved from organic matter, embedded in primordial darkness. Abstract elements such as rough and awkward lines that may seem obscure augment some of the richest lines of the New Testament. This is a conceptual image where *Christ* is a carrier of complex symbolic attributes, in what is at once a striking and simple design of profound depth, an icon in black and white, yielding to contemplation in the service of making meaning, of interpreting the Bible.

These designers have made use of a variety of resources at their disposal, the technological tools of sophisticated graphic-design computer applications and the traditional implements of chisel, awl, and woodblock, together with the intellectual resources of knowledge and understanding of the rituals of liturgy. They also garnered to their task color and silhouette to extraordinary effect. Both of the artists featured here have the benefit of theological study and varying degrees of formation and religious life in their own experience. This personal appreciation for and depth of knowledge of both the Scriptures and Christian liturgy no doubt influenced their graphic designs, enabling them to exploit the vast reservoir of semiotic potential constituted by those past uses of these iconic books, these lections, these liturgies, and other illustrations of these passages and events in a visual idiom that resonates with their viewers.

9.2. The Value of a Social Semiotics of the Visual for Biblical Reception

Applying a social semiotics of the visual analysis to these two designs demonstrates its great potential for bringing to the fore the ideational, interpersonal, and textual dynamics at work within an image. Semiotic resources such as the mode of color and the affordances of silhouette may be fundamental to the meaning potential of designs. Strikingly, both designs operate in the very lowest register of modality; the color is unmodulated and highly saturated, and the figures are silhouettes. There is no attempt at realism, and yet this does not detract from their capacity to make a truth claim, alongside the Scriptures they illustrate, in the social context of the corporate worship of the church. These designs, which may seem almost decorative at a first glance and perhaps not of sufficient visual complexity (modulated color, figurative landscapes and recognizable people, nuanced lighting, etc.) to warrant much scholarly attention, yield great insight and depths of meaning potential when analyzed through Kress and van Leeuwen's semiotic approach. Seeking to bring to the surface the many meaning potentials and affordances of a design, object, or event is in itself a generative process. There are other semiotic approaches to images, but this method offers an exciting, fruitful, convincing, and worthwhile way of exploring how meaning is made within an image. By opening up visual subject matter in this way, this approach has much to offer those exploring the visual receptions of biblical texts.

A social semiotics of the visual may be applied to any semiotic event, object, or resource. As a consequence of the hegemony of the verbal in Western cultures, far less emphasis has been placed on learning how to see images, how to apprehend the visual dynamics at play within them, how these work to construe meaning. In much the same way as one acquires verbal literacy, so too this approach offered by Kress and van Leeuwen can be learned with some time and effort. In turn it yields wonderful results, the joy of discovery and new insights that unfold as one begins to look deeper. Beyond the technical language of semiotics it is possible to apply this method fruitfully for a nonspecialist audience. This study has only touched on two examples—there are a great many artworks and artifacts yet to be explored that would benefit greatly from a social semiotics of the visual analysis, not least many superb graphic designs of the twentieth century. Bringing a social semiotics of the visual to the field of biblical reception history research makes a unique, timely, and significant contribution to knowledge in this area. This semiotic approach holds out great possibility to other adventurers in the field willing to engage with this method and demonstrate its powers in application to other semiotic productions, events, and artifacts.[4]

9.3. Proposals for Biblical Reception

The more history of reception of the Bible one reads, the clearer it becomes that the human importance of the Bible does not lie in a single foundational meaning that, by dint of scholarly effort, may finally be

---

4. By way of demonstrating its applicability to another very different type of artistic style, I looked at the art of Marc Chagall, known for his whimsical floating figures, enthusiastic use of many blended colors, and symbols and icons often incongruously juxtaposed. I applied a social semiotics of the visual method to his lithographic print *David et Bethsabée* (1956). See Amanda Dillon, "The Reception of King David in the Art of Marc Chagall," *PIBA* 40 (2017): 73–91.

revealed. This is not a resignation to postmodernism, but an acknowledgement that both inside and outside the doors of academia all of us live in a changing world in which engagements with the Bible are themselves ever changing. It is a world in which there are always new engagements between readers and the Bible (or "Bibles," as that text shifts according to manuscript translation and tradition), and those engagements will never stabilize. No amount of taxonomical or theological effort will alter this, as the matter is ontological, not pragmatic: individually and corporately, we change through time; in its singleness and multiplicity the Bible changes too.[5]

The social context of the liturgy is an environment where the Bible is received in simultaneously multimodal ways: it is read silently, read aloud, sung in hymns, chanted in psalms, inscribed into lintels, stitched into banners and altar cloths, illuminated in stained glass, acted out in nativity and passion plays—a mutually endorsing profusion of forms are to be found and experienced. Each of these is a semiotic production ripe for a reception history analysis. Beyond that, the confluence of these events, artifacts, performances, and productions is always changing and shifting, newly reconfigured from week to week, never repeating itself exactly. This is every bit as dynamic and interesting as the latest Hollywood blockbuster recounting a biblical epic. There is much material for further research for biblical reception scholars in this social context and environment.[6]

Likewise, there are many other graphic designers, Kacmarcik, Bethune, Eichenberg, Corbin, and Gill, among others, who have produced beautiful artworks illustrating biblical lections in different publications. These graphic designs, often encompassing verbal text, are another pro-

---

5. Roberts, "Introduction," 8.

6. James Bielo, in his anthropological investigations into Christian biblicism, observes, "The Bible is, after all, the transcendental logos for most Christians, a linguistic resource of habitual and strategic character, a semiotic object deployed by individuals and institutions, the subject of referential and performative discourse, and the recipient of all manner of hermeneutic imaginations." The anthropological study of how different groups of Christians make use of the Bible is another emerging area of research closely linked to biblical reception history that could greatly benefit from this method of multimodal analysis. See James S. Bielo, "Introduction: Encountering Biblicism," in *The Social Life of Scriptures: Cross-Cultural Perspectives on Biblicism*, ed. James S. Bielo (New Brunswick, NJ: Rutgers University Press, 2009), 4. See also James S. Bielo, *Ark Encounter: The Making of a Creationist Theme Park* (New York: New York University Press, 2018).

foundly rich and fertile area for research by biblical scholars. Art director Daniel Kantor's observation may be posed to those engaged with biblical reception scholarship too:

> The virtues of graphic design remain little celebrated. Rarely, if ever, has graphic design been formally called out as an essential art form of contemporary religious expression. We live in an age when new modes of communication are introduced at an alarming rate, and these media heavily rely on graphic design for their effectiveness. The question is not whether graphic design has a place in religious communications but whether religions, worshippers, and faith-based organizations are aware of graphic design's increasing presence, its strengths, its influences, and its vulnerabilities.[7]

Graphic design is not restricted to the material media of paint and ink, paper and print. The Bible in our current Western cultural context is increasingly no longer simply, or primarily, written or printed verbal text—but a multimodal semiotic production mediated to us as encompassing any variety of audio, visual, kinetic, moving-image (animation or video), and other elements simultaneously—possibly, but not necessarily, alongside the actual biblical text. The exponentially expanding arena of digital technologies and the many devices, applications, and platforms of media now in use are inherently multimodal in the way they present visual and verbal communications to the viewer/reader. Our new "pages"—democratically able to be designed by anyone with access to a tablet or computer—enable live-streamed videos embedded in verbal texts, scrolling bars of type, and spinning logos, accompanied by music and voiceovers. How are certain scriptural verses or passages received on Instagram or Pinterest, as two examples out of many?[8] How do these platforms or forums function as social-semiotic contexts for the reception of the Bible? What is their impact on the way the biblical text is represented, curated, mediated, and communicated? The "hegemony of the

---

7. Kantor, *Graphic Design*, 50.

8. I have explored the phenomenon of Bible journaling: the illustration of selected verses directly in Bibles by readers, then photographed and shared on Instagram and Pinterest. See Amanda Dillon, "Be Your Own Scribe: Bible Journaling and the New Illuminators of the Densely Printed Page," in *From Scrolls to Scrolling: Sacred Texts, Materiality, and Dynamic Media Cultures*, ed. Bradford A. Anderson (Berlin: de Gruyter, 2020), 153–78, https://doi.org/10.1515/9783110634440-008.

densely printed page" is well and truly past.⁹ As scholars of the Bible—a quintessential example of the authoritative densely printed page—a social semiotics of the visual equips us with a theoretical approach to analyzing new multimodal iterations of the Bible and biblical texts as they are received and presented in this new multimodal digital context. As with the liturgical context discussed above, this emerging multimodal digital-scape is another profoundly rich and varied site of biblical reception awaiting the attention of reception history scholars.

Finally, I endorse Exum's call for the adding of "visual criticism to other criticisms (historical, literary, form, rhetorical, etc.) in the exegete's toolbox—for making visual criticism part of the exegetical process, so that, in biblical interpretation, we do not just look at the text and the commentaries on the text but also at art as commentary."¹⁰ Visual exegesis, within the larger biblical reception history project, requires a methodological approach that opens up the affordances of meaning within visual content and a theoretical discourse for discussing the findings. A social semiotics of the visual offers a masterful approach to exploring in depth how meaning is made in visual interpretations of the Bible.

---

9. Kress and van Leeuwen, *Reading Images*, 178–79.

10. J. Cheryl Exum, "Toward a Genuine Dialogue between The Bible and Art," in *Congress Volume Helsinki 2010*, ed. Martin Nissinen, SVT 148 (Leiden: Brill, 2012), 475.

Appendix

A list of the lectionary readings from the respective lectionaries for the liturgical season of Easter, from Maundy/Holy Thursday through to Pentecost.

Evangelical Lutheran Church of America, *Revised Common Lectionary*	Roman Catholic Church, *Lectionary for Mass*
Maundy Thursday Years A, B, C	**Holy Thursday** Years A, B, C
Exodus 12:1–4 [5–10] 11–14 Psalm 116:1–2, 12–19 1 Corinthians 11:23–26 John 13:1–17, 31b–35	Exodus 12:1–8, 11–14 Psalm 115 1 Corinthians 11:23–26 John 13:1–15
Good Friday Years A, B, C	**Good Friday** Years A, B, C
Isaiah 52:13–53:12 Psalm 22 (1) Hebrews 10:16–25 *or* Hebrews 4:14–16; 5:7–9 John 18:1–19:42	Isaiah 52:13–53:12 Psalm 30 Hebrews 4:14–16; 5:7–9 John 18:1–19:42
Resurrection of Our Lord Vigil of Easter Years A, B, C	**Easter Vigil of Easter** Years A, B, C
1: Genesis 1:1–2:4a R: Psalm 136:1–9, 23–26	1: Genesis 1:1–2:2 R: Psalm 103 or Psalm 32
2. Genesis 7:1–5, 11–18; 8:6–18; 9:8–13 R: Psalm 46	2. Genesis 22:1–18 R: Psalm 15

3. Genesis 22:1–18
R: Psalm 16

4. Exodus 14:10–31; 15:20–21
R: Exodus 15:1b–13, 17–18

5. Isaiah 55:1–11
R: Isaiah 12:2–6

6. Proverbs 8:1–8, 19–21; 9:4b–6
or Baruch 3:9–15, 32–4:4
R: Psalm 19

7. Ezekiel 36:24–28
R: Psalms 42 and 43

8. Ezekiel 37:1–14
R: Psalm 143

9. Zephaniah 3:14–20
R: Psalm 98

10. Jonah 1:1–2:1
R: Jonah 2:2–3 [4–6] 7–9

11. Isaiah 61:1–4, 9–11
R: Deut 32:1–4, 7. 36a, 43a

12: Daniel 3:1–29
R: Song of the Three 35–65

Romans 6:3–11
John 20:1–18

Easter Day
A
Acts 10:34–43
or Jeremiah 31:1–6
Psalm 118:1–2, 14–24
Colossians 3:1–4
or Acts 10:34–43
Matthew 28:1–10
or John 20:1–18

3. Exodus 14:15–15:1
R: Exodus 15:1–6, 17–18

4. Isaiah 54:5–14
R: Psalm 29

5. Isaiah 55:1–11
R: Isaiah 12:2–6

6. Baruch 3:9–15, 32–4:4
R: Psalm 18

7. Ezekiel 36:16–17a, 18–28
R: Psalms 41 and 42

Romans 6:3–11
R: Psalm 117

A: Matthew 28:1–10

B: Mark 16:1–8

C: Luke 24:1–12

Easter Day
Years A, B, C
Acts 10:34, 37–43
Psalm 117
Colossians 3:1–4
or 1 Corinthians 5:6–8
John 20:1–9

B
Acts 10:34–43
or Isaiah 25:6–9
Psalm 118:1–2, 14–24
1 Corinthians 15:1–11
or Acts 10:34–43
Mark 16:1–8
or John 20:1–18

C
Acts 10:34–43
or Isaiah 65:17–25
Psalm 118:1–2, 14–24
1 Corinthians 15:19–26
or Acts 10:34–43
Luke 24:1–12 *or* John 20:1–18

Second Sunday of Easter
A
Acts 2:14a, 22–32
Psalm 16
1 Peter 1:3–9
John 20:19–31

B
Acts 4:32–35
Psalm 133
1 John 1:1–2:2
John 20:19–31

C
Acts 5:27–32
Psalm 118:14–29
or Psalm 150
Revelation 1:4–8
John 20:19–31

Third Sunday of Easter
A
Acts 2:14a, 36–41
Psalm 116:1–4, 12–19
1 Peter 1:17–23
Luke 24:13–35

Second Sunday of Easter
A
Acts 2:42–47
Psalm 117
1 Peter 1:3–9
John 20:19–31

B
Acts 4:32–35
Psalm 117
1 John 1:5–6
John 20:19–31

C
Acts 5:12–16
Psalm 29
Revelation 5:11–14
John 21:1–19

Third Sunday of Easter
A
Acts 2:14, 22–28
Psalm 15
1 Peter 1:17–21
Luke 24:13–35

B
Acts 3:12–19
Psalm 4
1 John 3:1–7
Luke 24:36b–48

C
Acts 9:1–6[7–20]
Psalm 30
Revelation 5:11–14
John 21:1–19

Fourth Sunday of Easter
A
Acts 2:42–47
Psalm 23
1 Peter 2:19–25
John 10:1–10

B
Acts 4:5–12
Psalm 23
1 John 3:16–24
John 10:11–18

C
Acts 9:36–43
Psalm 23
Revelation 7:9–17
John 10:22–30

Fifth Sunday of Easter
A
Acts 7:55–60
Psalm 31:1–5, 15–16
1 Peter 2:2–10
John 14:1–14

B
Acts 8:26–40
Psalm 22:25–31
1 John 4:7–21
John 15:1–8

B
Acts 3:12–19
Psalm 4
1 John 3:1–7
Luke 24:36b–48

C
Acts 9:1–6[7–20]
Psalm 30
Revelation 5:11–14
John 21:1–19

Fourth Sunday of Easter
A
Acts 2:14, 36–41
Psalm 22
1 Peter 2:20–25
John 10:1–10

B
Acts 4:8–12
Psalm 117
1 John 3:1–2
John 10:11–18

C
Acts 13:14/43–52
Psalm 99
Revelation 7:9, 14–17
John 10:27–30

Fifth Sunday of Easter
A
Acts 6:1–7
Psalm 32
1 Peter 2:4–9
John 14:1–12

B
Acts 9:26–31
Psalm 21
1 John 3:18–24
John 15:1–8

C
Acts 11:1–18
Psalm 148
Revelation 21:1–6
John 13:31–35

Sixth Sunday of Easter
A
Acts 17:22–31
Psalm 66:8–20
1 Peter 3:13–22
John 14:15–21

B
Acts 10:44–48
Psalm 98
1 John 5:1–6
John 15:9–17

C
Acts 16:9–15
Psalm 67
Revelation 21:10, 22–22:5
John 14:23–29
or John 5:1–9

Ascension of Our Lord
Years A, B, C

Acts 1:1–11
Psalm 47
or Psalm 93
Ephesians 1:15–23
Luke 24:44–53

Seventh Sunday of Easter
A
Acts 1:6–14
Psalm 68:1–10, 32–35
1 Peter 4:12–14; 5:6–11
John 17:1–11

C
Acts 14:21–27
Psalm 144
Revelation 21:1–5
John 13:31–35

Sixth Sunday of Easter
A
Acts 8:5–8, 14–17
Psalm 65
1 Peter 3:15–18
John 14:15–21

B
Acts 10:25–26, 34–35, 44–48
Psalm 97
1 John 4:7–10
John 15:9–17

C
Acts 15:1–2, 22–29
Psalm 66
Revelation 21:10–14, 22–23
John 14:23–29

Ascension
Years A, B, C
Acts 1:1–11
Psalm 46
Ephesians 1:17–23

A Matthew 28:16–20
B Mark 16:15–20
C Luke 24:46–53

Seventh Sunday of Easter
A
Acts 1:12–14
Psalm 26
1 Peter 4:13–16
John 17:1–11

B
Acts 1:15–17, 21–26
Psalm 1
1 John 5:9–13
John 17:6–19

C
Acts 16:16–34
Psalm 97
Revelation 22:12–14, 16–17, 20–21
John 17:20–26

Pentecost
Vigil of Pentecost
A, B, C

Exodus 19:1–9
or Acts 2:1–11
Psalm 33:12–22 or Psalm 130
Romans 8:14–17, 22–27
John 7:37–39

Day of Pentecost
A
Acts 2:1–21 or Numbers 11:24–30
Psalm 104:24–34, 35b
1 Corinthians 12:3b–13 or Acts 2:1–21
John 20:19–23 or John 7:37–39

B
Acts 2:1–21
or Ezekiel 37:1–14
Psalm 104:24–34, 35b
Romans 8:22–27 or Acts 2:1–21
John 15:26–27; 16:4b–15

C
Acts 2:1–21
or Genesis 11:1–9
Psalm 104:24–34, 35b
Romans 8:14–17
or Acts 2:1–21
John 14:8–17 [25–27]

B
Acts 1:15–17, 20–26
Psalm 102
1 John 4:11–16
John 17:11–19

C
Acts 7:55–60
Psalm 96
Revelation 22:12–14, (16–17), 20
John 17:20–26

Pentecost
Vigil of Pentecost (*simple form*)
Years A, B, C

Genesis 11:1–9 or Exodus 19:3–8
or Ezekiel 37:1–14 or Joel 3:1–5
Psalm 104:1–2, 24, 27–30, 35
Romans 8:22–27
John 7:37–39

Pentecost Sunday
Years A, B, C
Acts 2:1–11
Psalm 103
1 Corinthians 12:3–7, 12–13
John 20:19–23

Bibliography

"Ade Bethune Drawings." St. Catherine University Library and Archives. http://content.clic.edu/cdm/landingpage/collection/abcorig.

Aichele, George. *The Control of Biblical Meaning: Canon as Semiotic Mechanism.* Harrisburg, PA: Trinity Press International, 2001.

———. *Sign, Text, Scripture: Semiotics and the Bible.* Sheffield: Sheffield Academic, 1997.

Albers, Josef. *Interaction of Colour.* Rev. ed. London: Routledge, 2006.

Ambrose, Gavin, and Paul Harris. *Basics Design 05: Colour.* Worthing, UK: AVA, 2007.

Andreopoulos, Andreas. "Icons: The Silent Gospels." Pages 83–100 in *Imaging the Bible: An Introduction to Biblical Art.* Edited by Martin O'Kane. London: SPCK, 2008.

Arnheim, Rudolph. *The Power of the Center: A Study of Composition in the Visual Arts.* Berkeley: University of California Press, 2009.

Attrill, Martin J., Karen A. Gresty, Russell A. Hill, and Robert A. Barton. "Red Shirt Colour Is Associated with Long-Term Team Success in English Football." *JSportsSci* 26 (2008): 577–82. doi:10.1080/02640410701736244.

Baert, Barbara. *Interspaces between Word, Gaze and Touch: The Bible and the Visual Medium in the Middle Ages.* Leuven: Peeters, 2011.

———, ed. *The Woman with the Blood Flow (Mark 5:24–34): Narrative, Iconic, and Anthropological Spaces.* Leuven: Peeters, 2014.

Bal, Mieke. *On Meaning Making: Essays in Semiotics.* Salem, OR: Polebridge, 1994.

Bal, Mieke, and Norman Bryson. *Looking In: The Art of Viewing.* London: Routledge, 2001.

Balfour-Paul, Jenny. *Indigo: Egyptian Mummies to Blue Jeans.* Buffalo, NY: Firefly, 2011.

Barthes, Roland. *Introduction to the Structural Analysis of Narratives: Image—Music—Text.* London: Fontana, 1977.

———. *Writing Degree Zero and Elements of Semiology*. London: Vintage Classics, 2010.
Barton, Mukti. "I Am Black and Beautiful." *BlTh* 2 (2004): 167–87.
Batchelor, David. *The Luminous and the Grey*. London: Reaction Books, 2014.
Bauckham, Richard. "The Divinity of Jesus Christ in the Epistle to the Hebrews." Pages 15–36 in *The Epistle to the Hebrews and Christian Theology*. Edited by Richard Bauckham, Daniel R. Driver, Trevor A. Hart, and Nathan McDonald. Grand Rapids: Eerdmans, 2009.
Beal, Timothy. "Reception History and Beyond: Towards the Cultural History of the Scriptures." *BibInt* 19 (2011): 357–72.
———. *The Rise and Fall of the Bible: The Unexpected History of an Accidental Book*. New York: First Mariner, 2012.
Becker, Udo. *The Element Encyclopaedia of Symbols*. Translated by Lance W. Garner. Dorset, UK: Element, 1994.
Beckett, Wendy. *Sister Wendy Beckett Contemplates St Paul in Art*. London: St Pauls, 2008.
Belting, Hans. *The Image and Its Public in the Middle Ages*. New York: Caratzas, 1990.
Berger, Harry, Jr. *Figures of a Changing World: Metaphor and the Emergence of Modern Culture*. New York: Fordham University Press, 2015.
Bezemer, Jeff, and Gunther Kress. "Writing in Multimodal Texts: A Social Semiotic Account of Designs for Learning." *WC* 25.2 (2008): 165–95.
"The Bible and Women: An Encyclopaedia of Exegesis and Cultural History." Bible and Women. https://tinyurl.com/SBL6710f.
Bielo, James S. *Ark Encounter: The Making of a Creationist Theme Park*. New York: New York University Press, 2018.
———. "Introduction: Encountering Biblicism." Pages 1–9 in *The Social Life of Scriptures: Cross-cultural Perspectives on Biblicism*. Edited by James S. Bielo. New Brunswick, NJ: Rutgers University Press, 2009.
Bloedhorn, Hanswulf, and Gil Hüttenmeister, "The Synagogue." Pages 267–97 in *The Cambridge Companion to Judaism*. Vol. 3, *The Early Roman Period*. Edited by William Horbury, William D. Davies, and John Sturdy. Cambridge: Cambridge University Press, 1999.
Bockmuehl, Markus. "A Commentator's Approach to the 'Effective History' of Philippians." *JSNT* 60 (1995): 57–88.
Boer, Roland. "Against 'Reception History.'" The Bible and Interpretation, May 2011. https://tinyurl.com/SBLPress6701d1.

Bonfiglio, Ryan P. *Reading Images, Seeing Texts: Towards a Visual Hermeneutics for Biblical Studies*. OBO 280. Fribourg: Academic Press; Göttingen: Vandenhoeck & Ruprecht, 2016.

Bonneau, Normand. *The Sunday Lectionary: Ritual Word, Paschal Shape*. Collegeville, MN: Liturgical Press, 1997.

Boyd, Jane, and Philip F. Esler. *Visuality and Biblical Text: Interpreting Velazquez—"Christ with Martha and Mary" as a Test Case*. Florence: Olschki, 2005.

Boyd, Mary Petrine. "Red." *NIDB* 4:748–49.

———. "White." *NIDB* 5:844–45.

Bram, Jean Rhys. "Sun." *ER* 14:132–43.

Brand, Eugene L. "The Lutheran Book of Worship—Quarter Century Reckoning." *CurTM* 30.5 (2003): 327–32.

Breed, Brennan W. *Nomadic Text: A Theory of Biblical Reception*. Bloomington: Indiana University Press, 2014.

———. "What Can a Text Do? Reception History as an Ethology of the Biblical Text." Pages 95–109 in *Reception History and Biblical Studies: Theory and Practice*. Edited by Emma England and William John Lyons. London: Bloomsbury, 2015.

Brodie, Thomas L. *The Gospel according to John: A Literary and Theological Commentary*. Oxford: Oxford University Press, 1993.

Bruce, Frederick F. *1 and 2 Thessalonians*. WBC 45. Waco, TX: Word, 1982.

Bucklow, Spike. *Red: The Art and Science of a Colour*. London: Reaktion Books, 2016.

Bugnini, Annibale. *The Reform of the Liturgy 1948–1975*. Translated by Matthew O'Connell. Collegeville, MN: Liturgical Press, 1990.

Burch, Robert. "Charles Sanders Peirce." Stanford Encyclopedia of Philosophy. Fall 2010 ed. Edited by Edward N. Zalta. https://tinyurl.com/SBL6710u.

Burnette-Bletsch, Rhonda. *The Bible in Motion: A Handbook of the Bible and Its Reception in Film*. 2 vols. Berlin: de Gruyter, 2016.

Burnette-Bletsch, Rhonda, and Jon Morgan, eds. *Noah as Antihero: Darren Aronofsky's Cinematic Deluge*. London: Routledge, 2017.

Butler, Christopher S. *Structure and Function: A Guide to Three Major Structural-Functional Theories; Part 1: Approaches to the Simplex Clause; Part 2: From Clause to Discourse and Beyond*. Philadelphia: Benjamins, 2003.

Carey, John. "The Three Sails, the Twelve Winds, and the Question of Early Irish Colour Theory." *JWCI* 72 (2009): 221–32.

Chandler, Daniel. *Semiotics: The Basics*. 2nd ed. London: Routledge, 2007.
Charles-Murray, Mary. "The Emergence of Christian Art." Pages 51–63 in *Picturing the Bible: The Earliest Christian Art*. Edited by Jeffrey Spier. New Haven: Yale University Press in Association with the Kimbell Art Museum, 2007.
Cirlot, Juan E. *A Dictionary of Symbols*. 2nd ed. Translated by Jack Sage. London: Routledge & Kegan Paul, 1971.
Clague, Julie. "Divine Transgressions: The Female Christ-Form in Art." *CrQ* 47 (2005): 47–63. doi:10.1111/j.1467-8705.2005.00649.x.
Cohen, Shaye J. D. *From the Maccabees to the Mishnah*. 2nd ed. Louisville: Westminster John Knox, 2006.
Colledge, Gary. "White Throne." *NIDB* 5:845.
"Colour and Vision." National History Museum. https://tinyurl.com/SBL6710i.
"Comes Romanus Wirziburgensis." Universitätsbibliothek Würzburg. http://vb.uni-wuerzburg.de/ub/mpthf62/index.html.
Comfort, Philip W. *Encountering the Manuscripts: An Introduction to New Testament Paleography and Textual Criticism*. Nashville: Broadman & Holman, 2005.
"A Concise Dictionary of the Bible and Its Reception (Paper)." Westminster John Knox Press. https://tinyurl.com/SBL6710g.
Consultation on Common Texts. *Common Lectionary: The Lectionary Proposed by the Consultation on Common Texts*. New York: Church Hymnal, 1983.
Corrington, Robert S. *A Semiotic Theory of Theology and Philosophy*. Cambridge: Cambridge University Press, 2000.
Craighead, Meinrad. *The Litany of the Great River*. Mahwah, NJ: Paulist, 1991.
———. *Liturgical Art*. Kansas City, MO: Sheed & Ward, 1988.
———. "Lodestone." Pages 1–29 in *Meinrad Craighead: Crow Mother and the Dog God; A Retrospective*. San Francisco: Pomegranate Communications, 2003.
———. *Meinrad Craighead: Crow Mother and the Dog God; A Retrospective*. San Francisco: Pomegranate Communications, 2003.
———. *The Mother's Birds*. Worcester, UK: Stanbrook Abbey, 1976.
———. *The Mother's Songs*. Mahwah, NJ: Paulist, 1986.
———. *The Sign of the Tree*. London: Beazley, 1979.
———. *Sacred Marriage: The Wisdom of the Song of Songs*. London: Continuum, 1997.

Cramsie, Patrick. *The Story of Graphic Design: From the Invention of Writing to the Birth of Digital Design*. London: British Library, 2010.

Crossley, James G. *Reading the New Testament: Contemporary Approaches*. London: Routledge, 2010.

———. "The End of Reception History, a Grand Narrative for Biblical Studies and the Neoliberal Bible." Pages 45–59 in *Reception History and Biblical Studies: Theory and Practice*. Edited by Emma England and William John Lyons. London: Bloomsbury, 2015.

Crow, David. *Visible Signs: An Introduction to Semiotics*. Lausanne: AVA, 2003.

Davey, Nicholas. "Hermeneutics, Aesthetics and Religious Experience." Pages 1–26 in *Bible, Art, Gallery*. Edited by Martin O'Kane. Sheffield: Sheffield Phoenix, 2010.

———. "Hermeneutics, Aesthetics and Transcendence." Pages 191–211 in *Imaging the Bible: An Introduction to Biblical Art*. Edited by Martin O'Kane. London: SPCK, 2008.

———. "The Hermeneutics of Seeing." Pages 3–30 in *Interpreting Visual Culture: Explorations in the Hermeneutics of the Visual*. Edited by Ian Heywood and Barry Sandywell. London: Routledge, 1999.

"David Allan: The Origin of Painting ('The Maid of Corinth')." National Galleries Scotland. https://tinyurl.com/SBL6710q.

Davies, Rosemary. "The Struggle for Solitude." Pages 129–53 in *Meinrad Craighead, Crow Mother and the Dog God: A Retrospective*. San Francisco: Pomegranate, 2003.

Davis, Meredith. *Graphic Design Theory*. London: Thames and Hudson, 2012.

Declaissé-Walford, Nancy. "Tree of Knowledge, Tree of Life." *NIDB* 5:659–61.

Dillon, Amanda. "Be Your Own Scribe: Bible Journalling and the New Illuminators of the Densely-Printed Page." Pages 153–78 in *From Scrolls to Scrolling: Sacred Texts, Materiality, and Dynamic Media Cultures*. Edited by Bradford A. Anderson. Berlin: de Gruyter, 2020. https://doi.org/10.1515/9783110634440-008.

———. "The Reception of King David in the Art of Marc Chagall." *PIBA* 40 (2017): 73–91.

Dixon, Alex. "What Are HTML Color Codes?" https://tinyurl.com/SBL6710j.

Dowling Long, Siobhán. *The Sacrifice of Isaac: The Reception of a Biblical Story in Music*. Sheffield: Sheffield Phoenix, 2013.

Dowling Long, Siobhán, and John F. A. Sawyer. *The Bible in Music: A Dictionary of Songs, Works, and More.* New York: Rowman & Littlefield, 2015.
Drucker, Johanna, and Emily McVarish. *Graphic Design History: A Critical Guide.* 2nd rev. ed. Upper Saddle River, NJ: Pearson Prentice Hall, 2012.
Dunn, James D. G. *A Commentary on the Epistle to the Galatians.* BNTC. London: Black, 1993.
Ebeling, Gerhard. *The Word and Tradition: Historical Studies Interpreting the Divisions of Christianity.* Translated by S. H. Hooke. Philadelphia: Fortress, 1968.
Eco, Umberto. *A Theory of Semiotics.* London: Macmillan, 1977.
Edeline, Francis. "La Plasticité des Categories (2. Le Cas de la Coleur)." Pages 205–24 in *La Sémiotique Visuelle: Nouveaux Paradigmes.* Edited by Michel Constantine. Paris: L'Harmattan, 2010.
Eisenstein, Elizabeth. *The Printing Press as an Agent of Change: Communications and Cultural Transformations in Early-Modern Europe.* Cambridge: Cambridge University Press, 1980.
Elbogen, Ismar. *Jewish Liturgy: A Comprehensive History.* Translated by Raymond P. Scheindlin. Philadelphia: Jewish Publication Society, 1993.
Eng, Steve. "The Story Behind: Red Letter Bible Editions." International Society of Bible Collectors. https://tinyurl.com/SBL6710m.
England, Emma, and William John Lyons, eds. "Explorations in the Reception of the Bible." Pages 3–13 in *Reception History and Biblical Studies: Theory and Practice.* Edited by Emma England and William John Lyons. London: Bloomsbury, 2015.
English, Darby. "This Is Not about the Past: Silhouettes in the Work of Kara Walker." Pages 143–62 in *Kara Walker: Narratives of a Negress.* Edited by Ian Berry. Cambridge: Frances Young Tang Teaching Museum and Art Gallery at Skidmore College, 2003.
Evangelical Lutheran Worship. Minneapolis: Augsburg Fortress, 2006.
Evangelical Lutheran Worship Graphics. CD-ROM. Minneapolis: Augsburg Fortress, 2011.
Evans, Robert. *Reception History, Tradition and Biblical Interpretation: Gadamer and Jauss in Current Practice.* London: Bloomsbury T&T Clark, 2014.
Exum, J. Cheryl. *Fragmented Women: Feminist (Sub)versions of Biblical Narratives.* London: Bloomsbury T&T Clark, 2016.

———. "Lethal Women 2: Reflections on Delilah and Her Incarnation as Liz Hurley." Pages 254–72 in *Borders, Boundaries and the Bible*. Edited by Martin O'Kane. JSOTSup 313. London: Sheffield Academic, 2002.

———. *Plotted, Shot, and Painted: Cultural Representations of Biblical Women*. 2nd ed. Sheffield: Sheffield Phoenix, 2012.

———. "Second Thoughts about Secondary Characters." Pages 75–87 in *A Feminist Companion to Exodus to Deuteronomy*. Edited by Althalya Brenner. Feminist Companion to the Bible. Sheffield: Sheffield Academic, 1994.

———. "Toward a Genuine Dialogue between The Bible and Art." *Congress Volume Helsinki 2010*. Edited by Marti Nissinen. SVT 148. Leiden: Brill, 2012.

Exum, J. Cheryl, and Ela Nutu, eds. *Between the Text and the Canvas: The Bible and Art in Dialogue*. Sheffield: Sheffield Phoenix, 2007.

Felder, Cain, ed. *Stony the Road We Trod: African American Biblical Interpretation*. Minneapolis: Fortress, 1991.

Finaldi, Gabriele, ed. *The Image of Christ*. London: National Gallery, 2000.

———. "Seeing Salvation: The Image of Christ." *Pastoral Review* (June/July 2000).

Finlay, Victoria. *Colour: Travels through the Paintbox*. London: Sceptre, 2002.

Fitzmyer, Joseph A. *Acts of the Apostles*. New York: Doubleday, 1997.

———. *The Gospel according to Luke*. AB. New York: Doubleday, 1970.

Folsom, Cassian. "The Liturgical Books of the Roman Rite." Pages 258–61 in vol. 1 of *Handbook for Liturgical Studies: Introduction to the Liturgy*. Edited by Anscar J. Chupungo. Collegeville, MN: Liturgical Press, 1997.

Fontaine, Carole R. "Sophia." *NIDB* 5:356–57.

Forceville, Charles. "Metonymy in Visual and Audiovisual Discourse." Pages 56–74 in *The World Told and the World Shown: Multisemiotic Issues*. Edited by Eija Ventola and Arsenio Jesús Moya Guijjaro. London: Palgrave Macmillan, 2009.

Forgione, Nancy. "'The Shadow Only': Shadow and Silhouette in Late Nineteenth-Century Paris." *ArtB* 81 (1999): 490–512.

"Frank Kacmarcik—Uncle Frank." Pinterest. https://www.pinterest.ie/junierockmom/frank-kacmarcik-uncle-frank/?lp=true.

Gadamer, Hans-Georg. *Truth and Method*. Translated by Joel C. Weinsheimer and Donald G. Marshall. London: Bloomsbury, 2013.

Gage, John. *Colour and Culture: Practice and Meaning from Antiquity to Abstraction.* London: Thames and Hudson, 1995.
"Gallery." Rita Corbin. http://ritacorbinart.com/calenders/.
Gaventa, Beverly Roberts. *Our Mother Saint Paul.* Louisville: Westminster John Knox, 2007.
General Introduction to the Lectionary for Mass (LM), Ordo Lectionem Missae, Editio Typica Altera. Rome: Liberia Editrice Vaticana, 1981.
"Gérard Fromanger." Artnet. https://tinyurl.com/SBL6710p.
Gibbs, Raymond W., Jr. *The Poetics of Mind: Figurative Thought, Language and Understanding.* Cambridge: Cambridge University Press, 1994.
Gillingham, Susan. "Biblical Studies on Holiday? A Personal View of Reception History." Pages 17–30 in *Reception History and Biblical Studies: Theory and Practice.* Edited by Emma England and William John Lyons. London: Bloomsbury, 2015.
Goan, Sean. *Let the Reader Understand: The Sunday Readings.* Dublin: Columba, 2007.
Goldenberg, David M. *The Curse of Ham: Race and Slavery in Early Judaism, Christianity and Islam.* Princeton: Princeton University Press, 2009.
Gottdiener, Mark. *Postmodern Semiotics: Material Culture and the Forms of Postmodern Life.* Oxford: Blackwell, 1995.
Green, Joel B. *The Gospel of Luke.* Grand Rapids: Eerdmans, 1997.
Greimas, Algirdas J., and Julien Courtès. *Semiotics and Language: An Analytical Dictionary.* Translated by Larry Christ, Daniel Patte, James Lee, Edward McMahonII, Gary Phillips, and Michael Rengstorf. Bloomington: Indiana University Press, 1981.
Haas, David. *Biblical Way of the Cross, Based on the Stations Led by Pope John Paul II.* Music by David Haas and Marty Haugen. Images by Nicholas Markell. Chicago: GIA, 2005.
Hall, Sean. *This Means This, This Means That: A User's Guide to Semiotics.* London: King, 2007.
Hall, Stuart. "Encoding/Decoding." Pages 128–38 in *Culture, Media, Language: Working Papers in Cultural Studies.* Edited by Stuart Hall, Dorothy Hobson, Andrew Lowe, and Paul Willis. London: Hutchinson, 1980.
Halliday, Michael A. K. *Language as Social Semiotic: The Social Interpretation of Language and Meaning.* London: Arnold, 1978.

———. *On Language and Linguistics*. Vol. 3 of *The Collected Works of M. A. K. Halliday*. Edited by Jonathan J. Webster. London: Bloomsbury, 2004.

———. "Systemic Background." Pages 185–98 in *On Language and Linguistics*. Vol. 3 of *The Collected Works of M. A. K. Halliday*. Edited by Jonathan J. Webster. London: Bloomsbury, 2004.

Halliday, Michael A. K., and Christian Matthiessen. *Halliday's Introduction to Functional Grammar*. 4th rev. ed. London: Routledge, 2014.

Hansen, Bruce. *All of You Are One: The Social Vision of Galatians 3:28, 1 Corinthians 12:13 and Colossians 3:11*. LNTS 409. London: T&T Clark, 2010.

Hara, Kenya. *White*. Zurich: Müller, 2017.

Harvey, John. *The Art of Piety: The Visual Culture of Welsh Nonconformity*. Cardiff, UK: University of Wales Press, 1995.

———. *The Bible as Visual Culture: When Text Becomes Image*. Sheffield: Sheffield Phoenix, 2013.

———. "Framing the Word: Commentary, Context, and Composition." Pages 27–54 in *Bible, Art, Gallery*. Edited by Martin O'Kane. Sheffield: Sheffield Phoenix, 2011.

———. "Visual Typology and Pentecostal Theology: The Paintings of Nicholas Evans." Pages 123–42 in *Imaging the Bible: An Introduction to Biblical Art*. Edited by Martin O'Kane. London: SPCK, 2009.

Harvey, John R. *The Story of Black*. London: Reaktion, 2013.

Heffern, Rich. "Art and Spirituality: In the Name of the Mother." *National Catholic Reporter*, 18 July 2008. https://tinyurl.com/SBL6701c.

Helfand, Jessica. *Design: The Invention of Desire*. New Haven: Yale University Press, 2016.

Hestbaek Andersen, Thomas, Morten Boeriis, Eva Maagerø, and Elise Ship Tønnessen. *Social Semiotics: Key Figures, New Directions*. London: Routledge, 2015.

Hill, Russell A., and Robert A. Barton. "Red Enhances Human Performance in Contests." *Nature* 435 (2005): 293. doi:10.1038/435293a.

Hodge, Robert, and Gunther Kress. *Social Semiotics*. Cambridge: Polity, 1988.

Hogan, Martin. *Jesus Our Saviour: Reflections on the Sunday Readings for Luke's Year*. Dublin: Columba, 2006.

———. *Jesus Our Servant: Reflections on the Sunday Readings for Mark's Year*. Dublin: Columba, 2008.

———. *Jesus Our Teacher: Reflections on the Sunday Readings for Matthew's Year.* Dublin: Columba, 2007.
Holub, Robert C. *Reception Theory: A Critical Introduction.* New York: Routledge, 1984.
Hornik, Heidi, and Mikeal C. Parsons. *Illuminating Luke.* Vol. 1, *The Infancy Narrative in Italian Renaissance Painting.* New York: Trinity Press International, 2003.
———. *Illuminating Luke.* Vol. 3, *The Passion and Resurrection Narratives in Italian Renaissance and Baroque Paintings.* New York: T&T Clark, 2008.
———. *Illuminating Luke.* Vol. 2, *The Public Ministry of Christ in Italian Renaissance and Baroque Painting.* New York: T&T Clark, 2005.
Hurtado, Larry. "Tools of the Trade." Larry Hurtado's Blog, September 4, 2011. https://tinyurl.com/SBL6701d.
Huxley, Aldous. *The Doors of Perception and Heaven and Hell.* London: Flamingo, 1994.
"Images." Markell Studios. https://tinyurl.com/SBL6710t.
Iversen, Margaret. "Saussure v. Peirce: Models for a Semiotics of Visual Art." Pages 82–94 in *The New Art History.* Edited by Alan L. Rees and Frances Borzello. London: Camden, 1986.
Jasper, David. "Review of Jane Boyd and Philip F. Esler, *Visuality and the Biblical Text.*" *ACE* 44 (2005): 8–9.
Jauss, Hans Robert. *Aesthetic Experience and Literary Hermeneutics.* Minneapolis: University of Minnesota Press, 2008.
———. "Horizon Structure and Dialogicity." Pages 199–207 in *Question and Answer: Forms of Dialogic Understanding.* Edited and translated by Michael Hays. THL 68. Minneapolis: University of Minnesota Press, 1989.
———. *Toward an Aesthetic of Reception.* Translated by Timothy Bahti. Minneapolis: University of Minnesota Press, 1982.
Jauss, Hans Robert, and Sharon Larisch. "Job's Questions and Their Distant Reply: Goethe, Nietzsche, Heidegger." *CompLit* 34 (1982): 193–207.
"Jesus of the People." Janet McKenzie. https://tinyurl.com/SBL6710r.
Jewitt, Carey. "Different Approaches to Multimodality." Pages 28–39 in *The Routledge Handbook of Multimodal Analysis.* Edited by Carey Jewitt. London: Routledge, 2009.
———. "An Introduction to Multimodality." Pages 14–27 in *The Routledge Handbook of Multimodal Analysis.* Edited by Carey Jewitt. London: Routledge, 2009.

Jobson, Christopher. "The Rise of the Image: Every NY Times Front Page since 1852 in under a Minute." Colossal, February 22, 2017. https://tinyurl.com/SBL6710k.

Johnson, Elizabeth A. "Jesus of the People." Pages 69–73 in *Holiness and the Feminine Spirit: The Art of Janet McKenzie*. Edited by Susan Perry. Maryknoll, NY: Orbis, 2009.

———. *She Who Is: The Mystery of God in Feminist Theological Discourse*. New York: Crossroad, 1995.

Joynes, Christine E. "Changing Horizons: Reflections on a Decade at Oxford University's Centre for Reception History of the Bible." *JBRec* 1 (2014): 161–71.

Justin Martyr. "The First Apology." *ANF* 1:159–87.

Kahl, Brigitte. "The Galatian Suicide and the Transbinary Semiotics of Christ Crucified (Galatians 3:1): Critical Reimagination." Pages 195–240 in *The Art of Visual Exegesis: Rhetoric, Texts, Images*. Edited by Vernon K. Robbins, Walter S. Melion, and Roy R. Jeal. Atlanta: SBL Press, 2017.

———. *Galatians Re-imagined: Reading with the Eyes of the Vanquished*. Minneapolis: Fortress, 2010.

Kantor, Daniel. *Graphic Design and Religion: A Call for Renewal*. Chicago: GIA, 2007.

"Kara Walker." http://www.karawalkerstudio.com.

Keener, Craig S. *Acts: An Exegetical Commentary*. Vol. 1. Grand Rapids: Baker Academic, 2012.

Kentridge, William. "In Praise of Shadows." Pages 17–18 in *In Praise of Shadows*. Edited by Paulo Colombo. Milan: Charta, 2009.

"Kitchener: The Most Famous Pointing Finger." BBC, August 4, 2014. https://tinyurl.com/SBL6710s.

Knight, Mark. "Wirkungsgeschichte, Reception History, Reception Theory." *JSNT* 33.2 (2010): 137–46.

Koester, Craig R. *Symbolism in the Fourth Gospel: Meaning, Mystery, Community*. Minneapolis: Fortress, 1995.

Korte, Anne-Marie. "Madonna's Crucifixion and the Woman's Body in Feminist Theology." Pages 117–32 in *Doing Gender in Media, Art and Culture*. Edited by Rosemarie Buikema and Iris van der Tuin. London: Routledge, 2009.

Kottak, Conrad Phillip. *Cultural Anthropology*. 9th ed. New York: McGraw-Hill, 2002.

Kourdis, Evangelos. "Colour as Intersemiotic Translation in Everyday Communication: A Sociosemiotic Approach." Pages 736–46 in *New Semiotics between Tradition and Innovation: Proceedings of the Twelfth World Congress of the International Association of Semiotic Studies (IASS/AIS)*. Edited by Kristian Bankov. N.p.: NBU & IASS, 2017. https://tinyurl.com/SBL6710l.

Kress, Gunther R. *Multimodality: A Social Semiotic Approach to Contemporary Communication*. New York: Routledge, 2009.

Kress, Gunther, and Theo van Leeuwen. "Colour as a Semiotic Mode: Notes for a Grammar of Colour." *VisCom* 1 (2002): 343–68.

———. *Multimodal Discourse: The Modes and Media of Contemporary Communication*. London: Hodder, 2001.

———. *Reading Images: The Grammar of Visual Design*. 2nd ed. London: Routledge, 2006.

Kuhn, Thomas. *The Structure of Scientific Revolutions*. Chicago: University of Chicago Press, 1962.

Lacy, Marie Louise. *The Power of Colour to Heal the Environment*. London: Rainbow Bridge, 1996.

Lakoff, George, and Mark Johnson. *Metaphors We Live By*. Chicago: University of Chicago Press, 1980.

Lamb, William R. S. *The Catena in Marcum: A Byzantine Anthology of Early Commentary on Mark*. Leiden: Brill, 2012.

Lee, Dorothy. *Flesh and Glory: Symbolism, Gender and Theology in the Gospel of John*. New York: Crossroad, 2002.

Leeuwen, Theo van. *Introducing Social Semiotics: An Introductory Textbook*. New York: Routledge, 2005.

———. *The Language of Colour: An Introduction*. London: Routledge, 2011.

Legrand, Catherine. *Indigo: The Colour That Changed the World*. London: Thames and Hudson, 2013.

Lewis, Alan E. *Between Cross and Resurrection: A Theology of Holy Saturday*. Grand Rapids: Eerdmans, 2001.

Lifshitz, Felice. "Gender Trouble in Paradise: The Problem of the Liturgical Virgo." Pages 25–43 in *Images of Medieval Sanctity: Essays in Honour of Gary Dickson*. Edited by Debra Higgs Strickland. Leiden: Brill, 2007.

Light, Laura. "The Thirteenth Century Pandect: Bibles with Missals." Pages 185–215 in *Form and Function in the Late Medieval Bible*. Edited by Eyal Poleg and Laura Light. Leiden: Brill, 2014.

Lincoln, Andrew T. "Colossians." *NIB* 11:553–669.

———. *Ephesians*. WBC 42. Nashville: Nelson, 1990.

Liszka, James. *A General Introduction to the Semeiotic of Charles Sanders Peirce.* Bloomington: Indiana University Press, 1996.

Livingston, Alan, and Isabella Livingston. *Dictionary of Graphic Design and Designers.* London: Thames and Hudson, 2012.

Longenecker, Richard N. *Galatians.* WBC 41. Dallas: Word, 1990.

Louw, Johannes P., and Eugene A. Nida. *Lexical Semantics of the Greek New Testament.* Atlanta: Society of Biblical Literature, 1992.

Luz, Ulrich. *Matthew 1–7: A Commentary.* Translated by Wilhelm C. Luiss. Edinburgh: T&T Clark, 1989.

———. *Matthew 8–20: A Commentary.* Translated by James E. Crouch. Minneapolis: Augsburg Fortress, 2001.

———. *Studies in Matthew.* Translated by Rosemary Selle. Grand Rapids: Eerdmans, 2005.

Machin, David. *Introduction to Multimodal Analysis.* London: Bloomsbury, 2007.

Martín-Gil, Jesus, Francisco J. Martín-Gil, Germán Delibes-de-Castro, Pilar Zapatero-Magdaleno, and Francisco J. Sarabia-Herrero. "The First Known Use of Vermillion." *Experientia* 51 (1995): 759–61.

Matthews, Boris. *The Herder Symbol Dictionary: Symbols from Art, Archaeology, Mythology, Literature and Religion.* Wilmette, IL: Chiron, 1986.

McDannell, Colleen. *Material Christianity: Religion and Popular Culture in America.* New Haven: Yale University Press, 1995.

McDonough, Sean M. *YHWH at Patmos: Rev. 1:4 in Its Hellenistic and Early Jewish Setting.* WUNT 2/107. Tübingen: Mohr Siebeck, 1999.

McKinley, Catherine. *In Search of the Color That Seduced the World.* New York: Bloomsbury, 2011.

McLean, Bradley H. *Biblical Interpretation and Philosophical Hermeneutics.* Cambridge: Cambridge University Press, 2012.

McNamara, Martin. *Sunday Readings with Matthew: Interpretations and Reflections.* Dublin: Veritas, 2016.

Meggs, Philip B. *A History of Graphic Design.* London: Viking, 1983.

Meinrad Craighead: Praying with Images. Durham, NC: Resource Centre for Women and Ministry in the South, 2009.

Miles, Margaret. *Image as Insight: Visual Understanding in Western Christianity and Secular Culture.* Boston: Beacon, 1985.

"Mission and Values." Red Letter Christians. https://tinyurl.com/SBLPress6701d3.

Mitchell, William J. T. *Iconology: Image, Text, Ideology.* Chicago: University of Chicago Press, 1986.

———. *What Do Pictures Want? The Lives and Loves of Images*. Chicago: University of Chicago Press, 2005.

Moloney, Francis J. *The Gospel of John*. SP 4. Collegeville, MN: Liturgical Press, 1988.

Moore, Stephen D., and Yvonne Sherwood. *The Invention of the Biblical Scholar: A Critical Manifesto*. Minneapolis: Fortress, 2011.

Morgan, David. *The Embodied Eye: Religious Visual Culture and the Social Life of Feeling*. Berkeley: University of California Press, 2012.

———. *The Sacred Heart of Jesus: The Visual Evolution of a Devotion*. Amsterdam: Amsterdam University Press, 2008.

———. *Visual Piety: A History and Theory of Popular Religious Images*. Berkeley: University of California Press, 1998.

Moya Guijarro, Arsenio Jesús. *A Multimodal Analysis of Picture Books for Children: A Systemic Functional Approach*. Sheffield: Equinox, 2014.

New Oxford Dictionary of English. Oxford: Oxford University Press, 1998.

"Nicholas Markell." Gray's Sporting Journal. https://www.grayssportingjournal.com/nicholas-markell/.

"Nicholas Markell." Markell Wildlife Art. https://tinyurl.com/SBL6701b.

Nikolajeva, Maria, and Carole Scott. "The Dynamics of Picture Books Communication." *CLE* 31.4 (2000): 225–39.

———. *How Picturebooks Work*. New York: Routledge, 2006.

Nir-El, Yoram, and Magen Broshi. "The Black Ink of the Qumran Scrolls." *DSD* 3 (1996): 157–67.

———. "The Red Ink of the Dead Sea Scrolls." *Archaeometry* 38 (1996): 97–102. doi:10.1111/j.1475-4754.1996.tb00763.x.

Norris, Sigrid. *Analysing Multimodal Interaction: A Methodological Framework*. London: Routledge, 2004.

O'Halloran, Kay L. "Multimodal Analysis and Digital Technology." Pages 1–26 in *Interdisciplinary Perspectives on Multimodality: Theory and Practice; Proceedings of the Third International Conference on Multimodality*. Edited by Anthony Baldry and Elena Montagna. Campobasso, Italy: Palladino, 2007.

O'Kane, Martin, ed. *Bible, Art, Gallery*. Sheffield: Sheffield Phoenix, 2011.

———, ed. *Biblical Art from Wales*. Sheffield: Sheffield Phoenix, 2010.

———. "The Biblical Elijah and His Visual Afterlives." Pages 60–89 in *Between the Text and the Canvas: The Bible and Art in Dialogue*. Edited by J. Cheryl Exum and Ela Nutu. Sheffield: Sheffield Phoenix, 2007.

———, ed. *Borders, Boundaries and the Bible*. JSOTSup 313. Sheffield: Continuum, 2002.

———, ed. *Imaging the Bible: An Introduction to Biblical Art.* London: SPCK, 2008.
———. "Interpreting the Bible through the Visual Arts." *HBAI* 1 (2012): 388–409.
———. *Painting the Text: The Artist as Biblical Interpreter.* Sheffield: Sheffield Phoenix, 2007.
———. "*Wirkungsgeschichte* and Visual Exegesis: the Contribution of Hans-Georg Gadamer." *JSNT* 33 (2010): 147–59.
O'Mahony, Kieran. *Speaking from Within: Biblical Approaches for Effective Preaching.* Dublin: Veritas, 2016.
O'Toole, Michael. *The Language of Displayed Art.* 2nd ed. London: Routledge, 2011.
Page, Hugh R., Jr. *The Africana Bible: Reading Israel's Scriptures from Africa and the African Diaspora.* Minneapolis: Fortress, 2010.
Painter, Clare, James R. Martin, and Len Unsworth. *Reading Visual Narratives: Image Analysis of Children's Picture Books.* Sheffield: Equinox, 2014.
Parmenter, Dorina Miller. "How the Bible Feels: The Christian Bible as Effective and Affective Object." Pages 27–38 in *Sensing Sacred Texts.* Edited by James W. Watts. Sheffield: Equinox, 2018.
———. "The Iconic Book: The Image of the Bible in Early Christian Rituals." Pages 63–92 in *Iconic Books and Texts.* Edited by James W. Watts. Sheffield: Equinox, 2013.
Parris, David. *Reception Theory and Biblical Hermeneutics.* Eugene, OR: Pickwick, 2009.
Pastoureau, Michel. *Black: The History of a Color.* Princeton: Princeton University Press, 2008.
Patte, Daniel. *The Religious Dimensions of Biblical Texts: Greimas's Structural Semiotics and Biblical Exegesis.* Atlanta: Scholars Press, 1990.
Peirce, Charles Sanders. *Collected Papers of Charles Sanders Peirce.* 6 vols. Edited by Charles Hartshorne, Paul Weiss, and Arthur W. Burks. Cambridge: Harvard University Press, 1931–1958.
Perrot, Charles. "The Reading of the Bible in the Ancient Synagogue." Pages 137–59 in *Mikra: Text, Translation, Reading, and Interpretation of the Hebrew Bible in Ancient Judaism and Early Christianity.* Edited by Martin J. Mulder. Philadelphia: Fortress, 1988.
Plate, S. Brent. "What the Book Arts Can Teach Us about Sacred Texts: The Aesthetic Dimension of Scripture." Pages 137–59 in *Sensing Sacred Texts.* Edited by James W. Watts. Sheffield: Equinox, 2018.

Pontifical Biblical Commission. *The Interpretation of the Bible in the Church.* Boston: Pauline Media, 1993.

Pope John Paul II. "Address to the Kenyan Bishops." Nairobi, 7 May 1980. https://tinyurl.com/SBL6710n.

———. "Ekklesia in Africa." Yaoundé, Cameroon, September 14, 1995. https://tinyurl.com/SBL6710o.

Pope Paul VI. *Dei Verbum.* November 18, 1965. https://tinyurl.com/SBL6701h.

Porter, Stanley E., and Jason C. Robinson. *Hermeneutics: An Introduction to Interpretive Theory.* Grand Rapids: Eerdmans, 2011.

Quere, Ralph. *In the Context of Unity: A History of the Development of the Lutheran Book of Worship.* Minneapolis: Lutheran University Press, 2003.

Räisänen, Heikki. *Challenges to Biblical Interpretation.* Leiden: Brill, 2001.

Ramshaw, Gail. *Treasures Old and New: Images in the Lectionary.* Minneapolis: Fortress, 2002.

Rand, Paul. *Design: Form and Chaos.* New Haven: Yale University Press, 1993.

"Reception History." Blackwell Bible Commentaries. https://tinyurl.com/SBL6701e.

Reddish, Mitchell G. "Alpha and Omega." *ABD* 1:162.

Reif, Stefan C. "The Early Liturgy of the Synagogue." Pages 326–57 in *The Cambridge Companion to Judaism.* Vol. 3, *The Early Roman Period.* Edited by William Horbury, William D. Davies, and John Sturdy. Cambridge: Cambridge University Press, 1999.

Revised Common Lectionary. Nashville: Abingdon, 1992.

"Revised Common Lectionary." Vanderbilt Jean and Alexander Heard Libraries, Divinity Library. https://lectionary.library.vanderbilt.edu//search.php.

Robbins, Vernon K., Walter S. Melion, and Roy R. Jeal, eds. *The Art of Visual Exegesis: Rhetoric, Texts, Images.* Atlanta: SBL Press, 2017.

Roberts, Jonathan. Introduction to *The Oxford Handbook of the Reception History of the Bible.* Edited by Michael Lieb, Emma Mason, Jonathan Roberts, and Christopher Rowland. Oxford: Oxford University Press, 2013.

Rose, Gillian. *Visual Methodologies: An Introduction to Researching with Visual Materials.* 3rd ed. London: Sage, 2012.

Rowland, Christopher. "A Pragmatic Approach to Wirkungsgeschichte: Reflections on the Blackwell Bible Commentary Series and on the

Writing of Its Commentary on the Apocalypse." Paper presented at the Annual Meeting of the Society of Biblical Literature. San Antonio, Texas, November 2004. http://bbibcomm.info/?page_id=183.

Rush, Ormond. *The Reception of Doctrine: An Appropriation of Hans Robert Jauss' Reception Aesthetics and Literary Hermeneutics.* Rome: Gregorian & Biblical Press, 1997.

Sadler, Rodney S., Jr. "Black." *NIDB* 1:475.

"Saint John's University. Arca Artium." Collection at the Hill Museum and Manuscript Library. Saint John's University. https://hmml.org/collections/repositories/united%20states/saint-john-s-university--arca-artium/.

Saltzman, Lisa. "Faraway, So Close: Mythic Origins, Contemporary Art: The Case of Kara Walker." Pages 19–39 in *Contemporary Art and Classical Myth*. Edited by Isabelle Wallace and Jennie Hirsch. Surrey, UK: Ashgate, 2011.

Sandberg, Gösta. *Indigo Textiles: Technique and History.* London: Black, 1989.

Sandywell, Barry. "Seven Theses on Visual Culture: Towards a Critical-Reflexive Paradigm for the New Visual Studies." Pages 648–73 in *The Handbook of Visual Culture*. Edited by Ian Heywood, Barry Sandywell, and Michael Gardiner. London: Bloomsbury, 2012.

Sandywell, Barry, and Ian Heywood. "Critical Approaches to the Study of Visual Culture: An Introduction to the Handbook." Pages 1–56 in *The Handbook of Visual Culture*. Edited by Ian Heywood, Barry Sandywell, and Michael Gardiner. London: Bloomsbury, 2012.

Saussure, Ferdinand de. *Course in General Linguistics.* Translated by W. Baskin. Glasgow: Collins, 1974.

Sawyer, John F. A., ed. *Blackwell Companion to the Bible and Culture.* Chichester, UK: Wiley Blackwell, 2012.

———, ed. *A Concise Dictionary of the Bible and Its Reception.* Louisville: Westminster John Knox, 2009.

———. "A Critical Review of Recent Projects and Publications." *HBAI* 1 (2012): 298–329.

Schleifer, Ronald. *A. J. Greimas and the Nature of Meaning: Linguistics, Semiotics and Discourse Theory.* Lincoln: University of Nebraska Press, 1987.

Schmidt, Dennis J. *Between Word and Image: Heidegger, Klee, and Gadamer on Gesture and Genesis.* Bloomington: Indiana University Press, 2013.

Schneiders, Sandra M. "John 21:1-14." *Int* 43 (1989): 70–75.

———. *Women and the Word: The Gender of God in the New Testament and the Spirituality of Women.* New York: Paulist, 1986.

———. *Written That You May Believe: Encountering Jesus in the Fourth Gospel.* New York: Crossroad, 1999.

Schüssler Fiorenza, Elisabeth. *Jesus, Miriam's Child, Sophia's Prophet: Critical Issues in Feminist Christology.* New York: Continuum, 2004.

Schweizer, Eduard. *The Letter to the Colossians.* Translated by Andrew Chester. London: SPCK, 1982.

Sebeok, Thomas A. *Global Semiotics.* Bloomington: Indiana University Press, 2001.

Shepherd, David J. *The Bible on Silent Film: Spectacle, Story and Scripture in the Early Cinema.* Cambridge: Cambridge University Press, 2013.

———, ed. *The Silents of Jesus in the Cinema (1897–1927).* London: Routledge, 2017.

Shepherd, David J., and Nicholas Johnson. "The David Fragments—After Bertholt Brecht." Beckett Theatre (Dublin); Greenwood Theatre (London), 2017.

"Sister Wendy Beckett." Encyclopedia Britannica. 2015. https://tinyurl.com/SBLPress6701d2.

Sloyan, Gerard S. "The Lectionary as a Context for Interpretation." *Int* 31 (1977): 131–38.

Spier, Jeffrey. "The Earliest Christian Art: From Personal Salvation to Imperial Power." Pages 1–24 in *Picturing the Bible: The Earliest Christian Art.* Edited by Jeffrey Spier. New Haven: Yale University Press, 2007.

Sproul, Barbara C. "Sacred Time." *ER* 12:535–44.

The Sunday Missal. London: Collins, 1975.

Taussig, Michael. *What Color Is the Sacred?* Chicago: University of Chicago Press, 2009.

Taylor, Joan E. *What Did Jesus Look Like?* London: Bloomsbury, 2018.

Tertullian. "Treatise on Baptism." *ANF* 3:669–79.

Thiselton, Anthony. "Reception Theory, H. R. Jauss and the Formative Power of Scripture." *SJT* 65 (2012): 289–308.

Thompson, James W. *Hebrews.* PCNT. Grand Rapids: Baker, 2008.

Thurston, Anne. "Poetry as a Portal to Mystery." Unpublished paper presented at Arts and Spirituality Ireland conference "The Artist as Seer." Dublin, 15 October 2015.

Tilly, Michael. "Social Equality and Christian Life in Paul's First Letter to the Corinthians." *AcT* supplement 23 (2016): 225–37. doi:10.4314/actat.v23i1S.11.

Tollerton, David, ed. *Biblical Reception*. Vol. 4, *A New Hollywood Moses: On the Spectacle and Reception of Exodus: Gods and Kings*. London: Bloomsbury T&T Clark, 2018.

Tracey, Liam. "Word and Sacrament." Pages 53–62 in *The Study of Liturgy and Worship*. Edited by Juliette Day and Benjamin Gordon-Taylor. London: SPCK, 2013.

Turner, Victor W. *The Forest of Symbols: Aspects of Ndembu Ritual*. Ithaca, NY: Cornell University Press, 1967.

———. *The Ritual Process*. New York: de Gruyter, 1969.

Unsworth, Lee. "Explicating Inter-modal Meaning-Making in Media and Literary Texts: Towards a Metalanguage of Image/Text Relations." Pages 48–80 in *Media Teaching: Language, Audience, Production*. Edited by Andrew Burn and Cal Durrant. London: AATE-NATE and Wakefield Press, 2008.

———. "Multiliteracies and Metalanguage: Describing Image/Text Relations as a Resource for Negotiating Multimodal Texts." Pages 377–405 in *Handbook of Research on New Literacies*. Edited by Donald J. Leu, Julie Corio, Michele Knobel, and Colin Lankshear. Mahwah, NJ: Erlbaum, 2008.

———. "Towards a Metalanguage for Multiliteracies Education: Describing the Meaning-Making Resources of Language-Image Interaction." *ETPC* 5 (2006): 55–76.

Wagner, Anne M. "Kara Walker: The Black White Relation." Pages 91–101 in *Kara Walker: Narratives of a Negress*. Edited by Ian Berry. Cambridge, MA: Frances Young Tang Teaching Museum and Art Gallery at Skidmore College, 2003.

Walker Bynum, Caroline. *Wonderful Blood: Theology and Practice in Late Medieval Northern Germany and Beyond*. Philadelphia: University of Pennsylvania Press, 2007.

Walsh, Richard, ed. *T&T Clark Companion to the Bible and Film*. London: Bloomsbury T&T Clark, 2018.

Watts, James W. "The Three Dimensions of Scriptures." Pages 9–32 in *Iconic Books and Texts*. Edited by James W. Watts. Sheffield: Equinox, 2013.

Wedderburn, Alexander J. M. "The 'Letter' to the Hebrews and Its Thirteenth Chapter." *NTS* 50 (2004): 390–405.

Weems, Renita J. "Song of Songs." Pages 262–69 in *The New Interpreter's Bible: Old Testament Survey.* Nashville: Abingdon, 2006.

West, Fritz. *Scripture and Memory: The Ecumenical Hermeneutic of the Three-Year Lectionaries.* Collegeville, MN: Liturgical Press, 1997.

West, Gerald, and Musa Dube, eds. *The Bible in Africa: Transactions, Trajectories, and Trends.* Leiden: Brill, 2000.

Wharton, Annabel. "Icon, Idol, Totem and Fetish." Pages 3–11 in *Icon and Word: The Power of Images in Byzantium.* Edited by Anthony Eastmond and Liz James. Aldershot, UK: Ashgate, 2003.

Whelan, Thomas R. "Eucharist and Word." *MS* 4 (2014): 88–121.

"William Greenbaum Fine Prints: Fritz Eichenberg Prints." https://tinyurl.com/SBL6701a.

Yelle, Robert A. *The Semiotics of Religion: Signs of the Sacred in History.* London: Bloomsbury, 2013.

ANCIENT SOURCES INDEX

Old Testament/Hebrew Bible

Genesis
- 1:1–2:4   22, 149, 199
- 1:2   203
- 2–3   20
- 2:7   147
- 25:25   124
- 25:30   124

Exodus
- 3:1–4:17   149
- 4:6   112
- 15:4   124
- 20:4   152
- 24:12–31:18   149
- 34:1–34:28   149

Leviticus
- 13   112

Numbers
- 12:10   112
- 19:2   124

Deuteronomy
- 32:39   200
- 32:43   124

2 Kings
- 3:22   124
- 5:27   112

Esther
- 2:40   113

Job
- 16:16   124
- 38:4   22
- 38:19   22
- 38:38   22

Psalms
- 1   20
- 8:3   22
- 51:7   113
- 16:4   124
- 80:8–9   164
- 92:12   20
- 92:14   20
- 102   200

Proverbs
- 3:18   20
- 3:19   202
- 4:13   22
- 8:22–31   23, 202
- 9:1–6   23
- 23:31   124

Ecclesiastes
- 9:8a   113

Isaiah
- 1:18   113, 124
- 27:2–6   164
- 63:2   124

Jeremiah
- 2:21   164
- 31:35   22

Ezekiel
- 19:10–11 — 164
- 19:12–14 — 164
- 47:12 — 20

Daniel
- 4:10–12 — 2
- 7:9 — 112, 113

Jonah
- 1:14 — 124

Nahum
- 2:3 — 124

Zechariah
- 1:8 — 124
- 6:2 — 124

Deuterocanonical Works

Wisdom of Solomon
- 1:6 — 20
- 7:25–26 — 202
- 9:6–16 — 20
- 10:15 — 20

Sirach
- 1 — 20
- 24:8–12, 23–29 — 20

2 Maccabees
- 3:26 — 113

2 Esdras
- 2:40 — 113
- 6:45 — 22

Pseudepigrapha

2 Baruch
- 39.7 — 164

New Testament

Matthew
- 2:2–10 — 18
- 4:19 — 168, 169
- 6:11 — 141
- 13:47 — 169
- 14:17–19 — 168
- 14:28 — 170
- 15:34–36 — 168
- 16:2–30 — 124
- 17:2 — 113, 174
- 17:27 — 168
- 28:3 — 112, 113
- 28:9 — 141
- 28:16–20 — 141
- 28:20 — 164, 201

Mark
- 1:10 — 170
- 1:17 — 168, 169
- 6:38–43 — 168
- 8:7 — 168
- 13:24 — 174
- 16:5 — 113
- 16:9 — 141
- 16:12 — 141
- 16:14 — 141
- 16:19 — 162, 164

Luke
- 1:26–38 — 147
- 1:33 — 200, 202
- 4:15–21 — 85
- 5:6–9 — 167
- 5:10 — 168
- 8:23–25 — 170
- 9:13–16 — 168
- 22:20 — 22
- 23:45 — 174
- 24:13–24 — 141, 170
- 24:13–35 — 9
- 24:32–35 — 170
- 24:36–51 — 141

24:42–43	168	1 Corinthians	
24:51	153, 164	11:25	22
John		12:13	140
1:1–5	22, 174, 200, 203, 214	15:20	205
2:1–11	168, 170	15:49	202
3:19–21	174	2 Corinthians	
4:9	149	4:4	202
4:14	170	5:17	22
6:9–11	168		
7:38	170	Galatians	
8:11–12	174	3:28	140, 153
8:58	198	6:15	22
9:4–7	174		
11:9–10	174	Ephesians	
12:25–36	174	1:21	202
12:46	174	2:15	140
13:5	170	5:18–20	86
13:30	174		
15:1–11	164–166; 168	Philippians	
19:30	205	4:20	200, 202
19:34	170		
20:11–18	113	Colossians	
20:19–28	141	1:15	141, 145, 202, 203
21:1–14	9, 141, 170	1:15–20	23
21:15–17	183	1:16	200, 202, 203
		3:10	22
Acts		3:11	140
1:2	162, 164	3:16	86
1:10	113	4:16	86
1:11	162, 164		
1:22	162, 164	1 Thessalonians	
2:19–20	124	5:27	86
3:15	205		
5:28	124	1 Timothy	
10:30	113	1:17	202
13:32–33	205	4:13	86
15:21	85		
		2 Timothy	
Romans		1:9	202
1:25	200, 202		
8:11	205	Hebrews	
9:5	200, 202	2:14	205
11:36	200, 202	4:16	141
		8:8, 13	22

Hebrews (cont.)
8:8	22
8:13	22
9:15	22
12:24	22
13:8	200, 201
13:20	205
13:21	200, 202

1 Peter
1:19	124
2:9	145, 148

2 Peter
3:13	22

1 John
1:7	124
5:6	124
5:8	141

Revelation
1:4	200
1:5	124
1:8	200
1:10–12	200
1:14	112
2	20
3:4–5	113
4:8	200
4:11	199
6:4	124
7:9	113
7:13	113
7:14	113, 124
12:3	124
14	20
19	20
21:1	22
21:6	199
22:13	164, 199, 201

SUBJECT INDEX 261

Fresnault-Deruelle, Pierre, 59
gaze, 20, 21, 68, 140, 161, 172, 175–77, 196, 206
gesture, 17–18, 20, 22, 55, 66, 68–69, 129–30, 144, 148–49, 151, 159–61, 166, 171–72, 176–77, 179, 182–83, 185, 196–97, 210, 216
Gill, Eric, 50, 221
Good Friday, 89, 121–22, 191, 194, 214, 218, 225
graphic design, 1–6, 11, 17, 23–26, 35, 50–52, 55, 56, 69–74, 78, 83, 100, 103, 108, 116, 121, 132, 138
green, 110, 124, 126, 128
Halo, 6, 9, 160, 162, 173, 190
hermeneutics, 25, 26–29, 33, 46, 98. *See also* visual hermeneutics
Hjelmslev, Louis, 58
Holy Baptism, **152**
Holy Saturday, 121–22, 145, 153, 191, 194, 214, 218, 225
Holy Spirit, 83, 124, 127
Holy Thursday, 121, 155, 225
Honzl, Jindřich, 59
human, 23, 28, 46, 51, 55, 61, 63, 65, 71, 116–18, 123, 136, 140, 145, 147, 165–66, 175–76, 179, 182, 187–88, 196, 198–99, 202–3, 206, 208, 210–11, 220
ichthys, 215
iconography, 5, 45, 116
ideational metafunction. *See* metafunctions
imagination, 47–48, 50, 114, 149, 190, 210
incarnation, 18, 91, 98, 199
ink, 66, 116, 120, 129, 209, 211, 222
    Bible, 118
    carbon, lampblack, 120, 129
    iron-gall, 120
    oak-nut gall, 120
    red ink, 129
interpersonal metafunction. *See* metafunctions
Jakobson, Roman, 59
Jerusalem, 84, 114, 168, 172–74
Kacmarcik, Frank, 1, 50, 221

Kristeva, Julia, 58
Lacan, Jacques, 57
Lavater, Johann Caspar, 137
lectionary, 18–23, 35, 69, 76, 81–103, 108, 113, 118, 120, 130, 139, 155, 158, 215–17, 225. *See also* Book of Common Prayer; *Evangelical Lutheran Worship*; missal
    Revised Common Lectionary, 86, 93, 225
    Roman Catholic *Lectionary for Mass*, 81–82, 86, 90, 92–93, 113, 225
Lévi-Strauss, Claude, 57–58
light, 9, 11, 15, 21, 48, 112–16, 118, 127, 130, 136, 145, 153, 173–74, 178, 189–90, 194, 196, 201–4, 208, 214
Light (Craighead), 11, **13–14**, 115, 127, 153, **193**, 196–98, 203, **204**, 205, 207–8, 214, 218
Light (Markell), **8**, 9, 115, 127, **157**, 160–62, 172, 177, **178**, 185, 189–90, 218
liminality, 116, 119, 121, 153, 191, 204–5, 218
Lindekens, René, 59
liturgy, 69–70, 81–104, 125, 129, 139, 145, 148–49, 207, 216, 219, 221
literary theory, 29–31, 33, 37
male, 123, 134, 153, 177
Malinowski, Bronsiław, 64
Markell, Nicholas, 2, 4–9, 17, 19, 23–24, 50–51, 64, 70, 104, 108, 114–15, 119–20, 124–25, 127, 134, 139, 141, 148–53, 155–90, 196, 206, 209, 218
Mary, Virgin, 145, **147**
Mary Magdalene, 113
materiality, 58, 116, 209–11
Maundy Thursday. *See* Holy Thursday
mediator, 22, 51, 170, 187, 205, 207
metafunctions, 56, 62–67, 77, 108–9, 123
    color and, 109, 111–25
    Halliday and metafunctions, 62–67
    ideational, 63, 77, 78, 107, 109–10, 112–15, 118–119, 123, 128, 158, 159, 174, 177, 185, 195, 207, 210, 212, **213**, 219

metafunctions (cont.)
    interpersonal, 63–64, 77–78, 107, 109–11, 114–15, 119, 125, 127–29, 158, 175–77, 180, 182, 185, 190, 205–7, 210, 218–19
    textual (compositional), 63–64, 77–78, 107, 109, 111–12, 115–17, 120, 126, 158, 185–90, 207–8, 210
metonym, 131, 134, 137–41, 144, 151, 190, 217–18
Metz, Christian, 58–59
missal, 2, 4, 15, 23, 26, 35, 67, 69, 76, 82–84, 90, 95, 99–100, **101**, 108, **122**, 125, 129, 144–45, 209, 211. *See also* lectionary
    Missale Romanum, 89–90
    missalette, 99, 102–3
    Sunday Missal, 2, 4, 15, 69, 84, 100, **101**, 102, 104, 108, 121, **122**, 144, 148, 191, 194, 211, 214, 216
Morris, Charles, 58
Moser, Barry, 50
Moses, 85, 112, 137, 149, **150**
Muhlenberg, Henry Melchior, 96
Mukařovský, Jan, 59
multimodality, 29, 34, 40, 56, 63, 65–70, 74, 78, 99–100, 120, 144, 148–49, 195, 215–16, 221–23
narrative processes, 64, 121, 160–61, 174, 186–87, 190, 195–96, 218
Nattiez, Jean-Jacques, 59
Ogden, Charles, 58
Omega, 14–15, 164, 196, **197**, 198–200, **201**, 207–8
orange, 111
Outer and Inner Strands, 11, **12**, **14**, **193**, **197**, 198, 203–4, 206, 208
Paris school, 59, 61, 75
Paul, 32, 86, 140, 153, 202
Pentecost, 70, 91, 124, 127, 230
perception, 3–4, 30, 47
Peter. *See* Simon Peter
pink, 111, 128
Plato, 136
Pliny the Elder, 135–36

Prague school, 59
psychology, 31, 73, 167
Qumran, 120, 129
Quash, Ben, 25
reader response, 43, 125
reactional processes, 171–72
red, 6, 9, 18, 24, 70, 100, 108, 110–15, 118–32, 148–49, 161, 165, 177–78, 186–89, 217–18
red-letter, 123, 127–29, 131–32
    Bible, 123, 127–29
    Christians, 123, 128
    rubrics, 108, 123, 125, 129, 214, 218
Renaissance, 45, 47, 50, 52, 180, 186
represented participants, 6, 63, 160, 171, 175–77, 179, 182, 184, 196, 206
resurrection, 9, 21, 91, 98, 116, 121, 124, 140–41, 149, 152–53, 158, 168, 179, 186–87, 194, 199, 205–6, 214, 218, 225
    resurrection banner, 6, 186
Rezeptionsästhetik, 30
Rezeptionsgeschichte, 32
Richards, Ivor, 58
Rubrics, *See* red-letter
salience, 124–25, 161, 163–64, 185, 189, 207–8, 211
Schefer, Jean-Louis, 59
seasons, 18, 20, 22
    liturgical, 18, 23, 88, 91–92, 98–99, 113, 130, 158, 191, 194, 199, 225
Sebeok, Thomas, 58
shadow, 118, 136–37, 151, 174
sign, 55, 57–62, 64, 66, 69–77, 82, 110, 112–13, 137, 168–70, 215–17
Simon Peter, 168, 170, 183–84
semiology, 61, 73–74
semiotics, 4, 23, 25–27, 51, 55–62, 65–66, 71–78, 82, 220
semiotic resource, 56, 60, 62, 65–70, 74–75, 77–78, 83, 109, 132–34, 153, 175, 216–19
social semiotics, 4, 6, 17, 23–24, 26, 31, 52, 55–82, 107, 109, 158–59, 175, 195, 215–20, 223
sociochrome, 131, 217

SUBJECT INDEX 263

space, 20–21, 35, 68, 100–101, 112, 114, 116, 119, 121–22, 149, 151, 182, 185, 187–91, 203–5, 210
  black, 117, 119, 121–22, 203, 205, 214
  holding, 121–22, 191, 214
  liminal, 116, 119, 121, 203–6
  sacred, 20–21 114, 116, 203, 205, 214
  spatiality, 3, 20, 22, 49, 116, 180, 203, 206, 211, 213
  and time, 182, 203, 205–6
  white, 20–21, 100, 112, 114, 116–17, 161, 187, 190, 203, 217
spirituality, 11, 112, 134, 167
star, 17, 18, 20–22, 125, 147
Sunrise, **8**, 9, **157**, 160, 162, 173, 189
Sydney school, 61–62, 64, 68, 74
symbolic attributes, 17–18, 196–200, 214, 219
symbolic process, 17, 196
symmetry, 6, 9, 21, 161, 167, 186, 188, 197, 207
synecdoche, 138–39, 141, 144
Systemic Functional Grammar, 4, 56, 62–65, 75, 78, 215
Talmud, 84
Text, **13–14**, 15, **16**, **193**, 199, **201**, **204**, 207–8
textual metafunction. *See* metafunctions
texture, 17, 49
Tiberias, **8**, 9, 119, 131, 141, 161, 170–71, 173, 179–80, **181**, **183**, 189–90
time, 18, 20, 68, 85, 87, 116, 119, 121, 164, 188–90, 195, 196–203, 205–8, 210–11, 214, 218, 221
  beginning of, 20, 197–98
  end of, 20, 98, 174, 197–98
  liturgical, 92, 121, 127, 158. *See also* seasons
tomb, 121–22, 130, 140, 145, 153, 191, 194, 205–6
Torah, 20, 84–85, 87, 120
  haftorah, 85, 87
typography, 3, 71, 100, 107, 129, 131, 199, 210, 214, 217
Vatican II, 35, 86, 89–90, 93, 145, 148

Vatican II (cont.)
  Coetus XI committee, 90, 93
  Sacrosanctum Concilium, 148
vectors, 9, **159**, 160–62, 166, 169, 172, 176–77
Velázquez, Diego, 48–49
vine, 164–68, 218
  Sprouting Vine Shoot, 6, 119, 163, 165–69, 186–87
  Vine/Fish, 6, **8**, 9–10, 119, **156**, 163, **165**, 166–70, 174, 185–87, 189–90, 218
visual hermeneutics, 26, 29, 46
Walker, Kara, 135, 151
water, 6, 9, 70, 87, 110, 117, 119, 124, 147, 161, 167–71, 174, 180, 185, 188–90, 218
Waves/Net (Markell), **8**, 9, 119, 163, **169**, **178**, 180, **181**
Waves (Craighead), **13**, 14, **193**, 207–8
white, 6, 9, 11, 15, 18, 20–21, 24, 70, 100, 108, 112–32, 148–49, 153, 161, 163, 177–80, 183, 186–87, 190, 196–99, 203, 208, 210, 214–19
Wirkungsgeschichte, 29, 32, 34, 38, 41, 44, 81
wisdom, 20, 22, 202–3
woodcut, 15, 119, 144–45, 147, 153, 201, 209–10, 213
womb, 145, 153
Word, 22, 69, 83–84, 92, 97, 174, 214
yellow, 111, 126

www.ingramcontent.com/pod-product-compliance
Lightning Source LLC
Chambersburg PA
CBHW040747020526
44116CB00036B/2968